DEVOTED TO YOU

DEVOTED TO YOU

HONORING DEITY IN WICCAN PRACTICE

Judy Harrow

Alexei Kondratiev

Geoffrey W. Miller

Maureen Reddington-Wilde

CITADEL PRESS
Kensington Publishing Corp.
www.kensingtonbooks.com

CITADEL PRESS BOOKS are published by

Kensington Publishing Corp.
850 Third Avenue
· New York, NY 10022

Copyright © 2003, Judy Harrow, Alexei Kondratiev, Geoffrey W. Miller,
and Maureen Reddington-Wilde

All Kensington titles, imprints, and distributed lines are available at special
quantity discounts for bulk purchases for sales promotions, premiums,
fund-raising, educational, or institutional use. Special book excerpts or
customized printings can also be created to fit specific needs. For details,
write or phone the office of the Kensington special sales manager:
Kensington Publishing Corp., 850 Third Avenue, New York, NY 10022,
attn: Special Sales Department, phone 1-800-221-2647.

CITADEL PRESS is Reg. U.S. Pat. & TM Off.
The Citadel Logo is a trademark of Kensington Publishing Corp.

First printing: February 2003

10 9 8 7 6 5 4 3 2 1

Printed in the United States of America

Library of Congress Control Number: 2002113378

ISBN 0-8065-2392-1

Ron Parshley
Lord Sylvanus
11/17/43–11/12/01

I don't have the space here to relate Ron's many achievements. Long before anybody else, he hosted a Pagan radio talk show in central Massachusetts. He was one of the founders of the National Alliance of Pantheists. He was a community organizer and leader, first in the Northeast then later in Florida. Many a tale could be told of how he stood up for our rights, and for everybody's freedom of religion. You'll find a few of them at www.witchvox.com/passages/ronparshley.html.

I have a more personal story. Ron was a superb healer, compassionate and skilled. Once upon a time, in 1980, I had a frightening result from a Pap test. Shortly afterward, we were at a gathering that was held in an old barn, dorms on the ground floor and meeting space in the attic. I was napping. Ron took a bunch of people up to the attic and led a ritual that they tell me raised the roof. The next week, I went in for a biopsy. All clear. All clear ever since. Thank you, Ron!

—Judy Harrow

CONTENTS

ACKNOWLEDGMENTS

Thanks and praise to all those who have helped us find our own particular paths to our own particular Gods: to writers of books, to close kin and coworshippers, to friends we have met only on the Internet, to all those who collectively create the Pagan community within which we have found these good companions on the path.

Thanks to our teachers and students, too numerous to mention, for the sense of family and community that supports our personal explorations. Thanks to our own "home" groups: Daitales, Children of Memory, Garden Path, and Proteus. Abiding thanks to Iargalon, rootstock of three of those four. Thanks, Margot!

Thanks to our life mates and working partners—to Brian, Gwyneth, Jim, Kitty, Len, Rita, Roxanne.

Thanks to the erudite professionals who have generously shared their expertise: Dr. J the Egyptologist, Dr. Raven, and Sunfish. We can't thank any of them by name because public identification as Pagans would put their careers at risk. We ask you to ponder what that means for a country that prides itself on freedom of religion. May all people of good faith join in working for the day when unusual faith need not be hidden.

As always, Judy thanks Moose the instigator, Maury and Vivian the rescuers, and Little Judy for a cup of coffee on Fordham Road at the moment she needed it most. Although none of you had anything to do with this particular project, it would have been impossible without you.

Geoff and Judy join in thanking Renee for her sharp-eyed assistance at critical moments and for her steady emotional support.

Thanks to Jennie Dunham, our agent, for the core idea around which this book was built.

Thanks to Bob Shuman, our editor. We can't begin to tell you how helpful he has been.

Our deepest thanks go to Anubis, Aphrodite, Brigit, and Gaia, the Deities to Whom we are devoted. May this work, and the manner of its sharing, bring harm to none, good to many, and honor to You. So mote it be!

INTRODUCTION

Three friends and I decided to write a book sharing our experiences of working intensely with four specific Deities: Anubis, Aphrodite, Brigit, and Gaia.

This book is built around the Deity Focus exercise that we use in Proteus Coven (and that several other covens also use). Our intermediate students are asked to each choose one particular Goddess or God. They spend about a month researching the stories, symbols, correspondences (colors, incenses, flowers, animals, or anything else traditionally associated with that Deity), rituals—just gathering all the information they can about the Deity they have chosen. Then they spend a second month in a self-created immersion experience. They set up home altars, wear the colors, eat the foods, engage in meditative and ritual practices, do anything they can think of to make that Deity a focal point of their lives for that month, and a significant part of their lives from then on.

Half the purpose of the exercise is to help students establish close contact with the Goddess or God of their choice. The other half—if anything, more important—is to expose them to a method that they can use to establish contact with other Deities that they may feel drawn to in the future.

The four essays in this book all follow the same pattern as the Deity Focus exercise. First they tell stories and describe symbols and correspondences, giving you all the information they can. Then they suggest a range of practices that will help you connect more deeply with Anubis, Aphrodite, Brigit, and Gaia. Use these chapters to work with those four Deities, if you will, but also please use the book as a model to help you connect with any Deity you choose. Modern Paganism is a high-choice religion.

All four of us are Pagans. In general, Paganism is a polytheistic religion. Do we honor many different Deities, or do we honor Deity under many different forms? That fascinating philosophical discussion really makes no difference in practice.

What does matter is that people are unique as snowflakes are. We have different personalities, different interests, different life situations—and we all work within limitations of time and energy, balancing our spiritual lives with commitments to family, career, personal health, and more. So in living reality, we are *henotheists. Henotheism* is a theological term describing a religious practice that focuses on one Deity while acknowledging and even honoring the existence of the others. It's much like making a marriage commitment while still liking and respecting all the other people in your life.

We are four Pagan henotheists, each of whom has a long-standing devotion to the Deity he or she has written about here. We are devoted. We respect and admire one another's devotion. But our differences go way beyond the fact that we are devoted to four different Deities.

Since modern Paganism is a high-choice religion, we have a wide range of choices in our basic approach to religion itself. So another thing I would hope is that this book will show you something of the range of options available to you and help you find your own comfortable place within that range.

I am, for want of a better term, a serial henotheist. I have felt myself drawn to different Deities at different stages of my life, depending on which issues were focal for me at that time. In contrast, Geoffrey and Maureen write about long-standing primary connections with Anubis and Aphrodite respectively.

Alexei and Maureen are *reconstructionists*. That means they work with the myths and rituals of one particular ethnic group, staying as close to historically attested practices as makes sense to them.

They prize a sense of solidarity and continuity with the people who have worshipped these pantheons before. Both of them have gone to considerable effort to learn the original languages of their respective Deities, and both would urge you to do the same.

Alexei's chapter on Brigit explores the many ways that the spirit of Brigit the Goddess survived in the later worship of Brigit the Christian saint. Maureen, outrageous priestess of Aphrodite, describes how the sensibility that moved Aphrodite's ancient worship can be expressed through some very modern forms.

Geoffrey and I are Wiccans. He brings carefully researched understanding of the historical Anubis into a Wiccan ritual structure, while I am much more concerned with modern ecological consciousness than I am with Greek myth. I'm the most eclectic of the four by far, and yet I believe that reverence for Mother Earth lies at the very heart of my Craft.

Also, in reading these pieces, I get the impression that Geoffrey and Maureen perceive the Gods as self-aware entities that exist independently of humankind, while Alexei and I tend to perceive Them more as metaphors through which humans try to comprehend patterns of energy and meaning that are ultimately beyond our ability to define. Maureen writes about using rituals that Aphrodite will remember from ancient days, because that's the most likely way to attract Her presence. In contrast, I believe that Mother Nature is always present, and that the only thing that changes in ritual is my awareness of Her Presence.

Notice what I just said. I get this impression from reading their chapters. Although Alexei, Geoffrey, and Maureen are all friends of mine, I don't know for sure what their basic theological assumptions are. It doesn't matter, since modern Paganism is a high-choice religion, thankfully free of dogma. I invite you to compare and contrast what the four of us have written—and read and talk to many other thoughtful Pagans as well—and draw your own conclusions.

Many modern Pagans work with a festival cycle that we call the Wheel of the Year. You've probably seen this presented in many other books. It consists of eight evenly spaced festivals known as Sabbats. Four of these, the solstices and equinoxes, refer to events in the sky. The other four, sometimes called the cross-quarter days, refer to events on the ground.

Now, celestial events affect us all similarly, once you allow for the regular difference between Northern and Southern Hemispheres. But events on the ground, the terrestrial cycle, are different in different ecosystems. Our experience of the seasons is quite different in New Jersey or California or Hawaii. The cross-quarter days, our Earth Sabbats, originally celebrated significant turning points in the annual agricultural cycle of the British Isles.

It's very important to understand that the eight-spoked Wheel of the Year, as we now celebrate it, was created during the twentieth century by some of the pioneers of the Pagan Renaissance. No known historical Pagan culture had a calendar with eight, evenly spaced festivals. Not the Celts, or anybody else either. Our elders tell us that, in Gerald Gardner's first coven, there was an ongoing debate between members who wanted to celebrate the Sky Sabbats and others who preferred the Earth Sabbats. Then somebody noticed that people had better potlucks on the Sabbats than they did at other group meetings. The obvious win-win solution was to celebrate all eight of them.

The Earth Sabbats, which are also traditionally called the Greater Sabbats, are authentically Celtic and reflect the actual ways the seasons were experienced by the countryfolk of the British Isles. The solstices are important in Norse (Scandinavian) culture, which is the origin of the Anglo-Saxons, the other major group to settle in Britain. Even if your ancestors were not British, these six festivals at least are part of the cultural roots of all who speak English.

But only one of the Deities highlighted in this book is Celtic. None is Norse. However did we match these Deities from elsewhere to the four British Earth Sabbats?

The Earth Sabbats, which mark the stages of the agricultural cycle in Britain, present certain themes. These themes are universal and archetypal, even if they are most obvious at other times of the year in other ecosystems. We are devoted to four Deities whose myths and symbols seem compatible with those themes. Specifically:

- ⚘ Samhain (10/31) is the end of the harvest season, when excess flocks were slaughtered and farmers turned to hunting to supplement the stored crops. So it is associated with death, dying, and other uncomfortable but necessary transformations. Anubis as guide of the dead also works with those energies.

- ⚘ Imbolc (1/31) brings the very birth of the light, the earliest signs of life's return, the pregnant ewe's lactation. It is also the traditional feast of Brigit, midwife and foster mother, in Celtic culture.

- ⚘ Beltane (4/31) is the exuberant flowering of spring, when it seems that every bird, bee, and flower is seeking to mate, and humans are no different. Aphrodite radiates the energy of sensual attraction.

- ⚘ Lammas (7/31) is the beginning of the harvest, time to be sure we are on good terms with Earth Mother Gaia, by showing our deep appreciation for Her many generous gifts.

Remember, though, that out there in messy reality, babies are born in October and old folks die in May. Nobody tells them that this is symbolically inappropriate or that they should wait for the proper time of year. We all play the hands that the fates have dealt us. You may find yourself, at need, calling on these Deities out of season.

May all the Goddesses and Gods bless your path. May each of Them care for you and teach you the things you need to know, whenever you need to know them. Blessed be!

PART I

SAMHAIN

Geoffrey W. Miller has been a practicing Wiccan priest since 1984 and is one of three founders of the Garden Path Coven. He makes his home on the coast of Maine, where he works as a paramedic—a healing profession to which he felt guided. He regards his experiences with Anubis as evidence of the inexorable presence and inspiration of the Divine Spirit in his life.

Anubis

I do not do well in the bright sun, and the Egyptian desert is not known for its shady places. For some reason, however, I found myself bathed in shade as I worked on my latest project.

I was digging. Before me lay a tomb buried in sand. I had no idea who had left it here all those millennia ago. However, it was well known that the ancient Egyptians filled their tombs with magical texts. I was certain I would find them here. I was also determined to get my hands on them, to read them and understand what they had to offer. I had waited a long time for this opportunity. Thanks to Anubis, I would soon make my prize discovery.

This was not the first time that Anubis had visited me in my dreams, but as on all other occasions, He was not visible. He was sitting behind me, talking almost constantly. I had no idea what He was saying, or why. His words didn't come across as encouragement, more as a string of non sequiturs; comments that reflected on nothing—and everything— all at the same time. In any case, my enthusiasm for the project at hand turned my attention away from His words.

That is, until I was about to open the door of the tomb.

"There is nothing in there, I hope you realize," He said with disarming calm.

I froze. I would have turned to look at Him, but I had long since learned that such an action would bring the dream to an abrupt end. "What do you mean? This is a tomb! They are full of fascinating and important information such as coffin texts and burial papyri. That is why you brought me here!"

"No, I brought you here because you said you wanted to see one. You said nothing about content. This is a tomb, there's nothing inside." He paused, for effect I guessed. *"While you were so busy digging, however, I have been telling you things that no such text could ever relate. They are the sorts of details that you will hear only from the mouth of a God or Goddess, and you won't find them in any text. Can you repeat anything I have said to you?"*

No, I couldn't. I had been too busy unearthing an empty tomb. Curse my limited understanding of my own request. I could sense Anubis slowly shaking His head, and His sigh was thick with well-tested patience. Even when rebuking, He had a streak of compassion. "I thought not, and I'm not going to repeat what I said, either. Take that as your lesson now, and next time, listen to me."

That was when I woke up.

Of course, the great irony in this dream is that virtually all of the texts I sought have been published and are available in bookstores or libraries.

I am not certain why an ancient Egyptian Deity chose to connect with me, but some sixteen years ago while I was meditating on the Greek God Pan, that is what happened. Since then, I have been on a spiritual path that has been at times frustrating, fascinating, and ecstatic, but never boring.

How does it happen that a man raised an Episcopalian ends up venerating an ancient Egyptian Deity? Couched in those terms, that question isn't entirely fair.

The Egyptians were not linear in their beliefs. Their worldview was dualistic and allowed their Gods to take on seemingly contradictory aspects. That may seem odd, even foolish to some in this day and age. At the same time, however, none of us truly knows or understands the nature of the Divine. It is too big. Why would we want to limit its possibilities? We need not throw out the religion with which we were raised in favor of a new one. Instead, I see what has happened within me as a maturation, a new and different way of hearing and expression.

I was not raised to worship in one particular fashion. I was taught to make decisions for myself and be responsible for them. My religious instruction was intended to prepare me for that responsibility, not to relieve me of it. I was called to the Wiccan path, and I have never regretted answering that call. In the same fashion, Anubis called to me. From what I have seen, He has called to a lot of people.

Part of that call has been the discipline of reflecting on Anubis with modern eyes growing out of a culture different from the one from which He came. Most of what we learn from ancient Egyptian texts concerns the life and times of the ancient Egyptians. Learning to apply that knowledge to the modern world is a long process that will probably never cease. Yet, Anubis persists with me. It has been about a decade and a half now, so I have no reason to believe that this is either a phase or that it will end anytime soon.

In these pages, I hope to impart at least some of the knowledge I have gained along the way. Relating my experiences will not be easy because encounters with Deity are understood primarily in the deepest recesses of our consciousness where insight comes in the form of images, feelings, and intuition. They are extremely difficult to put into words, and I have yet to meet a God willing to sit at a word processor and spell it out. For those reasons, I am left with the task of communicating ideas that I received intuitively (sometimes with no apparent logic) in a limited language that demands precision. That requires the reader to understand my own position before I go any further, so I would like to make several points.

The ancient Egyptians were not Wiccan and I am not an ancient Egyptian. I am a contemporary American who has been a practicing Wiccan for almost twenty years. My worldview, religious beliefs, and ritual style are shaped by my training and research in a religion that I believe was founded in the early decades of the twentieth century. The age of a religion has nothing to do with its validity, and my growth as a spiritual being does not rely on the existence of ancient roots beneath my practices. In fact, I believe that creating our own symbols and liturgies strengthens our connection to Deity by making us rethink and reexamine our beliefs and assumptions. What follows here, while certainly influenced by the mythology and practices of the ancient Egyptians, is not at all what they practiced in their own time.

In some parts of this text, I have broken ranks with the Egyptians completely. While they sought to preserve the earthly remains of their deceased, the present concern with the health of our planet calls for a different action. In other ways (such as blowing on an image to instill it with breath and power), I have followed ancient Egyptian practice rather closely. The goal is always to make any observance relevant to me and to my times. That is the challenge I place before you.

I am also not a trained Egyptologist, nor am I a reconstructionist. Just as any healthy religion is a creative process, so are the rituals, meditations, spells, and observations included here. I am certainly not the only person to have contact with Anubis. I have met many such people and a search of the Internet turns up many more. My perspective is my own. My goal is to present you with material I wish I had had when my spiritual quest began. I hope you will take what you find useful and build on it.

Although I will be using the term *magic* in this text, my concept of it is close to the Egyptian concept of *heka*.[1] Magic was defined by Greek and Roman thinkers as something that:

[1]Robert Kreich Ritner, *The Mechanics of Ancient Egyptian Magical Practice, Studies in Ancient Oriental Civilization*, no. 54 (Chicago: Oriental Institute of Chicago, 1997). See chapter 6 for a discussion on the difference between the western concept of magic and *heka*.

- Stood outside the realm of cause and effect
- Violated the laws of God
- Violated the laws of man
- Was accessible only to the adept or initiate but was shunned by the pious
- Had no place in religious observance

The ancient Egyptians, however, saw *heka* as:

- The generative force behind cause and effect
- The force through which the cosmos was created and is sustained
- Accessible to Gods and humans at all levels of society
- Something to be mastered by the pious
- The link between theology and religious technique[2]

Most modern Neo-pagans will find this concept familiar to them. *Heka* is a force that we can access and direct at will. It is the energy raised in circle as a cone of power. *Heka* itself is amoral. The use to which we put it, not its essential nature, determines whether it is beneficial or harmful. A strong sense of ethics is important.

I will say a few words on the work of E. A. Wallis Budge. There is no doubt that Budge had a profound influence on twentieth-century occultism, whether or not he intended to. The papyri he published (especially the papyrus of Ani, published in 1895) were major foundational pieces in the development of magical systems from the Golden Dawn to Gardnerian Wicca. Magical Societies from the Hermetic Order of the Golden Dawn to many modern-day organizations still use Budge's work in developing their liturgies and rituals, and some of them are poetic things of beauty.

[2]Ibid. pp. 247–49.

Keep in mind, however, that Budge was a museum curator, not an Egyptologist. Even in his own time he was at odds with other scholars in the field on a number of points.[3] Egyptology is a rapidly evolving science and a lot has been learned over the last century—particularly in the area of language. Budge's work is primarily useful today in studying the history of Egyptology and tracing the development of twentieth-century occult practices. While we certainly shouldn't disregard liturgical work influenced by Budge, those seeking to deepen their understanding of ancient Egypt or to develop new liturgy based on sound scholarship would do well to consult more recent research for inspiration.

Finally, I make reference to a number of Egyptian source documents. Some explanation and a description of these are in order.

> ॐ **The Pyramid Texts.** The Pyramid Texts first appeared at the end of the Fifth Dynasty (ca. 2360 B.C.E.). They were so called because they were carved or painted on the inside walls of the royal pyramids, usually in the sarcophagus chamber. The texts consisted largely of a series of spells intended to assist the king on his journey to the sky after death. They are among the oldest religious texts known to humankind.
>
> The Egyptians believed that many dangers existed on the road to a happy afterlife. They also believed that provision needed to be made for the trip. The texts include spells to keep the body of the deceased intact, to restore his breath, to supply nourishment, and to assure the assistance of all necessary Deities. The names of guardians and ferrymen were included because it was believed the king would need to know them if he was to pass through their realms unscathed. Even common tools such as a ladder and animal forms with wings were added to make the flight into the sky more likely.
>
> The Pyramid Texts were available only to kings; those able

[3]Erik Hornung, *Conceptions of God in Ancient Egypt, The One and the Many*, trans. John Baines (Ithaca: Cornell University Press, 1982), pp. 24–25.

to have pyramids constructed for them. After 2200 B.C.E. they appeared in the pyramids of queens.

✧ **The Coffin Texts.** By the end of the Old Kingdom (ca. 2180 B.C.E.), the texts began appearing on coffins. Although the location of the texts changed, the content remained relatively stable.[4] The Coffin Texts appeared at the start of the Middle Kingdom (ca. 1987 B.C.E.). They were carved or painted on the coffins and tomb walls not only of kings but also of officials and subordinates. The ramifications of this were remarkable. Now, anyone who rated a tomb with a coffin had the potential to arise in the afterlife.

The content of the Coffin Texts was still heavily influenced by the earlier Pyramid Texts. New additions were included, however, such as writings pertaining to a reunion with one's family in the afterlife. Also appearing for the first time in the Coffin Texts was Apophis, the serpentine enemy of Re[5] who had to be defeated each night if the sun was to rise again.[6]

✧ **The Book of the Dead.** The period of the Coffin Texts was relatively short, lasting only about four and a half centuries. By the dawn of the New Kingdom in 1540 B.C.E., most funerary texts weren't written on the tomb or coffin itself; rather they were written on papyrus in various texts collectively called The Book of the Dead. This was then placed inside the coffin with the deceased. Like the Pyramid and Coffin Texts, The Book of the Dead focused on provisioning and protecting the deceased as he made his way through the perils and challenges of the underworld.

[4]Erik Hornung, *The Ancient Egyptian Books of the Afterlife*, trans. David Lorton (Ithaca: Cornell University Press, 1999), pp. 1–6.

[5]Re appears frequently in this chapter. He is a solar Deity and was probably the most important Creator God in ancient Egypt. He travels in His solar bark (boat) across the sky during the day and through the underworld during the night. In my practice, I see Him in four aspects: Re-Harakhti (Re of the Horizon) from dawn to noon, Re from noon to dusk, and Re-Atum (the undifferentiated one) in the evening. The fourth aspect is not covered in this chapter.

[6]Hornung, *Ancient Egyptian Books*, pp. 7–12.

Central to The Book of the Dead was the final judgment of the deceased's heart or soul. Many spells and amulets were enclosed with the body to assure that, when the time of judgment came, the deceased would be found worthy of a place in the House of Osiris.

Apparently, reuniting with one's family was of less concern by this period, as spells of this nature declined sharply in number. A new feature was the inclusion of vignettes or illustrations. At first, the vignettes served to illustrate only a few spells. In time, however, they became very common and even supplanted text in some cases. It is noteworthy that, although the vignettes were brightly painted from their beginning through the late period (ending ca. 332 B.C.E.), the Greeks of the Ptolemaic period and the Romans who followed them used no color at all (the reason for this isn't clear).

The Book of the Dead remained in use in one form or another through the Roman period of Egyptian history (ca. 30 B.C.E.–642 C.E.).[7]

☙ **Narrative stories.** Most of these stories appear in papyrus scrolls dating, usually, from later periods. Some stories are composed of bits and pieces collected from a number of different papyri. Often a story is missing its beginning or ending, or other parts that must be reconstructed. Stories that have survived completely intact are very unusual.

Ironically, the most complete tales that have come down to us from ancient Egypt were not told by the Egyptians. Instead, they were told by people from other cultures who visited Egypt starting in about the fourth century B.C.E. In many cases, the stories were culled from a number of texts set down by people many centuries earlier, with no apparent regard for consistency. The myth of Isis and Osiris is an

[7]Ibid., pp. 13—22.

example. The ancient Egyptians may have been less concerned with telling a cohesive story than with illustrating
important principles (such as the rule of kings, royal succession, proper social conduct, and so forth).

With all of this in mind, let's begin by looking at the mythology
that defines the sort of energy Anubis represents. There are two
tales that describe His character and tell us the most about Him:
the Tale of the Two Brothers and the myth of Isis and Osiris. I will
not attempt to tell them in detail here, but I will give enough
information to show how I have drawn my conclusions. I encourage you to read other versions and make your own decisions.

I want to warn you about one thing. As I said earlier, the
ancient Egyptian worldview often results in seemingly contradictory information about the Gods. You may find these stories con-
fusing or contradictory in some senses, but don't waste energy
trying to reconcile them. Take the information they contain and
make good use of it.

The Tale of the Two Brothers will require you to make some
choices. The version I present here is based primarily on a translation by Edward F. Wente Jr. but is written in my own words. I
hope this will provide a bit more narrative flow than a direct translation of the papyrus would allow.[8]

The original myth upon which this story is based was tradi-
tional in only one area of Egypt. More than one version of the
Two Brothers has weathered the centuries. Miriam Lichtheim cites
Papyrus D'Orbiney (currently in the collection of the British
Museum) as the source for her translation. Both she and Wente
also mention a late-period version in Papyrus Jumilhac that puts

---

[8]W. K. Simpson, ed., *The Literature of Ancient Egypt* (New Haven and London: Yale University Press, 1973), p. 92. The editor makes the comment that this story is written in the ver-
nacular of the time, seeming to indicate that, by the time it was written down, it was the
property of the common people and not primarily used for religious instruction. This may
make identification of the protagonists with their respective Deities problematic, but at the
same time it indicates that knowledge of the Gods was not, in fact, the sole purview of the
priests and scribes.

an entirely different spin on the nature of the brothers.[9] Virtually all of the primary research on the source papyri is written in either French or German, neither of which I read. All the sources I consulted seem to agree that the protagonists do represent their namesakes, even though that conclusion is not drawn from the story itself.

I have chosen, as have others, to identify the Anubis of the story with Anubis the God. I have also chosen to see the Tale of the Two Brothers as instructive not so much in the nature of Deity, but in the Deity of Nature. To explain, I interpret the actions and behaviors of the Gods in this story as being reflections of human nature. Like the Norse Gods, the Gods of the ancient Egyptian pantheon are born, have lives, and die. Like the Greek Gods, They have great sexual prowess. Like humans, They can be very benevolent or very cruel (more often than not with each other). Their behaviors also have consequences that serve to teach valuable lessons. In short, They are models of humanity in all its beauty and ugliness. We see ourselves in Them and may more easily learn to walk with Them. Through stories like this, we are able to see into ourselves and comprehend our essential divinity.

〜

THE TALE OF THE TWO BROTHERS

There once lived two brothers. The elder, Anubis, possessed a house and had a wife. The younger, Bata, lived with them. Although the brothers shared the same mother and father, Anubis raised Bata as his own son and provided for him. Anubis's wife was as a mother to Bata as well. Bata would labor in the fields for Anubis, bringing crops home to his house at day's end. He would also tend Anubis's cattle, taking them out to pasture at dawn and

---

[9]Miriam Lichtheim, *Ancient Egyptian Literature*, vol. 2 of *The New Kingdom* (Los Angeles: University of California Press, 1976), p. 203. See also Simpson, *Literature of Ancient Egypt*. P. Jumilhac identifies Bata with Seth and features Anubis as the hero in its version.

leading them back to the stables in the evening. Bata had a talent for speaking to the cattle. Each day they would tell Bata where the best grazing could be found, and Bata would take them there. Because of Bata's ability to understand them, Anubis's cattle were the healthiest and largest in the entire land. Bata was in every respect a perfect man, for he had the strength of a God within him.

One day, Anubis and Bata loaded their cart with seed and set out to plow and sow the fields with grain. Several days later, the seed was running low, so Anubis sent Bata back to the house to fetch more. When Bata arrived at the house, he found Anubis's wife plaiting her hair. Bata said, "Rouse yourself and fetch more seed for me as my brother is waiting for me." She replied, "Go to the storeroom and get what you need. Do not interrupt me while I am braiding my hair." Bata went to the storeroom and picked up five sacks of seed. When he returned to the house, Anubis's wife looked upon him carrying the great weight and suddenly desired to know him as a man. "Why don't you leave off and stay with me for one hour. We could lie together, and in return, I will make you fine clothing." Bata was angered by the suggestion and told her never to speak of it again. "How can you mention such things when you have been as a mother to me and my elder brother has been as a father? I will say nothing of this to anyone, but you must never speak to me like this again." Anubis's wife became fearful at Bata's anger, so she tore her garments and painted unguents on her skin to look like bruises. Then she swallowed a potion that made her vomit.

As was his custom, Anubis left the fields and went home before Bata while Bata stayed behind to drive the cattle back to the stable in the village. When Anubis arrived home, his house was dark and his wife did not greet him and wash his hands as she usually did. Instead, he found her in a terrible state and asked her what had happened. "Your brother, Bata, came to fetch seed, but while he was here, he bade me lie and take pleasures with him. I told him that we have been as mother and father to him and that he should never mention such a thing to me again. He became angry and beat me to prevent me from saying anything. You must avenge this wrong done to me, for I will take my life if you do not kill your brother." Enraged, Anubis sharpened his spear and hid behind the stable door waiting to kill Bata.

Bata was driving the cattle home from pasture when the lead cow said, "Beware, Bata. Your brother is behind the door to the stable waiting to kill you." Bata did not believe this until the second cow to pass through the door repeated the warning. Then Bata looked under the stable door and saw Anubis's feet. Bata realized the cows were telling the truth and fled with Anubis right behind him. As he fled, Bata called to Re asking that He intervene and judge the conflict. Re heard this prayer and placed a river full of crocodiles between the two brothers so that Anubis could not reach Bata. Frustrated at his failure to kill his younger brother, Anubis struck and wounded his own hand twice.

Bata then called to Anubis, "Wait until the dawn and Re-Harakhti will judge both of us. Then the guilty will be given to the just, for I must part with you and never again be in your presence."

On the dawn of the next day, the two brothers stood in the presence of Re-Harakhti and Bata said, "Why did you come after me in order to kill me unjustly? Why did you not ask me what had happened? Are you not a father to me? Is your wife not a mother to me? Am I not your younger brother? When I went to fetch the seed, it was your wife who asked me to take pleasures with her and I who refused." Bata told the whole story to Anubis and swore an oath to its truth before Re-Harakhti. Then he took a reed knife and cut off his phallus, throwing it into the water where it was devoured by a catfish. "You came after me with a spear to kill me all on the word of a filthy liar," he said. Bata became weak from loss of blood, and Anubis was overcome with remorse for he could not reach across the water to help his brother.

Bata then told Anubis, "I will go to the Valley of the Pine. There I will take out my heart and place it in a flower at the top of the pine tree. My only request of you is to care for me should something happen when I remove my heart. If the tree is cut down, you must come and search for it, and even if that search takes you seven years, do not be discouraged. When you find my heart, place it in a bowl of cool water and I shall come to life again and avenge the wrong done to me. You will know if anything has befallen me when a jug of beer in your hand begins to froth. Set out on that instant to find me." With these words, Bata turned and left for the Valley of the Pine.

In his grief, Anubis smeared dirt on his body and went home with his hands on his head. Once home, he killed his wife, throwing her body to the dogs. Then he sat and wept for all that he had lost.

Bata arrived in the Valley of the Pine and, true to his word, removed his heart from his body and placed it in a flower at the top of the tree. Then he set about rebuilding his life. He built a large house and hunted game everyday. Soon, he was living as happily as he could, but he was alone. One day, the Ennead[10] paid a visit to Bata and told him that Anubis now understood the truth and had avenged the wrong done to his younger brother. They also decided that Bata should have a companion, as this was the only thing he lacked. They called upon the God Khnum to craft a woman on His potter's wheel. When He had done this, the Seven Hathors came and, because they were the arbiters of fate, declared that this woman would die by the knife.

Bata lived happily with his wife, but he warned her never to leave the house. "If you go out from here, the sea will try to capture you. I will not be able to help you because I am now a woman like you, and I have no heart in me."[11] He then shared his deepest thoughts with her. Then, despite all his warnings, Bata's wife became bored and ventured out one day while he was hunting. As Bata had foretold, the sea rose to claim her. She did try to run for home, but the sea called to the pine tree asking it to hold her fast. The tree was able only to grasp a small lock of hair, however, and Bata's wife escaped. The sea took the lock of sweet-smelling hair and carried it to a place where laundrymen were washing Pharaoh's clothing. The perfume in the hair scented the garments. When Pharaoh put them on he summoned the servants who had washed them and quarreled with them about the mysterious scent. This

---

[10]An Ennead is a group of Gods and Goddesses. Anubis is descended from the Ennead of Heliopolis, which consists of Re, Shu, Tefnut, Geb, Nut, Osiris, Isis, Nephthys, and Seth.

[11]Both the Lichtheim and Wente translations have Bata referring to himself as female in obvious reference to his emasculation. It is interesting to note that the equation of maleness with the penis is very old, indeed.

went on every day until, vexed by the situation, the servants showed Pharaoh the lock of hair, which Pharaoh in turn showed to his scribes.

"Only a child of Re-Harakhti could have hair that smells so sweet," they declared. "This is a greeting from a far-off land. You must send out your men to search for that place!"

Pharaoh did as he was advised. Before long, his men returned from many foreign lands but they had nothing to report. Then, only one man returned from the Valley of the Pine; Bata had killed all the rest. Pharaoh sent soldiers and charioteers to the Valley of the Pine. With them he sent a woman with many jewels to convince Bata's wife to come to Egypt. Before long, Bata's wife arrived at Pharaoh's court. When Pharaoh saw her, he was taken with her beauty and made her his Queen. Pharaoh then spoke with her and caused her to speak of Bata and his secret. On her advice, Pharaoh's men cut down the pine tree and hacked it up. At that moment, the life went out of Bata's body.

At the same moment, Anubis was sitting down to a meal. When his beer was placed before him, it began to froth. When the beer was replaced by wine, the wine turned bad. Knowing that this was the sign that Bata had given him, and what it meant, Anubis immediately set out to find his brother.

Presently, Anubis found Bata's body lying lifeless on his bed. Anubis wept at the sight of his younger brother in death and then set out to find Bata's heart. For three years Anubis searched the place where the tree was felled, but he found nothing of Bata's heart. On the eve of the fourth year, Anubis longed to return to Egypt. I will search for one more day and then return to my home, he thought. On the next day, Anubis searched once again and found a pine cone. He returned home with the cone and Bata's body.

Once at home, Anubis dropped the pine cone into a bowl of water. Before long, the cone (which was actually Bata's heart) grew in size and Bata's body began to twitch. Soon, Bata turned his head and looked at Anubis. When Anubis saw this, he gave Bata the water to drink. In the process, Bata swallowed his heart and revived. The two brothers rejoiced at their reunion, but their joy was tempered by Bata's knowledge of his wife's actions.

"Tomorrow, I will turn myself into a splendid bull," he told Anubis. "You must ride me into the city and present me as a gift to Pharaoh. You will be rewarded for this with silver and gold. Then you must return to your home in the village."

At dawn of the next day, Bata transformed himself into a bull as he had said he would and Anubis rode the magnificent animal into the city. In all the land, nobody had ever seen such a wonder, and Pharaoh was indeed pleased with the gift as Bata said he would be. Anubis was given the bull's weight in gold and silver and, with servants and goods, returned to his village. Pharaoh made offerings to the bull and a great celebration took place throughout the land.

On the next day, the Queen, who had been Bata's wife, was in the kitchen of the palace when the bull entered and said to her, "Behold! I am still alive!" When she asked him who he was, he said, "I am Bata, and I know that you had Pharaoh's men cut down the pine tree on my account so that I would die. But as you see, I live as a bull." With that, he turned and left the kitchen.

Disturbed by this, the Queen caused Pharaoh to agree to do whatever she asked. He listened to all that she said and when he agreed, she said, "Sacrifice the bull and let me eat of its liver, for it will never amount to anything." Pharaoh was greatly troubled by this request, but he agreed. Offerings were made and the bull was sacrificed, but while Pharaoh's men were carrying it upon their shoulders, the bull shook its neck and caused two drops of blood to fall to the earth. One drop fell on each side of the doorway to the palace. In one night, a Persea tree grew where each drop of blood had fallen.

On the next dawn, Pharaoh was told of the great wonder that had occurred and he made an offering to the trees. Again, there was a celebration throughout the land. After a time, Pharaoh and his Queen went out of the palace to sit beneath the trees. As they sat beneath them, however, the Queen heard one of the trees call to her. It said, "Behold, I am Bata and still I live! I know that you had the bull sacrificed on my account, and I will see justice done." On hearing this, the Queen convinced Pharaoh to cut the trees down to make furniture for the palace. She came to watch as they were being cut down. As she watched, a splinter flew into her mouth and she swallowed it. In that moment, she became pregnant. She did not realize that it was Bata that she carried in her womb.

When the child was born, Pharaoh came to see his new son. He declared a day of celebration and held the child in his lap. Then Pharaoh named his son the Viceroy of Kush. A few days later, Pharaoh declared his son to be the Crown Prince of all Egypt. The child grew to manhood and eventually took the throne when Pharaoh died. One day, the king said, "Have my advisors come to me that I may give them a full accounting of all that has happened to me." He sent for his mother and, before his advisors, revealed that he was Bata. A consensus was reached that Bata's wife should be put to death for what she had done. The prophecy of the Seven Hathors had come to pass.

At long last, Bata sent for Anubis. Bata named his elder brother Crown Prince of all Egypt. With Anubis at his side, Bata ruled for thirty years. Anubis took the throne on the day that Bata died.

The myth of Isis and Osiris tells the story of Anubis's birth, or at least one version of it. He is seen as the son of Osiris here, but this is only one possibility (albeit my personal favorite). Egyptian texts list other fathers for Anubis. Those will be discussed later.

THE MYTH OF ISIS AND OSIRIS

In the very beginning, there was Nun, the great, primordial sea. Nun could not be thought of as darkness, for as yet light itself did not exist. Nothing had been called into being actually and Nun was but the endless potential waiting to emerge into form.

Within the heart of Nun, the great creator Re-Atum began to stir. He called out His deepest, most secret name and arose out of the sea. As He emerged, a vast hill formed beneath His feet. He was one with Nun and separate from Him as well.

The self-creation of Re-Atum brought order to the chaotic sea that was the universe, but the God stood alone within it. In His first act of creation, Re took His phallus into His own hand and embraced His shadow. When His seed poured forth, Re took it into His mouth where His two children were conceived.

The first child to be spat from Re's mouth was Shu, the God of air. After Him came Tefnut, the Goddess of mists. Re delighted in Their presence and wept with joy. His tears fell to the ground beneath His feet and became humankind. Re then busied Himself calling other Gods and Goddesses into being.

Shu and Tefnut soon had children of Their own. Geb was the God of the earth and Nut was the sky Goddess covered with stars. These two were born of Tefnut's womb and were locked in an embrace when They emerged. Soon, Their father Shu interceded and separated Them, but by this time Nut was pregnant. Nut's pregnancy infuriated Re because He considered Nut to be His own wife upon Her birth. Re placed a curse on Nut so that She could never give birth to Her children during the day or night.

Nut appealed to Thoth, a wise God that Re had created, and asked for His help. Thoth was a cunning sort, and had invented a game called draughts, which He played with the Moon. The wager between Them was that Thoth would gain one seventy-second of a day each time He won. The Moon was not very good at draughts, and soon Thoth had enough time to equal five whole days. Because this time was not day, it did not belong to Re. Because Thoth had won it in a wager, it did not belong to the Moon either. It now belonged to Thoth to do with as He pleased. We still experience this time during the nights of the New Moon when the sky is completely dark. Thoth gave His five days to Nut, who was then able to give birth to Her children.

The first child of Nut was Osiris. Being born first, He was destined for kingship. The second child was Isis. She was the sister-wife of Osiris (the relationship having been consummated in Nut's womb), wiser than all humankind, and knowledgeable in the ways of magic. The third child was also the second son, Seth. Unlike His two siblings before, Seth tore Himself free of His mother's womb and caused Her great pain. This was an unfortunate portent for the future. Seth was jealous of Osiris, and His jealousy would only increase as time passed. Finally, Nut gave birth to the second daughter, Nephthys. As with Isis and Osiris, Seth and Nephthys were married. Unlike the older couple, however, there was no love between Them.

Osiris journeyed far and wide, teaching agriculture to people and bringing them knowledge of art and government. He was fair in His dealings with everyone and was just in sorting out their differences. By the time Osiris arrived home in Egypt again, He was very popular and well loved. Isis was happy because She had dreamed that She would have a son one day who would take the throne after Osiris and rule Egypt in the same manner as His father.

Osiris's success had a different effect entirely on Nephthys. She longed to have a loving husband who was popular among the people. Seth, who ruled over the lifeless desert and all it represented, was more feared than loved. He was lightning and thunder, the burning sun of the desert under which no life can thrive. As a lover, He was forceful, caring only for His own pleasure without regard for His wife. All of this left Nephthys with a great longing to know the touch of a gentle and considerate man. She also wanted to bask in the light of Osiris's popularity. When She could bear it no longer, She sought Osiris out.

Little did Nephthys realize just how receptive Osiris would be to Her suggestion. In one afternoon, They made love many times. Nephthys's joy and pleasure were mixed with sadness and dread. She knew She would probably not feel these sensations again. She feared Seth's reaction if He found out what She had done.

Nephthys conceived with Osiris. The child could not possibly be Seth's, for the ruler of destruction was unable to spark life in any womb. Her dread of Seth deepened. Although Nephthys did manage to keep Her pregnancy a secret from Her husband, when the child was born, She looked upon it with despair. He did have the body of a perfect human, but His head and face were those of a dog. Fate had been worse than cruel to Her. Nephthys carried the child into the desert and left Him there to die. She could never love Him as a mother should, so She was determined to be rid of Him.

Nephthys would struggle with Her fear and conscience for a long time, but Seth was so involved with His own plans that She needn't have worried. Seth's jealousy of Osiris had reached a terrible peak by this time. His attention was focused on a plot to murder the king. Seth had a cabinet constructed to the exact measurements of Osiris's body. When it was finished, Seth held a party for all of the Gods. He invited each God to lie down in the cabinet and see if it fit, declaring that the one who fit would possess it. Only when Osiris lay in the box was it seen to fit Him perfectly. In that same instant, Seth slammed the cover down and sealed it shut. His henchmen then carried the box with Osiris inside to the river Nile, where they dumped it. The box was carried off and drifted across the sea until it came to rest at Byblos (in modern-day Lebanon).

Isis's anguish over Her husband's death knew no bounds. Not only had She lost Her greatest love, She would never have a son by Him. It was then that She learned of Nephthys's attempt to destroy Her own child. Determined to raise a child of Her husband's seed, Isis took the infant's birth wrappings and gave them to Her hounds. It did not take long to find Him. Although He would serve as a constant reminder of Her husband's weakest moment, Isis took up the child. She named Him Anubis and took Him home to be raised as Her own son.

In the years that followed, Anubis could always be found at Isis's side. In time, She taught Him the magical and healing arts. She gave Him the ability to speak and understand human speech—a gift those with a canine mouth and ears are not likely to possess at birth.

When Isis set out to find the body of Osiris, Anubis accompanied Her. The search was long and arduous, but it was successful. On the return voyage, Isis used unguents made from scorpions to revivify Osiris. They made love one final time and Isis became pregnant with Horus. Knowing that Seth would try to destroy the body as well as any heir to Osiris, Isis hid in the marshes, where She concealed the body of Osiris and Her newborn son.

While hunting with His hounds one day, Seth chanced to discover Horus and the body of Osiris in the marsh where Isis had hidden them. He seized the body of His dead brother and hacked it into fourteen pieces, scattering them to the most distant parts of

Egypt. He also poisoned Horus, but Isis appealed to Re and Horus was cured.

Isis was devastated at the second loss of Osiris. Her lamentations were carried to the ears of the other Gods. It was not likely that They would help Her, though. Many feared Seth. Still others openly backed Him. Isis again set out to recover Her husband's body and Anubis again accompanied Her. The journey took some fourteen years, but in the end, every part of Osiris was found except for His phallus, which had been devoured by a fish.

Under the direction of Isis, and with the assistance of Nephthys and Horus (who by now had grown to manhood), Anubis assembled and embalmed the body of Osiris. This was the first embalming, and it established Anubis as the protector of the deceased from that time on. So skilled was His work that Osiris was resurrected in the underworld as Lord of the Dead.

Anubis served Osiris as Lord of the Necropolis (the place of embalming and internment) and Judge of the Soul. From the moment a deceased arrived in His realm, Anubis would assure breath for him and protect his body. Once in the halls of judgment, Anubis would weigh the heart of the deceased against the feather of Ma'at, the Goddess of Truth. If the heart balanced, Horus would lead the deceased into the company of Osiris, there to dwell in happiness for eternity.

This is one way the myth ends. In another myth, Horus goes on to avenge His father's death in an epic battle with Seth, but Anubis plays virtually no role in that version.

The misogyny in these two tales is unmistakable, although it is difficult to say how much of it was in the original Egyptian texts or how much was brought about because of later cultural influence. Women are certainly not the only troublemakers in Egyptian mythology, as Seth's persecution of Isis attests. There are other examples of male troublemakers, such as the story of Truth and Falsehood—another tale of conflict between two brothers. The schools of thought hailing from Greece and Rome were focused on rationality and carried their own cultural bias. This, no doubt, influenced their retelling of the Egyptian stories.[12]

The Pyramid Texts mention Anubis as a cosmic God in His own right, although there are many inconsistencies with regard to His parentage and specific attributes. I have found no references to Anubis as a self-created Deity. In his book *A Dictionary of Egyptian Gods and Goddesses*, George Hart, a scholar of Egyptian art and architecture and a staff lecturer at the British Museum, notes that, depending on the text, Anubis is seen as the son of Re, Osiris, or Seth. Interestingly, His mother is said to be Nephthys in each of these cases. These seeming contradictions did not bother the ancient Egyptians, but by the time of the Coffin Texts Anubis appears to have been more fully absorbed into the myth—and family—of Osiris.[13]

That does not mean that He has to stay there. If we avoid the trap of rational thought and its desperate need to categorize everything logically, we are free to see Anubis as the son of all three parental combinations. Instantly, His range of possible attributes broadens and deepens. So much the better for us. After all, each of us is capable of carrying the attributes of many different Gods in our personalities. The most successful of us will merge them into a cohesive personality over which we exert control. When we focus on a particular aspect of our own psyche that can be personified as a God or Goddess, we can be thought of as a "child" or manifestation of that particular Deity.

In the same way, pondering different myths of Anubis's origins helps us understand different aspects of His character. These are some of my own reflections.

[12]Hornung, *Ancient Egyptian Books*, pp. 237–41. This is a fascinating discussion of the problem that logic and rationale create in a system of belief that is based in large part on dualistic thought. It is well worth studying.

[13]George Hart, *A Dictionary of Egyptian Gods and Goddesses* (1986; reprint, London: Routledge & Kegan Paul, 2000), p. 25. More specifically, Anubis was supplanted by Osiris as Lord of the Underworld.

ANUBIS AS THE SON OF RE

Because Re is seen as the primal creator Deity, this would seem to give Anubis a profoundly cosmic aspect. In a sense, that is true. However, even though His father is a creator, Anubis was not simply created by the breath and words of Re's mouth as were Thoth and Hathor. He is also the son of Nephthys. Thus the realm of Anubis remains a part of the life cycle and is essentially earthbound.

Initially, the Pyramid Texts mention Anubis as Lord of the Underworld. This would have placed Him in the seat that Osiris eventually came to occupy, where it would have been His function to reward or punish the deceased appearing before Him. Even with Osiris as Lord of the Underworld, however, Anubis remains the Judge of the Scales, weighing the heart of the dead against the feather of truth. His judgment is recorded by Thoth and is used to determine whether the soul should be resurrected in the afterlife or destroyed utterly.

These functions would seem most suited to a cosmic figure—one that could be all-seeing and all-knowing, a Deity that possessed the power to look deeply within and tell your story. Anubis certainly has those capabilities, so His aspect as a son of Re seems justified to me.

ANUBIS AS A SON OF OSIRIS

I confess to a preference for this aspect of Anubis. The rich symbolism in the tale of His birth allows a more complete understanding of His nature. In most literature, we find that Anubis is primarily the God of the necropolis, of all cemeteries, and of embalming. All of this is true, but in my mind Anubis is not so monolithic.

We discover in the myth of Isis and Osiris that Anubis learned a great deal more in life than embalming and protecting the dead. He also learned the arts of magic and medicine. Other Gods and

Goddesses have these skills as well, but each rules a different aspect. The Egyptians were careful to draw distinctions. For example, both Anubis and Seth have associations with death. Anubis, however, is the compassionate receiver of the deceased. Seth, on the other hand, is an uncompassionate taker of life, seen early in His career destroying the enemies of Re. Later on, He is reduced to the rank of a murderer.

Until 1970 when the Aswan High Dam was completed, Egyptians had to contend with the annual inundation that resulted when the Nile overflowed its banks. As troublesome as this was, the water would irrigate large areas of land and deposit black silt that was very fertile. This made farming possible in the Nile Valley.

In terms of symbolism, I see Seth as the hostile desert where life is precarious, Osiris as the Nile's fertilizing power, and Nephthys as the land between that would lie fallow in the dry season and erupt with life after an inundation. The silt deposited on the land was Anubis—the child of river and land. That is one reason why the canine animal representing Anubis has a black coat.[14]

The meaning of Anubis's name in Egyptian—a matter of some conjecture—may also reflect this aspect. In his book *Conceptions of God in Ancient Egypt, The One and the Many*, Erik Hornung defines the name *Anpu* as possibly meaning "puppy." He also notes that the Egyptians were very fond of wordplay in their sacred names. Apparently, one possible meaning for the name *Anpu* in the Ptolemaic period (305–30 B.C.E.) was "Wind-Water-Mountain."[15] Playing with this in my own mind produces the idea of Anubis as the child of the arid winds from the land of Nephthys and the fertile waters of the Nile (Osiris), and as He who stands on a high precipice watching over the necropolis, becoming *Tepy-*

---

[14]Hart mentions the association of the color black with fertility in the Egyptian mind because it is the color of the fertile silt. He does not, however, draw a direct line between the soil and Anubis. That is my connection. As with Osiris, any fertility with which Anubis was associated probably had more to do with resurrection in the afterlife.

[15]Hornung, *Conceptions of God*, p. 67.

Dju-Ef or "He who is upon His mountain" (one of the ancient titles for Anubis).[16]

So it isn't just about death and embalming. Anubis holds the key to renewed life and potential by virtue of this parentage.

ANUBIS AS THE SON OF SETH

Early in the Tale of the Two Brothers, Anubis's rash decision to turn on the brother He loves displays His heritage from Seth. He could be seen as trusting His wife's word, which might be noble if not for the fact that Anubis attempts to murder Bata. This is part of the nature of Seth: a base, animal instinct that takes action first and asks questions later, if at all.

Often we find that we have done wrong. It is almost a truism that most harmful magic is accidental and intended for the best reasons. For example, a spell intended to stop someone's self-destructive behavior could result in that person's total incapacitation. The behavior stops, but at a terrible cost. As aware as we believe ourselves to be, taking the correct action in any situation requires thought, patience, and care. We get into trouble when we act in haste or anger, out of passion, or in response to base instinct. Any action that presents itself as the easiest, most practical or obvious solution to a problem should send up a red flag.

Seth energy responds quickly to those heated moments and does not consider the consequences. The story of Anubis and Bata shows what happens when we give in to that energy. It also shows the transformation of a man undone by base instinct, although the transformation is by no means clean. Standing at the river of crocodiles, Anubis is tormented by the result of His actions, but that does not stop Him from going home and killing His wife.

Later in the story, Anubis displays a change when He revives His brother's dead body by restoring His heart. Here, He takes on

[16]Hart, *Dictionary*, p. 23.

His aspect as the son of Osiris bringing life where there was none. Later in the story, Anubis takes the throne of Egypt after His brother's death. In this aspect, He appears as a son of Re. Purged of the last vestiges of Seth's influence, Anubis achieves Godhead.

Because the influence of His cult changed over time, Seth's devolution from a protector of Re to a God of chaos probably had more to do with human politics than anything divine. It is interesting, however, that He never disappeared from the pantheon. The forces Seth represents are a part of the human experience regardless of how we feel about it. He is anger, rage, intensity (in all its flavors), drive, determination, ferocity, passion (if not fecundity), and the will to survive. He is an aspect of ourselves with which we must all make peace lest it consume us. Seth's realm is human just as Anubis was the human brother.

As the son of Seth, Anubis symbolizes the internal struggle we face as we try to respond to a world in almost constant turmoil. Every time we must decide on a course of action, we must remain aware that Seth is always there, ready with a fast answer that will easily achieve our goals. He will not, however, tell us the price we may pay—not because He is trying to mislead us purposefully, but because He doesn't care.

In ritual and magical work, then, Anubis is the perfect vector for approaching Seth energy. In this aspect, Anubis does not *manifest* Seth energy, he *understands* it. As the son of Seth, Anubis can help us deal with emotions such as anger and rage. In His aspect as Observer of the Balance (described later), the son of Seth can help us channel strong emotions into constructive action as an alternative to unthinking reaction.

ANUBIS AS THE SON OF NEPHTHYS

Nephthys is enigmatic as a mythological character. According to Hart, Her name means "Lady of the Mansion." She has funerary functions and is said to weep for the king after his death (the king being identified with Her brother Osiris in the afterlife). References in Egyptian texts are not very helpful, though they do indicate that Nephthys may have held a prominent position early on.[17]

So we are left to decide for ourselves what qualities personify Nephthys. Because Nephthys may be seen as that land between the fertile Nile and the arid desert, the place of ebb and flow, She speaks to change and flux. It is an intersection not only of natural forces, but of thoughts and ideas. When a decision or choice must be made, we are confronted by Nephthys.

In Her funerary aspect, Nephthys is identified with the bandages used in mummification. Although these wrappings are an essential part of the process, the deceased must free themselves from the wrappings after death.[18] Anything that is necessary but that has the potential to become an impediment is also the realm of Nephthys. Remember, She not only gave birth to Anubis, She also tried to destroy Him.

As with *heka*, there is nothing inherently good or evil in the nature of Nephthys. She represents the choices that we must make in life. What we do when confronted with a choice is up to us, and we must accept the consequences of our actions.

With Nephthys as His mother, Anubis arises as the nexus between Her power and the powers of His respective fathers. Remember that Anubis is the child of a sexual union. According to Egyptian belief, any substance emanating from the body of a God contained the essence and power of that God. Those would accrue to His offspring or to whoever subsequently possessed that bodily substance.[19] It makes sense to apply this same principle to the mother with whom the child shares the most intimate of connections. Anubis possesses the powers of His fathers. As the child of Nephthys, He represents the choice we make when we exercise those powers.

[17]Ibid., p. 136.
[18]Ibid.
[19]Ritner, *Mechanics of Ancient Egyptian Magical Practices*, p. 78.

ANUBIS AS THE SON OF ISIS

Few Goddesses in Egyptian mythology possessed a power equal to or greater than that of Isis. Examples of such Goddesses include Tefnut, Hathor, Sakhmet (an aspect of Hathor, actually), and Ma'at. They were directly created by Re and were powerful because His essence was within Them.

In contrast, Isis, great-granddaughter of Re, obtained His essence and power by poisoning Him in a successful attempt to obtain His secret name. Because Re is the highest and most cosmic of the creator Gods, knowing this name would cause all of His power and knowledge to accrue to Isis. Only when Re concedes defeat and tells Isis His true name does She neutralize the poison and spare His life. Instead of looking at this through modern eyes, we should consider that Her son's place on the throne of Egypt would be more secure if She could pass the secret name of Re to Him.

I have said that the rescue of Anubis by Isis in the desert was motivated by compassion. There is ample evidence that Isis was a doting and fiercely protective mother. Indeed, She was regarded as the symbolic mother of the king. Her love for Osiris certainly knew no bounds, and Her love for Her people may have been just as strong.

At the same time, Isis displays a cool practical nature in Her decision making. She may have been a loving wife and caring mother; She was also politically astute. Her rescue of Anubis not only assured His survival, but did the same for Her by providing Her with an heir to Osiris.

Anubis's illegitimate birth certainly left Him little in the realm of kingship. How many tales exist detailing the evil deeds of the bastard son (for example, Edmund in Shakespeare's *King Lear*)? These usually focus on the desire of the unrecognized son to usurp the father's position at the expense of the legitimate heir. That doesn't happen in these myths. Horus is heir to the throne of Egypt, yet Anubis makes no play for His position. He makes no claim of His own. At the same time, Isis (unlike Hera of Greek mythology) sees the inherent value in the progeny from Her husband's dalliance and raises Him as Her own.

Just as Anubis remained a symbol to Isis of Osiris's infidelity, so too can He be a symbol to each of us of our own imperfection and humanity (as in the Tale of the Two Brothers). This reminder can instill a spirit of compassion and tolerance for one another. He becomes that divine spark of inspiration that drives our need and desire to care for others. At the heart of it all, we are connected to each other and our world in very profound ways. An awakening to those connections leads to an important realization: the most vital task we have before us is ministering to others.

As the adopted Son of Isis, Anubis has the power to strengthen us to our caring nature. His rescue is our inspiration for the correct treatment of our world and its people. We don't need the power of the Gods to serve. We need only the conviction of our hearts. His knowledge of healing, exemplified in His rescue, is the inner, spiritual drive that sets us on the course of caring and service. It gives us purpose.

ICONOGRAPHY

Because the ancient Egyptians made no attempt to create a single symbol to represent a God or Goddess, Thoth was seen as an ibis, a baboon, the moon, a human, or any combination of these. Hathor could be seen as a human, a cow, a wildcat, and more. Isis also had a wide variety of forms including bird, scorpion, snake, human, and even as other Goddesses.[20]

With all of this confusion, it is interesting that Anubis appears to be one of a very small handful of Deities whose iconographic representations are relatively static. He is shown either as a dog

[20]Hornung, *Conceptions of God*, pp. 125–26.

(usually in a crouching position) or a human with the head of a dog. Nobody will ever really know how this particular form arose, although theories abound. One of the most common is that people observed desert jackals marauding the graves of the recently buried and chose a jackal Deity as a figure of propitiation to prevent disturbance of the deceased.[21] Whatever its origins, the form of Anubis remained stable throughout its history possibly because of the limited number of (primarily funerary) functions He represented (embalmer, Protector and Judge of Souls, Lord of the Necropolis, and so forth).

As I noted in the dream story that began this chapter, any attempt on my part to see Anubis results in a disruption of the dream. If the dream does not actually end, I find myself, within the dream, staring at a statue or a work of art representing the God based entirely on my own perceptions. Those perceptions, however, are the key to understanding the very symbolism I see. The desert jackal is not a resident of my home state of Maine (although coyotes certainly are), and neither are the other canine species that may or may not make up the image commonly associated with Anubis. No single animal can be said to represent Him, as He has the tail of a desert jackal, the body of a greyhound, and very tall, pointed ears that fit no animal.

This may not bear any relevance to someone living in twenty-first-century America, however, so the question of what Anubis represents to *me* needs to be addressed. Certainly, Anubis's functions in the afterlife—as a guide, and protector of the soul—remain elemental to me, although the funerary customs of my culture (and the degree to which I believe in a judgment in the afterlife) are different from those of an ancient Egyptian. Below are some of the additional aspects of Anubis's character that I have gleaned from the stories related in this chapter, and after many years of personal work with His energy.

[21] Hart, *Dictionary*, p. 22. This would support Anubis as a very ancient Deity indeed.

Manifestations

Lord of Between Places. As the son of Nephthys and Osiris, Anubis represents the potential in all things. He is the death and decay—also represented in the black color of His fur—that must occur in order for new growth to emerge. Anubis would receive the deceased in a place between this world and the next. As a practicing Wiccan, I regard my circle space as occupying just such a realm—a place between the worlds and touching all worlds. From that vantage, the ability to reach out in any and all directions is limitless.

As Lord of Between Places, Anubis's most powerful times are noon, dusk, midnight, and dawn. The time of the new moon is also best for work calling upon this aspect: this is a good time for divination and searching out possibilities. In this aspect, Anubis's ears represent all that is heard and understood. They remind us that no issue is one-sided, and that nothing exists without duality to define it.

Protector of Travelers. Anubis is responsible for protecting and defending the soul as it travels through the underworld on its way to the House of Osiris. Just as He is able to protect souls on their final journey, so may He extend that protection to people traveling in this world. Travel need not be actual physical movement. We travel in figurative terms when we contemplate a change of heart or mind—especially on issues dear to us. As we move from one place to another, or from one way of thinking to another, the stress of change may be eased by contemplating His protection. It may not (in fact, it will not) make the process easier, but it will strengthen the traveler and that is the most important thing.

Patron of the Oppressed and of Lost Causes. Because of Her fear of Seth, Nephthys attempted to destroy Anubis before His birth could be discovered. Nothing is as helpless as a newborn infant, and the odds of surviving such treatment are slim, yet Anubis survived.

Isis was a childless widow at that time. Anubis was the son of Her beloved Osiris, albeit by a different mother. Her compassionate rescue of the foundling fulfilled a great need for Her. Of course, Isis was subsequently able to conceive Horus with Osiris through the use of Her magic, thus supplanting Anubis as the heir to the throne. Yet Anubis did not turn on Horus.

Rather than attempt to find a reason for this lack of animosity, I see it as an inspiration for people to choose the peaceful course of action. Anubis chose rash action against Bata, and apparently never forgot the pain that choice caused. We live in a world rife with oppression and injustice. Many people facing these troubles have done so with courage and determination, choosing the peaceful and diplomatic (if agonizingly slow) road to change. Others have chosen a path that might seem faster, but which often results in suffering, violence, and terror. By His example, Anubis clearly points the way to the peaceful path as a conscious choice. Here the canine symbolism again asserts itself—there are few animals willing to love as unconditionally as a dog.

Observer of the Balance. Anubis determines the deceased's worthiness for life in the realm of the blessed. The idea of a final judgment does not resonate with me. I do not hold with the idea of a system of rewards and punishments in the afterlife. A healthy religion teaches that we should choose the right course of action because it is the right choice to make in the here and now, not because of any perceived rewards that accrue to us later.

Still, balance has always been a cornerstone of my training, and there is more than enough room for a Deity who is able to tell us how the cosmic balance is tipping. Careful thought and consideration (even debate) are crucial before most magical workings, and divination is often a good idea as well.

In the last twenty years, I have seen and read more spells than I can count intending to bring justice or a favorable result to any situation. There are spells to win in court, to prevail over an enemy, to end a quarrel, and so on. Humans, however, are not usually equipped with eyes to see the whole picture and tend to focus on their own, highly subjective impressions. A spell for justice may bring the painful realization that the one doing the working is, in fact, in the wrong! Before such workings are undertaken, therefore, ritual intended to divine the state of the cosmic balance is in order. An example of such a ritual will be found later in this chapter.

Lord of the Necropolis and of Embalming. This was one of the ancient Egyptian titles for Anubis.[22] In this role, Anubis watched over the necropolis (the "city of the dead" usually located on the west bank of the Nile) and those within. Death remains a part of the life cycle, and the role of Anubis in that process is as relevant today as it was at the dawn of civilization. Not only does He watch over the deceased, He is also the patron of those who attend to the dead.

Up until recently, Pagan literature had little to say on the subject of funeral and memorial ritual even though it is an essential part of any spiritual life.[23] Such ritual primarily benefits the bereaved by providing a space for saying farewell. Egyptian funerary rites, however, were intended to preserve a place for the deceased not only in the afterlife, but on this plane of existence as well. The Egyptians believed that actions taken in this life would have a direct correlation to the next. Therefore, anything done to the body of the deceased (for example, preservation through mummification) is how his body would be in the afterlife.[24]

[22]Ibid, p. 23, *Neb-Ta-Djeser*, or "Lord of the Sacred Lands," indicating the desert to the west of the Nile where the necropoleis were usually to be found.

[23]Thankfully, as we mature as a religion, this is changing. See Starhawk and M. Macha NightMare, eds., *The Pagan Book of Living and Dying* (San Francisco: HarperSanFrancisco, 1997), JH.

[24]Hornung, *Ancient Egyptian Books*, p. 6 regarding the opening of the mouth. Also see Ritner, *Mechanics of Ancient Egyptian Magical Practice*, ch. 4 regarding execration texts and rituals used to curse and defeat enemies. Images of the enemy were often buried upside down with the belief that they would suffer the same fate after death. As with magic practiced today, the nature of Egyptian *heka* was bivalent—able to bless or cures equally.

As the one primarily responsible for embalming, Anubis assures preservation and memory not only of the deceased but of that person's life, works, and gifts. Many modern Neo-pagans feel that it is important to let go of the departed, thus allowing them to move on. This is a different paradigm from the Egyptian, which placed so much importance on having a place in this world and the next for the *ba* (soul) of the departed to reside.

A good modern adaptation of this idea might be to create a vessel for holding our memories of a loved one. Such a vessel could contain something that once belonged to that person as well as small token gifts from us. An appeal to Anubis for protection of the memories would be spoken in a ritual to seal the container, which could be kept in the home. This adaptation of the canopic jar (the jars used for storing the organs of the deceased during mummification) is not intended as a means to hold the spirit of the departed in our world. Rather, it is a way of keeping the memory of that person alive in our hearts until we pass ourselves.

Patron of those who serve. Anubis also learned the arts of magic and medicine from Isis. These capabilities, like all of His other attributes, were generally used in service to others. From His assistance to Isis in searching for Osiris to His assistance in restoring Bata to life (recovering Bata's heart for Him) to His protection of the deceased, Anubis clearly concerns Himself with the needs of others. In the acknowledgment section of his book *Gods and Myths of Ancient Egypt*, Robert Armour notes that Anubis is the "watchdog of all those who serve others."[25] I agree.

Anubis knew desertion, fear, anger, compassion, and love. All of these went to form His character and His courses of action. They made Him into a Deity that I have experienced as compassionate, patient, sardonic, and at times darkly humorous. He is an intellectual wit who, while expecting me to keep up, is very forgiving when I do the human thing and trip up instead.

[25]Robert A. Armour, *Gods and Myths of Ancient Egypt*, 10th ed. (Cairo: American University in Cairo Press, 1999), p. 5.

For easier reference, I have to put all that I've discussed into a table format along with some correspondences. You might find these useful in creating rituals and exercises for working with Anubis. For example, let's suppose you want to do a ritual to protect yourself while traveling. Find the aspect you need (Protector of Travelers) in the first column. The second column tells you that this aspect rules the body and the life cycle among other things. In the third column you will find information regarding what time of day is best to perform the ritual (sunset in this example), what color to use (black), and what incense to burn (sandalwood). Some of the rituals in this chapter require that you insert the aspect of Anubis that you are seeking. This table is one place to find them. Remember, these are suggestions. A little research and experimentation on your part may yield different ideas.

ATTUNEMENT

I believe that a God's energy will most often seek out people whose life experiences will make them able to understand and comprehend that energy. I have known fear, isolation, pain, and anger. As well, I have known great love, joy, acceptance, and community. I also have the blessing of a wonderful family. Beginning in my college years, I devoted most of my time in service to others, and I currently work in that capacity as a paramedic. A job like that requires no small amount of compassion. If you have ever had to jump out of a warm bed at two o'clock in the morning to care for someone complaining of sore hair for the third time in one week, you know what a challenge it can be to reach in deeply to understand what that person's real needs are and then minister to them. At times like that, Anubis can provide just the right energy to keep my mind focused on the real issues.

Different people have different life experiences and nobody will ever truly understand how a relationship with a particular Deity

Aspect/Manifestation	Rules	Correspondences
Son of Re and Nephthys • Observer of the Balance	Order Philosophy Intellect	*Time:* Morning *Color:* Gold *Element:* Water *Life aspect:* Creativity *Magical aspect:* Divination *Direction:* East *Moon phase:* New *Incense:* Frankincense

Son of Osiris and Nephthys
• Protector of
  Travelers
• Lord of Between
  Places
• Patron of the
  Oppressed
  and of Lost Causes
• Lord of the
  Necropolis and
  Embalming
	Body
	Life cycle
	Memory
	Love
	Abstraction
	  and the mind
	Thought
	Potential
		Time: Sunset
		Color: Black
		Element: Earth
		Life aspect: Birth,death
		Magical aspect: Protection
		Direction: West
		Moon phase: Waxing to full
		Incense: Sandalwood

Son of Seth and Nephthys	Animal instinct Anger Action Survival Storms	*Time:* Noon *Color:* Black, red *Element:* Fire *Life aspect:* Struggle *Magical aspect:* Banishing *Direction:* South *Moon phase:* Waning *Incense:* Dragon's blood
Son of Isis • Patron of Those Who Serve	Compassion Health Magic Wit Guile Leadership	*Time:* Night *Color:* Black, gold *Element:* Air *Life aspect:* Service *Magical aspect:* Healing *Direction:* North *Moon phase:* Full *Incense:* Sandalwood

develops or why it does. It does not, however, surprise me that Anubis found me even though I was looking elsewhere at the time.

Connecting and working with Anubis is a process that requires patience. Like other Egyptian Deities, He does not freely associate with humans on the mundane level.[26] In my experience, Anubis has manifested in three types of situations only: ritual designed for that purpose (such as the rituals in this work), deep trance, and dreams. In each case, I have not been able to look directly at Him, but still His presence is palpable. I may hear His voice or feel His presence in my heart. Often, images are all that appear in dreams or trance, and, although they are clear and long lasting, I am left to interpret the experience in my own, imperfect terms.

The single rule that seems to apply in every case is that the more effort I put into the experience, the better the contact will be. For instance, a simple request made at bedtime for a visit during sleep will always result in dreams full of rapid-fire images that stick with me for many months. On the other hand, rituals preceded by preparations such as fasting (even for just a few hours), careful planning, and contemplation will result in a powerful experience.

Even in different worldviews, everything and everyone in creation can be seen as either a work of divinity or a manifestation of it. Some might say we are both. The common thread in these viewpoints is a deep, unbreakable connection to the Gods that can inform our thoughts and actions as we go about our daily lives. This somewhat "general" connection is different from a personal encounter with a particular Deity for a specific purpose. In the latter case, there may be rules to follow and observances to be honored.

The simplest of these observances is to repeat the phrase, "Anubis, guide my thoughts and actions." Speak quietly and direct the thought within. In time, it will build up energy, as will any prayer spoken over and over.

[26]See Hornung, *Conceptions of God*, p. 128. This had always been my own personal experience of Anubis. It was validating to find that the ancient Egyptians had the same experience.

Rituals for protection are more involved procedures, but once such work has been done, reinforcing it is a small matter that you can do frequently. Brief prayers to "remind" the Gods of your objective will strengthen the actions you undertook in the first place. Here is an example of a prayer to charge a protective spell after it has been worked:

> *I call upon Anubis,*
> *He who is upon His mountain,*
> *He who extends His hands and protects,*
> *He who has the magic of Re within Him,*
> *And is cloaked in the colors of night.*
> *Give the breath of your mouth to this work,*
> *Confirm and strengthen it.*
> *May day and night pass without mischief,*
> *And may the light return.*

This same sort of formula is applicable to any aspect of life or to any form of ritual work. I advise using not only the proper name but also the titles, which identify the specific aspect to which you are appealing. This focus and clarity adds strength to your work.

As I have described, dreams are fertile ground for interaction with Anubis. He has shown a predilection for them over the years. A polite request at bedtime is all that is needed, and Anubis will visit while you sleep. With time, this practice will bring about dreams containing images relevant to Anubis that will remain with you. Record your dreams in a journal.

The power of dream work cannot be overstated. The realm of dreams is a liminal space where the power of the mind can create a reality that transcends our own physical world. In that place, the Gods can talk to us and we can learn from Them.

Trance is another means of access to that liminal space of consciousness. Trance is not difficult, but it does take some practice to learn how to change consciousness and then be able to observe and remember what happens. Here's a trance journey to make contact with Anubis.

Use any form of trance induction you wish (there are many good trance inductions available on tape or CD). Record the following on a tape and play it while you enter trance.

THE VISIT TO THE NECROPOLIS

Feel the surface beneath you melting away. You remain suspended. You are weightless, floating. You are adrift on the Celestial Sea that is Nun. There is no light or dark here. Nun is neither warm nor cold. Nun simply is, and you are supported by the endless, boundless nonexistence that is Nun. Take time to float here. This is the place from which all arose. It is pure potential without form. From here, anything is possible.

We are at the beginning. Remember to breathe.

(Pause here for a few minutes.)

Now, the Celestial Sea that is Nun begins to recede. As it does, you find yourself lying upon solid ground. It is comfortable and warm. You are lying in the sand of a desert oasis. A gentle breeze passes over your body. It is lightly scented with flowers. Take a moment to smell the breeze. The sun is shining, but it is not too hot for you. Remain relaxed, and take the time to feel the sensations of the warm desert: the sand, the sun, the breeze, the gentle scent of flowers.

(Pause briefly.)

Arise and look to your right. Before you is a small pool fed by a spring. The pool has water lilies floating in it. The water is crystal clear and cool to the touch. Dip your hand into the pool and gently splash some cool water on your face. Take a moment to notice how this feels.

Now look again into the pool. The water is rippling where you dipped your hand. Within the concentric circles of the ripple, you see the image of a man. He is tall and muscular. He wears a white-and-gold linen kilt about His waist and carries a staff in His left hand. In His right hand, He holds an ankh. Most stunning of all, He has the head of a desert dog. It is jet black with eyes that are deep and soulful. This is the image of Anubis. You cannot tell if He smiles at you or not, but He is not threatening to you. Take time to observe Him.

(Pause briefly.)

Now, Anubis points to your left. You turn to face your left and see the Necropolis in the west. The City of the Dead is bordered by a high wall with a large gate. The gate is open, and you see torch light inside. It is not far away. Move in that direction until you reach the gate.

(Pause briefly.)

Now you stand at the gate to the Necropolis. Before you lies the City of the Dead. It is dark within, for the sun has now set, but the narrow pathways between the many buildings are well lit with torches. You step through the gates. Once you are inside, you are aware of a presence behind you. You turn and behold Anubis. He looks exactly as He did in the water pool, but now He seems real to you. He tells you that you are still seeing an image, for you cannot see His true form. He passes by you and bids you follow Him.

(Pause briefly.)

Anubis tells you that the Necropolis is not only a place on Earth, but also a place in our minds. It is this place to which you have come. It is a place of many secrets, even if it does belong to you alone.

Anubis leads you down a deserted path to a wall with a large door. With a tap of His staff, the door opens to reveal a small room with another open door beyond. This door is open as well, and leads to another room and another door. In fact, as far as you can see, there is a never-ending chain of rooms and open doors.

Breathe in, breathe out. Relax.

Anubis tells you that this is the Vault of the Past. In each room you will find a moment in your life, an event that left its mark upon you and changed you in some way. This may have been for better or for worse. In this place, it is all the same.

You step in and find the first room empty. You look and see that there is yet another chain of rooms and doors in each of the walls. Without doubt, the pathways through this vault are endless, and it would be easy to get lost here forever.

The lesson of this vault is that there are many events that shape who we are and how we behave. The first room is empty because it is the moment at hand. It has not yet affected us. The endless honeycomb of rooms in the Vault of the Past contains each and every hurt and happiness that made us who we are now. Some stray into this place and wander its paths for long periods of time—even a lifetime. They dwell on moments that belong in their past and do not progress. We should not forget our past, but we should not live in it, either. Take time to contemplate the Vault of the Past. Remember to breathe.

(Pause for a few minutes.)

Step out of the Vault of the Past, watch its door seal itself, and follow Anubis down another path to another door. Another tap of the staff, and the door disappears to reveal a great hall full of furniture, art, people, music, and everything else that can stir the senses. No sooner do you step through the doorway than you are overcome with a sense of familiarity. Well you should be. Anubis tells you that this is the Vault of Remembrance. It is different from the Vault of the Past because you have consciously stored what you find here. These are the people, events, and various items that you have chosen to remember for one reason or another. Not all of them are pleasant. You notice both sweet and noxious odors. You hear music that you enjoyed and some that you loathed. You see people you would like to hug, and some you want to avoid.

Nothing is solid here. If you attempt to touch something, your hand passes through it. Anubis tells you that these are memories. As such, they are but images in the mind—your mind. These are the thoughts, images, people, and sensations that you have imbued with special meaning. Take some time to look around. You need not pay attention to anything you would rather ignore. These are your memories, and what you recall here is your decision.

Now you want to take a few steps farther into this vault. A giant, golden cobra rears before you. Its movements are slow, graceful, and nonthreatening. It slowly raises its head and looks at you with its hood open. It is getting the measure of you and looks at you quizzically. Remember, Anubis is with you. No harm will come to you. Breathe!

The serpent is a magnificent creature. He is gold and deep blue. He appears fearsome, but his voice is gentle and warm. With a polite nod to Anubis, he addresses you.

"In days long past, the dead were buried with all of their possessions intact. We believed they would have need of them in the afterlife. To this day, we do not know if that is correct. It is unlikely that we will know until we ourselves pass to the land of Osiris. So we continue with our ancient practice.

"You, however, live in the world of form. This place is filled with the many things you have stored because you thought they would be needed at some point in time. Every day you live, you add to this collection. It has grown ponderous, even burdensome, yet still you add to it.

"Look about you. Do you truly need all that is kept here or are you hoarding unnecessarily? Is there anything that you can release? Perhaps a wrong done to you that is as worn as an old sandal now? Even a pleasant memory can outlive its welcome if we pay it too much attention.

"Does anything hold you back? Tell me what you wish to have removed from this place. I will take it to the Vault of the Past where it truly belongs. Free yourself of your burden now!"

Take some time to ponder the serpent's words. Is there something getting in your way? Are there memories—good or bad—that intrude in your life? Which memories are those? Recognize them and tell the serpent about them.

(Pause for a few minutes.)

Anubis tells you that it is time to move on. The blessing of the Vault of Remembrance is that you are free to return at will. These images are all part of your inner landscape. Keeping track of them is important if you are to live a conscious and deliberate life. Yet beware the temptation to spend too much time in your memories. If you do that, they will keep you from moving forward. Balance is critical. Remember both the pleasant and the unpleasant, for both have contributed to your makeup. Reflect often on how that has happened in your life. Then release what you no longer need.

Remember to breathe.

(Pause briefly.)

With a tap of His staff, Anubis closes and seals the Vault of Remembrance and leads you down yet another path.

(Pause briefly.)

Anubis now tells you that He will take you to a remarkable vault. It is the most stunning place in the Necropolis and holds its greatest treasure. This is the Vault of the Future. Few who enter the Necropolis ever find this gift, and fewer still have used it to full advantage. Now, you will be given a chance to do so.

You wind up one sandy street and down another. Anubis seems to be moving in random directions, but He never appears lost. Door after door appears, and yet you pass them by. You notice that they are more and more splendid looking. Truly, you must be heading into the very center of the city's heart.

(Pause briefly.)

At long last, Anubis stops before a very large door. It is golden in color and has magnificent torches to either side of it. Anubis tells you that this door leads to the greatest treasure that any can possess and commands that the door be opened.

As it slowly swings away, the door opens onto a familiar sight. Beyond lies the desert where your journey began. Out there lies not your past, but your future. For the Necropolis is about the past and those who live in the world of form cannot stay here. Before you lies total potential. It is a challenge, but also an opportunity.

You are welcome to visit the Necropolis when you have need. It offers a close look at what has gone before. Take what you learn here and move forward in your life. That is the gift of this place, and why the world beyond is such a great treasure. Knowledge of the past can inform the future without holding it a prisoner. Go forward from here and meet that challenge.

(Pause briefly.)

Leave the Necropolis now. Anubis will remain behind for this is His domain, but His spirit is with you. Walk across the sand as you think about what you have seen. Slowly, the oasis comes into view. Take your time getting there.

(Pause briefly.)

When you have arrived, splash cool water from the pool over your face. Feel the warmth of the day just ended as it radiates from the sand beneath your feet. When you are ready, lie down on the sand and close your eyes. Feel the sand becoming liquid again as Nun rises to lift you up. Once again, you float on the Celestial Sea as a babe floats in its mother's womb.

(Pause for a few minutes.)

Now, feel the waters recede as the floor solidifies beneath you. You have returned to this room. When you are ready, open your eyes.

RITUAL OBSERVANCE

The rituals laid out in this chapter are my own creation. They are not attempts to reconstruct Egyptian practice. They are what one friend of mine calls "Egyptian-flavored Wicca." Still, they all contain some elements of historical ancient Egyptian practice. Some of these elements are used as they were thousands of years ago, but most have been reinterpreted symbolically. When these practices are used, I will explain my intention. For the moment, however, a brief overview of them will prove useful.

⚶ **Magic by contagion.** This refers to the use of any part of the body, or its emissions, in the process of a ritual. Classically—and today—such substances have included hair and nail clippings, which are intended to create a bond between the donor and a magical object. The Egyptians also included all substances emanating from the body with connotations that are fairly predictable even in the twenty-first century. These included saliva, sweat, tears, blood, sexual fluids, and bodily wastes.

The theory is that any substance coming from the body is still an essential part of that person or God and carries his or her power. It is unique to that individual and can be mistaken for no other. Thanks to modern science, we know this to be true. Anything that originates in or on our bodies carries our unique genetic signature.

Re created Shu and Tefnut either by an act of masturbation or by *spitting* Them from His mouth (my version of that story incorporates both ideas).[27] As such, they became the very images of the creator. When Isis poisons Re to obtain His secret name, She uses His spittle to create a poisonous serpent that bites Him, thus turning His essence in on itself.[28]

Spittle was particularly singled out as a means of creation and of healing or harming. Egyptian texts make frequent reference to spitting and spittle besides that in the story of Shu and Tefnut. Mythological texts also feature the use of spittle as a cure for blindness among other things.[29]

Try as hard as I might, it is difficult to find a context in my own cultural frame that would see spitting as socially acceptable in a public ritual. What can modern Pagans do that transfers power but doesn't inspire revulsion? In my coven, we always pass our ritual cup to the next person with a kiss. If one of us is at all ill with, say, a cold, then we kiss the cup instead of drinking from it and pass it along with a peck on the cheek. Either way, we transfer something of our essence and power from mouth to mouth around the Circle.

The ancient Egyptians themselves also provided a good adaptation, whether or not that was their intention. The act of *blowing* on an object or person is an act of spitting without

---

[27]Ritner, *Mechanics of Ancient Egyptian Magical Practice*, pp. 75–76. Ritner also points out the parallels in French and English expressions, "describing a child as the 'spitting image' of its parent."

[28]Ibid., p. 83. In the story, Re is very old and the spittle Isis used to create the serpent is actually drool. This would indicate that the spittle of Re was an agent of disease in this case.

[29]Ibid., pp. 78–82.

the saliva. Breath was extremely important in various texts, including the Pyramid Texts mentioned at the beginning of this chapter. According to Ritner, the Egyptians saw "expectorated breath" as essentially identical to spitting in magical effect.[30] This may be the most useful adaptation to a modern Pagan, given the importance placed on breath control by many groups and traditions.

We are also free to substitute one substance for another. Blood is a bodily, and therefore magical, fluid. While I believe blood to be a powerful agent, I generally do not encourage its use in anything other than a private ritual. In our time, blood is a risky substance. A lot of my day-to-day energy in my work as a paramedic is spent shielding myself from it, and that is a behavior I do not wish to alter.

To this point, I have touched on only the active transfer of power. The receptive aspect of this transfer also figures in Egyptian magical practice in the form of *swallowing*. In the Tale of the Two Brothers, Bata must swallow His heart to be revivified. Later in that story, Bata's wife swallows a splinter from the Persea tree and becomes pregnant with Him. In both cases, some part of a God's body is ingested to rejuvenate Him.

A portion of the Pyramid Texts that comes to us under the somewhat alarming title of the *Cannibal Hymn* describes how the king arrives in the heavens and proceeds to hunt, cook, and devour the Gods in order to gain Their powers.[31] Extreme as this may be to our modern sensitivities, we certainly ingest the power and virtues of animals and plants. While these provide us with the means of biological survival, the Gods can do the same for our spirit.

The idea of ingesting the body of a God to receive power or blessings need not be repugnant. Anyone raised a Christ-

---

[30]Ibid., p. 88.
[31]Simpson, *Literature of Ancient Egypt*, p. 269.

ian has encountered the sacred body and blood of Jesus in the Eucharist. Whether we believe that the ritual food we share is the symbolic or literal body of the Gods is irrelevant. What we do in our rites is to invest the power and spirit of the Gods in the ritual food and drink. Ingesting food that has been blessed in this fashion imbues us with the aura of the sacred. By partaking of the feast, we don't just honor the Gods—we become Them.

⚜ **Circumambulation.** The concept of circumambulation (walking in a circle around something) had a broad range of meanings for the ancient Egyptians. The word for "encircling" was also the root word for "remedy." Later, it became associated with the Demotic and Coptic words meaning "to enchant."[32]

Encircling provided a means of purification, establishing boundaries, protection, and control. The Egyptians seemed to have a great fondness for processions of every sort and size. Ritual processions could be public, as with the coronation of a king, or private, as in a spell to protect the home. In coronation ceremonies, the procession would encircle the walls of the city, magically establishing the boundaries of the king's universe.[33]

The solar God Re also travels in a circuit each day. In the morning, He rises as the sun and travels the sky. At night, the Solar Bark travels the underworld fighting off the enemies of Re, only to rise again the following morning. By this action of encircling, Re establishes not only the boundaries of the universe, but His place as its ruler and defender.[34]

The concept behind Circle Casting is nothing less than the use of our will to create sacred space. Every time we walk the

---

[32]Ritner, *Mechanics of Ancient Egyptian Magical Practices*, pp. 57–61.
[33]Ibid., p. 58.
[34]Ibid., p. 62.

Circle, we turn our living rooms, bedrooms, backyards, cellars, gardens, or other secular spaces into temples for sacred worship. When we are finished with our rituals, we take the Circle down and return those spaces to their regular uses.

Circumambulation can also be used effectively in the creation of images. By walking around an object as you speak, the power of your will as expressed in your words can be brought to bear on it.

☙ **Use of images.** This is another practice that is well known in the Neo-pagan and Wiccan world. An image is created in cloth or wax; finished, it is ritually linked to the person it represents. The idea is that anything done to the image will happen to the target individual.

In my own practice, such images are used almost exclusively for healing purposes. This technique should be used only with the approval of the person whose image is being created. Creating an image without the target's consent is asking for trouble.

In Egyptian-inspired practice, such images might instead be made of clay, reflecting the myth of the God Khnum, who created human beings on a potter's wheel.[35] Clay is an easy material to use. If you choose to use clay for making images, get earthenware clay at a pottery or potters supply store. (Clay sold in craft stores is often polymer-based or "self-hardening." This is fine for sculpting images you intend to keep. It's less earth-friendly, though, and impossible to dissolve or reuse.) Also, be careful with clay images. They can break easily and will fall apart in water. That may be part of your ritual plan (after any ties between the image and the target individual are severed), but when it happens by accident, it can cause some consternation.

[35]Hart, *Dictionary*, p. 110.

✤ **Use of red.** The color red was associated with Seth. It was used with various other demonic beings as well. Further, the names of these characters were often written in red ink.[36] This association gives red negative connotations.

Red is also the color of blood. Blood is the stuff of life. The Egyptians acknowledged Seth as an unavoidable fact of life. We would do well to do the same.

It is not necessary to limit red to undesirable aspects of life. I have used it successfully (while calling on Anubis, no less) in Samhain rituals where we painted red ocher on the faces of the participants. In the ritual, Anubis led those gathered to the underworld to visit with the Crone. The red ocher served as a mark of death for the people wearing it. Any entities seeing the mark (including the Crone) would know that the wearers were in the care of Anubis, and would welcome them.

Again, this is a matter of reinterpretation. In rituals appealing to Anubis as the son of Seth, red may be entirely appropriate—especially if the goal is to rid yourself of excess anger. Words of anger can be painted or written on papyrus (which is easily found in occult and specialty paper stores) and burned in a fire to release them. The only limit is the boundary of your creative spirit.

✤ **Breaking of vessels.** In Egyptian sacrificial practice, a vessel used to offer food or drink to the Gods would be destroyed immediately afterward. Robert Ritner notes that breaking of vessels was a component of both offering and execration rituals.[37] The Pyramid Texts make clear that the action was intended to terrify enemies. The rite of breaking (in this case,

---

[36]Ritner, *Mechanics of Ancient Egyptian Magical Practices*, p. 147. Ritner goes on to make an interesting observation. Modern scientists have deduced that Ramses II was redheaded. This has led to speculation that his great achievements may have been inspired, at least in part, by his desire to compensate for that "defect."

[37]Ibid., p. 146.

"Breaking the Red Vases" as part of a funerary offering meal)
was accompanied by the slaughter of a bull elsewhere in the
pyramid temple, and the two acts served to mirror each
other.[38]

Once again, reinterpretation of this action allows a new
avenue for religious expression. In the Offering Meal below,
an offering of food is made to Anubis. His portion of the
meal consists of foods He prefers (meats, cereal grains, and
beer).[39] These are placed on unfired clay plates and dedicated
to Him. After the Circle is opened, the plates are carried out
of doors. The meal is tossed into the woods (Anubis having
dined on its essence). The plates are then smashed and
dropped to the ground.

I break the plates so that, once the Gods have been offered
the meal and accepted it, they cannot be used for any other
purpose. The food belongs to the Gods; so do the dishes.
Because they are made of unfired clay, the plates will dissolve
and rejoin the Earth. Of course, any other material that will
break down is fine for constructing the ritual vessels. Just
make certain that they are destroyed and unusable after the
ritual.

 ✦ **Use of sand.** It doesn't take an Egyptologist to predict that
sand would play some role in Egyptian magical practice.
Sand was used heavily in architectural work, and figures
prominently as an agent of purification.[40] Ritual uses of sand
included sprinkling during processions of the Gods, and as
an offering.

As one might expect, sand also had its negative connotations. These focused primarily on sand's ability to blind an

---

[38]Ibid., p. 146.
[39]I took this inspiration from The Tale of the Two Brothers in which Anubis raises cattle
and grain. In addition, He takes beer with His meals in that story. The offerings made to
Deities by the ancient Egyptians would make a good subject for research.
[40]Ritner, *Mechanics of Ancient Egyptian Magical Practices*, p. 155.

enemy if it got into his eyes. This property also made it something for the deceased to fear in the afterlife.

I live on the coast of Maine where sand is a fact of life. It is useful for many mundane and ritual purposes. Sand may be used instead of salt to ground the Circle with the power of Earth in outdoor rituals. Scattering sand also may not be a good idea indoors, however. A small amount of fine salt will work just as well, or you can reduce the amount of sand you scatter. Quantity is not the issue. The ritual action is.

Egyptian magicians could punish demons or even threaten Gods if they felt they had reason.[41] I choose to avoid such violent actions. Throwing sand in someone else's eyes—even ritually—cannot be expected to produce positive results. However, you may on rare occasions want to do this to banish some undesired and objectified aspect of yourself.

These ritual examples are not exhaustive. There is nothing particularly "Wiccan" about them. They are well suited to almost any Pagan path that can accommodate a cross-cultural influence. If you feel these rituals will work for you, adapt them and make them your own.

THE BOUNDARY RITUAL

The Boundary Ritual is used to clear a ritual space before casting a Circle. It is entirely optional. It is also designed to acknowledge those entities (Gods, Goddesses, and such) that will *not* be invited to your ritual. The goal is to clear the space of any unwanted influence so that you may focus on your ritual with greater clarity.

You will need a candle, a bell, a bowl of sand, and some incense. I prefer dragon's blood incense for banishing simply because its perfume speaks to me of cleansing. Follow your own

---

[41]Simpson, *Literature of Ancient Egypt*, pp. 276–77. These passages come from Pyramid Utterances 310 and 569. In them, the Gods are threatened with curses and with the prevention of Their births if They do not cooperate with the deceased.

tastes. Finally, you will need a small offering of food and drink. It should be the same offering you are planning to use in the ritual(s) later on.

Place all items for the ritual on the altar. Include not only those materials and tools required for the Boundary Ritual, but also the items for the ritual(s) to follow.

Ground and center.

Light the candle and the charcoal. Say

> *The fires are lit. The first rite has begun.*

Take up the bowl of sand. As you walk the space, scatter the sand around the boundary and say

> *Substance of the Gods,*
> *Ground and basis,*
> *Define and mark this space.*
> *Establish the boundary and set the limit.*
> *Prevent that which I (we) do not desire here and keep*
>   *close that which I (we) do.*
> *By the power of Re and Nephthys,*
> *And by my (our) will,*
> *So mote it be.*

Put some incense on the charcoal. When the smoke rises, take up the censer and walk the space clockwise. With your hand, fan the smoke around the boundaries of the space as you say

> *Perfume of the Gods,*
> *Strength and purification,*
> *Free this place of all influence.*
> *Remove hindrance and harmful energy.*
> *Restore the cosmic balance.*
> *By the power of Thoth and Ma'at,*
> *And by my (our) will,*
> *So mote it be.*

Take up the candle. Walk the space again holding the light before you and say

Light of the Gods,
Illumination and vision,
Cleanse and purify this space.
Remove all false motive and doubt.
Restore the Great Light that I (we) may see.
By the power of Osiris and Isis,
And my (our) will,
So mote it be.

Take up the bell. Walk the space once again. Stop at each of the cardinal points, trace a banishing pentagram with the forefinger of your dominant hand and ring the bell. After each ring, say

Hear me, O Gods;
Hear me, O great ones!
This place is claimed by me (us),
It is claimed in Your honor!
It is cleansed for Your entry!
By the power of Anubis, the Lord of these places,
I (we) will welcome You.
So mote it be!

Lastly, take up the ritual food and drink. You have not created Sacred Space yet, but bow respectfully when you leave the area. Scatter the food in a place that is outdoors and well removed from the ritual space. If you are working indoors and will be moving right into the purification or Circle Casting, simply leave the food in a spot outside the ritual space. Say

You who were removed from the temple,
And told to leave that place,
Know that I (we) recognize and honor You.
Accept this gift of my (our) ritual meal.

It is what I (we) will eat.
It is what I (we) will drink.
Share in it and be joyful.
You are not forgotten or neglected.
Accept this gift, and go in peace.

Move on to the Purification Rite or the Circle Casting.

THE PURIFICATION RITE

This ritual is to be performed after the Boundary Ritual and before the Circle Casting. It is an optional ritual that I would recommend for special occasions such as funerary rites or any rituals of personal importance to you.

This is an adaptation of a censing prayer from the Pyramid Texts.[42] The lines may be read responsively with the celebrant saying the first line of each couplet and the participants saying the second.

Preparation. In addition to the altar setup for the basic Circle Casting (below), you will need a bowl of sand.

If you haven't done so already, ground and center.

Light the charcoal in the censer and say

The fire is laid, the fire shines.

Add the incense. When the smoke begins to rise, say

The incense is laid on the fire, the incense shines.

Take up the censer and walk clockwise as you say this prayer:

Your perfume comes to me (us), O Gods;
May my (our) perfume come to You.
May I (we) be with You, ancient ones;
May You be with me (us).

[42]Ibid., p. 275.

May I (we) live in You, O Gods;
May You live in me (us).
May You receive my (our) love, ancient ones;
May I (we) receive Yours.
Blessed Be.

Return to the altar. Place the tip of the athame in the water and
say

The water is poured out for me (us), the water shines.

Put three measures of salt into the water and say

The salt is dissolved in the water, the salt shines.

Stir the salt water with the athame as you say

Your purification comes to me (us), O Gods;
May I (we) be worthy of it.

Put the athame on the altar. While the responses are spoken,
the cup may be passed around the Circle for each to sip. Alternatively, the celebrant may walk the Circle and sprinkle each person.

May I (we) be with You, Ancient Ones;
May You be with me (us).
May I (we) cleanse Your way, O Gods;
May You cleanse me (us).
May You receive my (our) love, Ancient Ones;
May I (we) receive Yours.
Blessed Be.

Return the water to the altar and take up the bowl of sand. Walk
the circle once again and sprinkle sand on the feet of each participant. If you are working indoors, take the bowl of sand to each
participant. Each person should hold his or her hands over the
bowl while the celebrant drizzles sand over them and back into
the bowl.

The Circle is cleansed, the Circle shines.
I (Those who gather here) am (are) cleansed, I (they) also
  shine.

Walk the Circle.

May I (we) be with You, Ancient Ones;
May You be with me (us).
May I (we) defend You, O Gods;
May You protect me (us).
May You receive my (our) love, Ancient Ones;
May I (we) receive Yours.
Blessed Be.

When you are finished, place the sand on the altar.

CIRCLE CASTING

There are many ways of creating sacred space for ritual, and as
many sources of instruction for doing so. For that reason, I will
forgo such instruction here except to give you the wording I use
when Casting Circle.

For blessing the water, dip the tip of your athame in the cup
and say

Blessed Be, creature of Water
May Shu of the Air and Tefnut of the Mists be in you.

Next, the tip of the athame is placed in the salt cellar with the
words:

Blessed Be, creature of Earth
May Geb of the Earth and Nut of the Sky be in you.

Three measures of salt are then added to the bowl with appropriate words to this effect:

Salt and water, Inner and Outer
Body and Soul be cleansed.

I cast out all that is harmful,
And conjure all that is healing within you.
I make of you the Great Celestial Sea that is Nun,
And invest you with the Power that is Re.
By my will and the will of those present,
So mote it be.

If you desire, the people gathered may be sprinkled with the salt water, or, alternatively, the cup may be passed around with each person taking a small sip from it.

In establishing sacred space, the Circle should be walked seven times. With the first four circumambulations, bless the space with each of the elements (Water, Fire, Earth, and Air). On the fifth, call the quarters with the following (the words in parentheses can be changed depending on your correspondences):

Hail, Guardians of the (East), Power of Water!
Wellspring and inundation.
Emotions that ebb and flow.
We ask that you join in our circle and witness our rite.
Bring to us your special power, the power to dare.
Come to us now, Hapy, one of the four Sons of Horus.
We welcome you.
Blessed Be!

Hail, Guardians of the (South), Powers of Fire!
Hearth and conflagration.
Passion, desire, and zeal.
We ask that you join our circle and witness our rite.
Bring to us your special power, the power to will.
Come to us now, Duamutef, one of the four Sons of
    Horus.
We welcome you.
Blessed Be!

Hail, Guardians of the (West), Powers of Earth!
Shelter and tomb.
Strength and solidity.
We ask that you join our circle and witness our rite.
Bring to us your special power, the power to keep silent.
Come to us now, Imsety, one of the four Sons of Horus.
We welcome you.
Blessed Be!

Hail Guardians of the (North), Powers of Air!
Breath and whirlwind.
Thought, mind, and limits.
We ask that you join our circle and witness our rite.
Bring to us your special power, the power to know.
Come to us now, Qebehsenuef, one of the four Sons of
   Horus.
We welcome you.
Blessed Be!

The God and Goddess are then called to the space as follows:

HIGH PRIESTESS:
   Great Mother Isis,
   You in whose mouth are the Sacred Names of Re,
   Wisest of the Wise,
   Daughter, Sister, Wife, Mother, Queen!
   Come to us in this our Circle,
   Bring your society, knowledge, and wisdom.
   Witness all that we do and celebrate with us.
   We who are your children call to You!
   Blessed Be.

HIGH PRIEST:
   Lord Osiris,
   He who dwells in Orion,

With a season in the Sky and a season on the Earth,[43]
Son, Brother, Husband, Father, King!
Come to us in this our Circle,
Bring your society, words, and blessings.
Witness all that we do and celebrate with us.
We who are your children call to You!
Blessed Be.

After calling the Deities, the Circle is traced a sixth time while all
in the Circle join in chanting

By Water, by Fire, By Earth, by Air,
By the Goddess, by the God, and by the will of all
*   gathered here.*
This circle is cast!

The HPS or other celebrant walks the circle for the seventh and
final time as she says

We stand now in a time that is no time,
And in a place that is no place.
We stand on the same sacred ground that our ancestors
*   stood upon,*
And that our descendants will stand on after us.
May our work be worthy of them,
And theirs of us.
So mote it be!

If Anubis is to be called as a third Deity, it should be done here. It
is a good idea to have an image of Anubis on the altar when inviting Him so that He has a place to reside while He is with you.

Invitation to Anubis

If you are inviting Anubis to your Circle, stand facing the altar
with your arms raised and your hands empty. Put your hands

---

[43]Hart, *Dictionary*, p. 153.

together with the palms facing each other and the fingers extended. Tap the index fingers against your forehead, then your mouth, then your heart. Bow to the altar.

Stand once again before the altar and hold your arms out at your sides but below the level of your shoulders. If you wish to use a tool of the Craft, pick up your wand or staff. Do not call upon Anubis while holding a blade. Speak these words with a clear voice.

> *I call upon Anubis,*
> *Lord of Between Places,*
> *Foremost among the Westerners,*
>   (if performing a funeral/memorial)
> *He who is Upon His Mountain,*
> *Son of _____,*
> *(Re, Osiris, Seth)*
>   (name of father depending on the nature of the ritual)
> *Son of _____,*
> *(Nephthys, Isis)*
>   (name of mother depending on the nature of the ritual—
>   call upon additional aspects as necessary)
> *Silent, strong, and compassionate one,*
> *Keeper of Secrets and Teacher of Magic.*
> *Come now and be with me (us)!*
> *Speak with the words that are in your mouth,*
> *That I (we) may hear.*
> *Act with the Magic that is in your body,*
> *And be my (our) example.*
> *Bring your guidance, wisdom, and knowledge to me (those*
>   *gathered here).*
> *And reside with me (us) for a time.*
> *I am (we are) prepared. Guide my (our) thoughts and*
>   *actions!*

When you are finished, bow politely and resume your place in the Circle.

Because Anubis has so many different aspects and manifestations, it is best to call upon Him not by His proper name, but by His titles. This allows us to focus on those aspects of Deity we wish to call and avoids confusion. Simply calling on "Anubis" means too much all at once.

THE OFFERING MEAL

The Offering Meal should be shared after the body of any ritual. In the case of the Requiem it is an intrinsic part of the ritual. When we call upon our Gods, it is only right to offer Them a portion of our ritual food. More than this, it is hospitable to provide foods that are to Their liking.

Just which foods those are depends on the Gods and Goddesses involved. In my own experience, I find that Anubis is fond of meat, cereal grain, and beer. I am not a beer drinker and, therefore, do not tend to have beer in the house. I do, however, like other beverages made from grain, so I offer those. To date, I haven't noticed any protest from the Divine quarter.

A look at the mythology reveals that Egyptian Deities live in abundance and do not require our offerings.[44] They do not make demands of tribute, and would probably be distressed if we felt They did. In the true spirit of Ma'at, our offerings are *gifts*. They are freely given without expectation, much like the gift you bring to friends when they have you over for dinner.[45] We enjoy the abundance of creation that is the gift of the Gods and return the fruits of our labors to Them. Thus, the Circle that is Ma'at is complete.

What is more important to the Gods is that we respond to Their presence and actions. The worst fate (and greatest insult) for an

---

[44]Simpson, *Literature of Ancient Egypt*, p. 55. In the myth of the Shipwrecked Sailor, a God in the form of a serpent is offered incense and myrrh as a tribute. He declines the gifts for they are His already. All this God asks is that His name be remembered to Egypt when the sailor returns there.

[45]Hornung, *Conceptions of God*, p. 203.

Egyptian Deity is to have His shrines ignored.[46] It is important that we make Them an essential part of our lives. One of the most socially binding rituals that humans practice is the sharing of food. How wonderful to practice that same sharing with our Gods.

Preparation for the offering meal is simple. You should have a loaf of bread and a cup of drink on your altar at the start of the ritual. If you wish, other foods may also be included. If the Offering Meal will be part of a Requiem, add some barley, oats, or rye in a separate dish. These can be added to the offering and given to the deceased, the Gods, and any uninvited entities (as in the Boundary Ritual). Finally, you will need a plate made from unfired clay or other material that will break down in contact with soil. Again, if this is a Requiem, you will need three plates: one for the Gods, one for the deceased, and one for the uninvited.

As with Circle Casting, there are many scripts available for these blessings. Follow one of those or use your imagination in creating one of your own.

This is a good time for sharing stories, music, poetry, and other creative work. Pass the bread and the cup around until everyone is ready to close the ritual.

The offering meal concludes your ritual. When it is completed, open the Circle.

Carry the offering plate containing the food and drink for the Gods outdoors to a relatively wild spot. That may be a city park or the woods behind your house or your garden. It may even be a window box. The size is not important.

Scatter the offering meal and break the plate on which it was carried (see the notes on the breaking of vessels earlier in this chapter).

---

[46]Ibid., p. 112. In the myth of the Contendings of Horus and Seth, Re is determined to put Seth on the throne of Egypt despite demands by the Goddess Neith and the rest of the Ennead. In His anger, a God named Bebon tells Re, "Your shrine is vacant!" This insult so saddened Re that He spent the entire day sick in His tent. Bebon fared less well. As angry as They were with Re, the rest of the Ennead threw Bebon out of the tribunal.

THE IN-DRINKING SPELL

This spell takes advantage of the magical act of swallowing, and provides a means of "borrowing" the power of a God or Goddess. With the In-Drinking spell, you call upon a specific aspect of Anubis and use it for a *finite* period of time.

Use a small statue of Anubis. Many occult supply stores and catalogs carry statues made of stone, silver, alabaster, and other such insoluble materials. Fired clay is also an option. (Avoid polymer substances and statues with paints that may be toxic.) Make sure the statue is clean of dust and dirt before beginning the ritual.

When the time comes to call Anubis into the object, use the Invitation to Anubis and call only the aspect you wish to absorb. Focus your intention on the statue and allow Anubis time to inhabit it.

Preparation. Prepare the ritual space for Circle Casting. In addition to the regular tools on the altar, you should have:

- ⚜ A small image of Anubis
- ⚜ A bowl large enough for the image to stand in—preferably black in color
- ⚜ A small pitcher of water
- ⚜ A clean cloth

Step 1: Cast a Circle or create sacred space as you normally would. Call upon a God and Goddess other than Anubis.

Step 2: Call Anubis into the image. Take some time after the invocation—perhaps a few minutes—during which you should focus on your intent and the use to which you will be putting the energies you will absorb. Visualize the image as animated and shimmering with divine light. Take a deep breath and exhale in its direction.

Step 3:

With the first pinch, say: *This to awaken the spirit of Light and Beauty!*

With the second pinch, say: *This to open the ways!*

With the third pinch, say: *This to acknowledge that death and decay will follow!*

Step 4: Declare your intentions. Even though you have already called a specific aspect of Anubis into the image, you should be prepared to explain your reason for the In-Drinking ritual. Tell the Gods what brought you to this point and what you hope to accomplish. There is no need to engage in theatrics at this point. Plain language will do nicely. When you have made your declaration, stand before the altar with your empty hands out to your sides and say the following:

> *I stand before You,*
> *I have declared my intentions.*
> *You know what is within me,*
> *And your understanding is beyond mine.*
> *Guide my thoughts and actions.*
> *Instill in me your power as* [state the aspect you have called],
> *That I may* [state *exactly* what you intend to do].
> *I seek this boon for* [state the period of time],
> *And ask that the Work be done by that time.*

Step 5: Take up the pitcher and pour a small amount of water over the image and into the bowl seven times. With each pouring, say the following (if this is a group, these may be spoken responsively):

- First pouring: *Let this give substance to my request.*
  May Anubis be in it.

- Second pouring: *Let this purify my motives.*
  May Anubis be in them.

- Third pouring: *Let this make of me a vessel of the Gods.*
                      May Anubis be in me.

- Fourth pouring: *Let this open my heart.*
                      May Anubis find me justified.

- Fifth pouring: *Let this open my eyes.*
                      May Anubis grant me insight.

- Sixth pouring: *Let this open my mouth.*
                      May Anubis give me breath and words.

- Seventh pouring: *Let this open the way.*
                      May Anubis bless this work.

Step 6. Remove the image from the bowl and place it on the cloth. Dry it completely before continuing.

Step 7. Take up the bowl of water. Visualize it glowing with intense, divine light. After a moment of reflection, lower the bowl to your mouth. Drain the bowl in seven sips. After each sip, repeat one verse of the prayer you spoke while pouring water over the image. If you are performing this ritual with other people, pass the bowl around the circle seven times with each person taking a sip. The first person should speak the prayers before passing the bowl.

Step 8. When the bowl is empty, place it on the altar. Take a deep breath, let it out, and say the following:

> *I am but flesh and blood,*
> *But I carry a God's powers within me.*
> *That which hinders will not stand before me,*
> *And none of good heart shall be harmed.*
> *Anubis guides me and protects me,*
> *And I have no fear within me.*
> *I am blessed.*

Step 9. Release the image. Anubis will come and go as He sees fit, but a word of thanks will never go amiss. Direct these words to the image:

Thanks be to the Gods who dwell with us.
Thanks be to Anubis who is in me.
Thanks be to the skilled one who created this work of art.
May it be now a thing of beauty.
May Anubis dwell here as He will, when He will,
And may He be welcomed always.
Blessed Be.

Step 10. If there is further work to be done, do it now. If not, move on to the Ritual of Offering.

Step 11. Perform the Offering Meal.

THE MA'AT RITUAL

The Ma'at (mah-áht) Ritual celebrates cosmic balance. It serves as a means for recognizing and understanding the flow of energy in the universe and the part we play in that process. The Egyptian Goddess Ma'at personifies the principle of cosmic harmony and the notion that what moves in one direction is counterbalanced by movement in the other.

Ma'at is the mirror of Truth that permits no illusion. She is also the arbiter of Justice who sees all that happens, and is completely impartial to the concerns of any but the universe itself. She gives us a clear vision of the morally correct path of action.[47] It is our choice and our challenge to act according to Her revelation, which may not suit our preconceived notions or our convenience. We can ignore Her—but only at great risk.

In the Hall of the Two Truths, the feather of Ma'at lies in one pan of the scale opposite the pan with the heart of the deceased. The Truth of the deceased's life is measured against the Truth of Ma'at. Only if Anubis decides that the two are in perfect balance may the dead person move forward.

The concept of the Ma'at Ritual follows the weighing of the heart. A scale is used to balance our own goals, desires, or bless-

[47]Hart, *Dictionary*, p. 116.

ings on one side with our actions and talents on the other. When
the two sides balance, we are said to be justified.

This is not payment for services rendered. The Gods have no
need for such a system. After all, what we have flows from Them
and is a part of the universal equation. The real balance being
struck is between the gifts we receive and the use to which we put
them. If you seek clear vision into a matter in one pan of the scale,
you must weigh that against what you will do with that vision in
the other pan. The two must balance.

There are many conceivable uses for the ritual, and I offer two
suggestions here:

- **Thankfulness.** You may wish to perform this ritual to give
  thanks for a blessing you have received. It is a good ritual for
  marking life passages such as birthdays, graduations, initia-
  tions, job changes, marriages, and so forth.

  In the case of birthdays, you would balance the year you
  just completed with what you have done in that time. You
  may also wish to state your intentions for the coming year.
  The other observances would follow in the same manner. If
  you will begin by stating what you have received, the balancing statement should begin not with how you earned it,
  but with what you did with it.

  Remember, the gifts of the Gods are free. What returns to
  Them should be equally so.

- **Observation.** This form of the Ma'at Ritual focuses on the
  here and now. It recognizes a situation that currently exists
  and weighs it against the actions you are currently taking.
  This allows insight into effectiveness of your efforts both in
  terms of quality and quantity. If the scales do not balance,
  you will need to adjust something on one side or the other.
  The exact nature of that adjustment is up to you, but you
  may wish to empty the scales and try a petition (or propitiation if appropriate).

These are just some of the ideas for the Ma'at Ritual. A little creative thinking will undoubtedly find more.

Anubis should be called to the Circle. It is His judgment that determines the balance of the scales. The best way for this to occur objectively is to perform the In-Drinking spell as a group (calling on the Observer of the Balance) and rely on the combined judgment of everyone in the Circle to serve as Anubis's word on the balance. If people are capable of being honest (and they shouldn't be Circling with you if they aren't), they will tell you what they see.

To prepare for this ritual, have the altar set up as usual for Circle Casting. At the center of the Circle space, have a small table with a two-pan balance, a container of sand, and some feathers. You may also include an image of Anubis, although this isn't absolutely necessary. You should also have an offering meal ready.

Perform a Purification Ritual.

Cast the Circle.

Call upon the God and Goddess. The best choices for the Ma'at Ritual in my mind are Ma'at and Thoth, but follow your own heart.

Perform the In-Drinking spell as a group or call upon Anubis as follows:

> *I call upon Anubis,*
> *Observer of the Balance,*
> *Keeper of the Gates in the West.*
> *Before you we stand prepared for your insight.*
> *We have called to Ma'at and opened our hearts.*
> *We have called to Thoth to hear our case.*
> *Let your sharp sight find the balance,*
> *And may we be justified in the eyes of the Gods.*
> *Come and be with us, Bright One!*
> *Blessed Be!*

The first person approaches the scale and states before the Gods his or her reason for being there. Here is an example:

I have come before the Gods to thank them for another
  year of life.

Add some sand to one pan of the scale. Sand should be added just until the scale tips.

In that year, I have worked to support my family.

Add a feather to the opposite pan.

I have volunteered my time in service to my community.

Add another feather.

I have brought honor and offerings to the Gods.

Add another feather.

And so on until the scales tip back and balance. The celebrant says

Well met, my child.
The scales have balanced and you are justified.
Well have you used the time you have been given.
May you see many more years,
For the world is blessed with your presence.

The sand may then be tipped into a charm bag for that person's later use. The feathers are removed and placed back on the table for the next person to use.

When everyone has completed this segment of the ritual, the table should be moved to one side of the space.

Perform the Offering Meal.

Open the Circle.

REQUIEM

This chapter would not be complete without a funerary ritual. As receiver and protector of the deceased, Anubis can be an important focus when the time comes to lay a loved one to rest. Although we may not hold the same views as the ancient Egyptians with regard to the afterlife and its challenges, there are reasons for crafting a farewell ritual from this perspective.

While the Egyptians performed their funerary rites for the benefit of the deceased, we in the twenty-first century generally do so for those who survive. In our grief, we are very open and in need of a healthy means of expression. The Gods can be a great source of strength to us at such a vulnerable time. In our memorial rituals, we comfort each other and say good-bye to the departed. We reaffirm our connections both to the deceased and to each other. We share tears, stories, laughs, and a few hugs.

At the same time, a funeral based on the ancient Egyptian view of death gives us a chance to provide for the spiritual creature comforts of the departed. We may write stories about the person passing to his new life, defeating his enemies along the way, and ultimately enjoying a life of splendor in the hereafter. We may take this opportunity to write one last letter to a loved one knowing that it will remain forever between the two of us. These exercises have the potential to comfort us as much as any ritual.

The ritual presented here has a number of elements based on Egyptian practice and belief. Some of them, such as Letters to the Dead and the Opening of the Mouth, have not yet been discussed and will be covered afterward. Others are familiar.

This ritual requires some preparation and is fairly lengthy as written. There are items that you may wish to leave out or change, which is your prerogative. There are some elements, however, that I would urge you to follow closely.

1. Be certain to perform the Boundary and Purification Rituals at the beginning. This is an emotionally charged time for the people involved, so clearing the air of any uninvited influence is that much more important. Pay extra attention to the liminal stages of this ritual. The more energy you put into establishing the sacred space, the better the ritual will be.

2. The ritual beverage should not be sweet. Water with lemon in it will do nicely. If you use an alcoholic beverage, an ale with a bitter flavor is a good choice. Another good choice would be an anise-flavored drink. Anise is the flavoring in licorice, which is characteristically black in color. You can take the symbolism from there.

3. Make the image out of unfired earthenware clay. In this ritual, you will bury it. You want to be sure that once interred it will gradually merge into earth once again. For this reason, do not use polymer or self-hardening clay (see the notes on clay under "Use of Images"). The idea is to keep the image as earth-friendly as possible. Where I live, it is possible to dig clay right out of the ground and use it. That way, what was taken is literally returned to the source in the end.

4. At the conclusion to the interment, there is a short banishing ritual to ward off any hindrance against the departed. It is not absolutely necessary to perform this part of the ritual, and should you choose to leave it out, I suggest some sort of prayer for smooth passage to the afterlife. I have included a suggested wording.

The two influences present in this ritual are The Book of the Dead and Letters to the Dead.

❧ **The Book of the Dead.** The Egyptians developed texts intended to assist the deceased in the afterlife. These included the Book of Breathing and the New Kingdom Books of the Netherworld.[48] I would suggest an approach derived from, but not identical to the Egyptian Book of the Dead.

In preparation, each participant should sit down with a piece of paper and take time to reflect on the journey of the

---

[48]Hornung, *Ancient Egyptian Books*. Beginning on page 23, Hornung details these texts.

deceased to the next life. Consider the deceased person's fears and hopes, likes and dislikes, and so forth.

After some time, decide what would help the deceased make a smooth transition between the worlds and how those needs can be symbolically provided. Use words, pictures, poetry, and so on to represent on paper the things that would aid and comfort the deceased on his or her journey. For example, if the deceased loved music and never went anywhere without it, draw musical notes or instruments on the paper. If, for instance, Dylan Thomas was a favorite poet, copy down one of his poems.

This ritual also involves the use of a small roll of gauze or cloth bandage. If it's possible, have one person do artwork or writing on that.

Roll the paper into a tight scroll and bring it with you to the Requiem.

Letters to the Dead. The ancient Egyptians believed that the spirit of the deceased could function as an intermediary before the Gods and spirits of the underworld. As such, the spirit could convey the desires and requests of people in this life very effectively. Letters to the Dead were essentially petitions seeking that kind of aid.[49] We should add one for our ritual here.

Often, the requests were malevolent, seeking curses against either the living or the Gods Themselves. However, they could be used to solicit good fortune, justice, health, or a number of other helpful—if somewhat self-interested—ends.

I think of the possibilities for letters of this sort, and I come up with some different uses. Perhaps a letter could serve as a final, deeply personal farewell, realizing that only you and the deceased will know what it contains. Just the process of writing such a letter could be cathartic for a person

[49]Ritner, *Mechanics of Ancient Egyptian Magical Practice*, pp. 180–83.

grieving a loss. Think of the things you always wanted to say but didn't. If your last words to the deceased were angry ones, now would be a good time to restore the balance.

Of course, a request to the deceased for assistance, or to carry a message to the Gods, is also a possibility. Asking the person to "poke Harry in the eye when you see him," however, is bad form.

When you have written your letter, roll it into a scroll and bring it to the Requiem.

Preparation for the Requiem should begin some days before you intend to perform it. The version I am including here does not have the actual body present. Instead, a clay image is sculpted to represent the deceased. It is identified with the deceased during the ritual and is laid to rest in his or her stead. This way, it does not matter what choice the deceased made regarding disposal. Performing the ritual in this manner may also help avoid painful conflicts between the deceased's legal family and his or her coreligionists.

Sculpt the image a few days before the ritual will take place. You don't need to be an artist. The rough outline of a human body will be quite sufficient for the purpose. *Do not* include any items belonging to the deceased. Unlike the image in other rituals, the image in the Requiem is entirely symbolic. The spirit of the recently departed usually spends some time between this life and the next. Overidentifying the image with that person could serve to trap the spirit in this world for some time, preventing the deceased's necessary progress.

The image should be small enough to fit comfortably in your hand. When you have finished sculpting, place it aside in a safe place and allow it to dry.

With the same clay, make three flat disks. These will be the offering plates for the ritual meal. One plate is intended for the

Gods, the second for the deceased, and the third for opposing forces (more on that later).

Perform the Boundary Ritual well ahead of time and prepare the ritual space. This version is written for an outdoor space; a little modification is required if you are going to work indoors. The primary concern is the interment. That will have to be done at another time if you are indoors. For this reason, the interment is written in stand-alone fashion. If it is done as part of the larger ritual, there is no need to cast a Circle again.

The Circle should be located where the image and all its accompanying documents will be interred. If that is not possible, perform the interment as though you were doing the Requiem indoors. If you will bury the image during the Requiem, dig a hole at the western compass point. The hole should be just outside the area where participants will gather but inside the area established by the boundary ritual.

The ritual space should be well decorated. Flowers are always a welcome sight at a funeral, so there should be plenty of them. Pictures of the deceased are also a good idea, as are favorite music and colors. Black is not a requirement, although you may wish to drape the altar that way. If the deceased didn't like black, on the other hand, then don't.

In addition to the usual setup for Circle Casting, the altar should have the image, the gauze bandage, the plates, and some offering food on it (see the Offering Meal Ritual for advice on this). To one side, you should have the scrolls and letters that participants have brought with them.

When all is prepared, everyone should gather in the Circle.

Perform the Purification Ritual.

Cast the Circle. Call on Osiris as Lord of the Underworld and Isis as the Goddess of Magic.

Call upon Anubis as indicated for funerals.

When the Circle is cast, the celebrant says

Greetings, children.
We come together in a time of great sadness,
For one of us has departed this life.
The burden of such a loss is difficult.
Everything changes now, and we must change with it.
The place that (name) held in our hearts is changed, for
*   what lies there is memory now.*
There are no magic words or incantations that will drive
*   out your sorrow.*
It is a wound that must heal like all others.
But know this, (name) shall rest happily among the
*   blessed when he (she) enters into the house of my*
*   Father, Osiris.*
Rejoice in his (her) good fortune, for he (she) is beyond
*   want.*
Let us reflect on the blessing of having known (name),
And speed his (her) journey to the land of the blessed.

Turn to the altar. Take the image and lift it up for all to see.

Behold, O creature of art!
Fashioned by steady hands,
And in a spirit of love.
You are now changed by the love of many,
Whose memories fill you,
And whose breath will wake you!
You are not mere clay,
You are flesh and blood.
You are consecrated by Water,
*   (Sprinkle the image with water.)*
You are consecrated by Fire,
*   (Wave the image over the source candle.)*
You are consecrated by Earth,
*   (Sprinkle a little salt or sand on the image.)*

And you are consecrated by Air.
  (Wave the image over the censer.)
You are spirit.
We here name you (name).
You are he (she) between the worlds and in all worlds.
We greet you!

The celebrant turns and faces into the Circle.
Hold the image for all to see. Say

Before you I stand, bearing (name).
He (she) is under my protection on this journey.
Naught will befall him (her) that is harmful.
Take heed, for this is your beloved departed.
So mote it be!

The image is returned to the altar. The celebrant stands before
the altar, hands out to his or her sides, and says

Well met, you who are newly deceased and have entered
  into the House of the Blessed.
You are well known of the Gods and will share all that is
  within them on your journey.
When you come to the Boat of a Million Years,
May you find your place among the stars.
Be known now by all the Gods.

These verses are adapted from the Pyramid Texts and may be
read responsively. They are not a literal translation by any means,
but they are close. While these lines are being read, the image is to
be wrapped in the cloth bandage. This action provides a symbolic
encircling, much like circumambulation.

He (she) who is newly arrived in the Great Hall stands before the
Ancient Ones. He (she) raises his (her) eyes to them and says:

CELEBRANT: *Be not unaware of me, O Re;*
GROUP: *If you know me, I will know you.*
CELEBRANT: *Be not unaware of me, O Re;*
GROUP: *Of me it is said, "Greatest of all who have passed."*
CELEBRANT: *Be not unaware of me, O Thoth;*
GROUP: *If you know me, I will know you.*
CELEBRANT: *Be not unaware of me, O Thoth;*
GROUP: *Of me it is said, "He (she) who rests."*
CELEBRANT: *Be not unaware of me, O Dweller in the
    Netherworld;*
GROUP: *If you know me, I will know you.*
CELEBRANT: *Be not unaware of me, O Dweller in the
    Netherworld;*
GROUP: *Of me it is said, "He who wakes healthy."*
CELEBRANT: *Be not unaware of me, O Bull of the Sky;*
GROUP: *If you know me, I will know you.*
CELEBRANT: *Be not unaware of me, O Bull of the Sky;*
GROUP: *Of me it is said, "He (she) is a star in the heavens."*

Now it is time to open the mouth of the deceased. In my coven, the wand is the tool of Air. Many groups attribute the athame to Air. The celebrant takes up whichever tool is attributed to air.

He or she holds it aloft and says

> *Blessed Be, O tool of the Art!*
> *Touched by the Spirit of Air.*
> *You are breath and breath is life.*
> *Cleave now the mouth of* (name),
> *And assure his (her) breath in the Great Hall.*

The celebrant touches the tool of Air to the mouth of the image.

> *Now is the mouth opened again.*
> *Receive our breath and be blessed with it.*

The celebrant turns and faces into the Circle again, holding the image as the group breathes in unison. People should breathe out in the direction of the image and imagine their breaths moving in and out of it. Each person should visualize the deceased breathing deeply.

After about a minute, the celebrant returns the image to the altar and says

> *He (she) lives now among the blessed!*
> *So mote it be!*

The mouth having been opened, it is now time to present offerings of food and assistance to the deceased. The image should still be on the altar. Place one of the offering plates beside it. Put a small amount of offering food on the plate. Say

> *On your journey, be fed with our love.*
> *May you never hunger.*

Dip the tips of three fingers into the offering drink. Sprinkle a few drops on the offering plate and say

> *On your journey, drink deeply of our affection.*
> *May you never thirst.*

Celebrant now turns and faces the group. It is time for people to present their scrolls. Say

> *Beloved children,*
> *Here is your newly departed.*
> *He (she) is revivified and prepared for the journey,*
> *There is food and drink,*
> *And the protection of Anubis encircles him (her).*
> *Bring now the gifts of your love and labor.*
> *And state your final farewells.*

One at a time, each member of the group takes up his or her scrolls to the altar. This is a private moment between the deceased and the presenter. Nothing need be said, but a short explanation of The Book of the Dead scroll would be appropriate. Here is an example of one possibility:

Presenting The Book of the Dead scroll:

> *Here on this scroll I present music. You were a lover of*
> *music, and you should have it on your journey. May it*
> *sing to your heart and uplift your spirit.*

Presenting a Letter to the Dead:

> *Here I present my last letter to you. You will understand*
> *its meaning as only the two of us could. Take it and be*
> *comforted. I will go on.*

When the scrolls and letters have been presented, perform the Offering Meal, adding a plate for the deceased and any possible hindering forces.

Then it is time for the interment. The celebrant should take up the image and cradle it gently. Another person takes up the offering plate, and a third takes up the scrolls. They form a line in that order with the rest of the group behind them. The group should chant, sing, play percussion instruments, or make joyful noises of any kind while the procession goes forward. Walk the circle at least three times in this fashion, coming to a halt at the western point. The celebrant should open a gate through the Circle boundary through which all pass. All gather around the interment site.

The celebrant says

> *We gather now at the vault. This is the place between this*
> *world and the next. We cannot follow or share in the*
> *journey ahead. That is for* (name) *alone.*

Address the image:

> (Name), *go forth with our love.*
> *Remember those present when you come to the Great Hall.*
> *May you enjoy the great favor of the Gods,*
> *And come to a new life refreshed.*
> *It is not meet to keep you here,*

Desire it though we may.
We sever now the connection between you and this image.
It is clay, but you are spirit.
Take the gifts we have bestowed,
And go as you will.

Lay the image in the hole. The next person adds the offering meal for the deceased and breaks the plate. Finally, the scrolls are added. Carefully fill in the hole.

The offering for the hindering forces is now scattered with these words:

You who would stand in the way of (**name**),
You who we do not know,
Be gone from this place and this person.
Leave him (her) alone on the road to the Great Hall.
You shall have no power,
And you shall be as sand beneath his (her) feet.
Take this meal and be satisfied.

Break the plate and scatter its pieces.

Return to the Circle space after a few moments. When all are gathered again, the celebrant says

And now, it is done.
Let us share with our Gods,
And welcome them into our hearts.

Take up the food and drink from the offering meal and share it. Open the Circle.

The power of a ritual is greatly affected by the amount of effort that goes into designing and performing it. The Requiem has the potential to be very powerful, indeed.

As I said earlier, it is not necessary to do everything exactly as laid out here. You may have other ideas and inspirations that will make the ritual more pertinent for you. In addition, those who knew the deceased may choose a completely different flavor for the ritual atmosphere. Even in grief, we can laugh if that is what the departed enjoyed. Often, memories will spark spontaneous observances as well.

FINAL REFLECTION

I will close with one final reflection. It has been many years since the dream that started this chapter. In that time, I have come to understand something.

Anubis was being impish.

It is true that I did not pay attention to what He was saying. It is also true that if I had paid attention I would not have comprehended Him. Because those words are not of this earth, they cannot be passed along from mouth to ear. Instead, they are planted like seeds in the soil of our very being. It's like being told a parable. On the surface of it, we were told a story. Down deep, we know we have been taught a lesson, but we can't put it into words of our own. Over time, however, the true meaning of the story comes through to us as we experience insights and moments of spiritual clarity in response to seemingly mundane events and situations. With time and care, the lessons will bear fruit and make of us an example for others to follow. To the extent that this chapter has proven of use to you, it is an example of that fruit.

Merry meet, merry part, and merry meet again.

GODS AND GODDESSES

My primary source for this information is George Hart's *Dictionary of Egyptian Gods and Goddesses*. This book is invaluable as an approachable source of information that is succinct yet thorough. Hart's bibliography is excellent as well.

In secondary terms, I have added some observations of my own from various readings. All of these materials are listed in the Resources.

Amun-Re	Syncretized form of the supreme God of the pantheon (Amun) with the ancient solar God of Heliopolis (Re).
	"Syncretized" does not mean that either God is subsumed in the other. Rather, They are joined but retain Their own identities.
Anpu	Ancient Egyptian name for Anubis.
Anubis	Ancient Egyptian God of the Necropolis and embalming.
Bata	Lesser-known God of Upper Egypt. Bata (or Bet) is often pictured as a bull. Precisely what His attributes were is unclear although He is mentioned in several texts.
	Bata's primary claim to fame is the part He plays in the Tale of the Two Brothers.
Geb	Primeval earth God, child of Shu and Tefnut and father of Osiris, Isis, Nephthys, and Seth.
Hathor	Daughter of Re, Goddess of women, joy, and sexuality. In her aspect as the Eye of Re, Hathor becomes Sakhmet. Her ferocity in this form is such that Re will steer clear of Her. (See Sakhmet.)
Isis	Daughter of Geb and Nut, sister-wife of Osiris, and mother of Horus. Isis also raised Anubis after Nephthys rejected Him.
	Isis is the Goddess of wisdom, magic, and healing. She also has a strong political streak.
Heliopolis	Greek meaning "sun-city." Heliopolis was the center of sun worship (primarily in the forms of Re and Atum) in ancient Egypt.
Khnum	Creator God of Elephantine. Khnum was said to have created all life on His potter's wheel. He is pictured as a man with the head of a ram.
Ma'at	Goddess of universal harmony and balance.
Nephthys	Daughter of Geb and Nut, sister-wife of Seth, and birth mother of Anubis.

Nun   The primeval celestial sea out of which Re is said
               to have risen. Nun (pronounced "noon") is
               nonexistence and was not worshipped as other
               Gods in Egypt.

Nut   Sky Goddess, daughter of Shu and Tefnut, sister-
               wife of Geb. Her name is pronounced "noot."

Osiris   Firstborn son of Geb and Nut, brother-husband of
               Isis. Osiris is the God primarily associated with
               kingship and the afterlife.

Re   Primary creator God of Heliopolis. Re may be seen
               as the sun at midday.

Re-Atum   Syncretized form combining Re and Atum. In this
               aspect, the God arose from the sea of Nun and cre-
               ated His first children by masturbating.
                   This form of the God may be seen as the sun
               in the evening.

Re-Harakhti   Syncretized form combining Re with Harakhti
               (Horus of the Horizon). In this aspect, the God
               represents the sunrise.

Sakhmet   Lion-headed Goddess, daughter of Re. Sakhmet
               carried the wrath of Re against His enemies but
               almost destroyed humankind in the process. She
               was stopped only after Re mixed red ocher with
               beer and got Her drunk.
                   She is also known as the Eye of Re and is
               an aspect of Hathor. Her center of worship was
               Memphis.

Seth   Second son of Shu and Tefnut, brother and mur-
               derer of Osiris. Seth (Set, Sutekh, later called
               Typhon by the Greeks) ruled the destructive and
               chaotic forces of nature as well as the burning
               desert.
                   Seth is mentioned as an enemy of Re in some
               texts, but He is charged with the responsibility for

destroying Apophis each night. In Papyrus Chester Beatty I, however, Re is determined to see Seth enthroned before Horus.

Seth should not be written off as purely evil. His character is far more complex than that.

Shu

First son of Re-Atum, brother-husband of Tefnut. Shu is the primeval God of air and is often depicted as separating Geb (earth) and Nut (sky).

Tefnut

First daughter of Re-Atum and sister-wife of Shu. Tefnut is the Goddess of the primeval mists. She is the mother of Geb and Nut.

Thoth

Ibis-headed God of scribes, writing, and knowledge. Thoth is also pictured as a baboon and is considered a lunar Deity.

Depending on the legend you read, Thoth is either a son of Re or was born by parthenogenesis when He sprang from the head of Seth. Papyrus Chester Beatty I states that the seed of Horus came from Seth's head (much to Seth's chagrin) and became the lunar disk that Thoth placed on His own head.

Thoth was a peacekeeper among the Gods. In one tale, He took the form of a baboon and approached Sakhmet (a dangerous thing to do) in an effort to persuade Her to return to Re as Hathor.

Resources

Armour, Robert A. *Gods and Myths of Ancient Egypt.* 10th ed., Cairo: American University in Cairo Press, 1999.

Harris, Geraldine, and O'Connor, David. *Gods and Pharaohs from Egyptian Mythology.* New York: Peter Bedrick Books, 1998.

Hart, George. *A Dictionary of Egyptian Gods and Goddesses.* London: Routledge & Kegan Paul, 2000.

Hornung, Erik. *Conceptions of God in Ancient Egypt, The One and the Many.* Trans. John Baines. Ithaca: Cornell University Press, 1982.

————.*Ancient Egyptian Books of the Afterlife*. Trans. David Lorton. Ithaca: Cornell University Press, 1999.

Lichtheim, Miriam. *Ancient Egyptian Literature*. Vol. 2, *The New Kingdom*. Los Angeles: University of California Press, 1976.

Meeks, Dimitri, and Christine Favard-Meeks. *Daily Life of the Egyptian Gods*. Trans. G. M. Goshgarian. Ithaca: Cornell University Press, 1996.

Ritner, Robert Kriech. *The Mechanics of Ancient Egyptian Magical Practice, Studies in Ancient Oriental Civilization* No. 54 (third printing). Chicago: Oriental Institute of Chicago, 1997.

Simms, Maria Kay. *Circle of the Cosmic Muse, A Wiccan Book of Shadows*. St. Paul: Llewellyn Publications, 1994.

Simpson, William K., ed. *The Literature of Ancient Egypt*. New Haven and London: Yale University Press, 1973.

Starhawk and NightMare, M. Macha, eds. *The Pagan Book of Living and Dying*. San Francisco: HarperFrancisco, 1997.

Wood, Robin. *When, Why . . . If*, Dearborn, MI: Livingtree Books, 1996.

PART II

IMBOLC

Alexei Kondratiev teaches Irish language, Celtic mythology, Celtic Christianity, and other topics related to Celtic tradition at the Irish Arts Center in New York City. He gained his passionate interest in Celtic lore during his formative years in rural France. After majoring in anthropology and linguistics at Columbia University, he studied Celtic philology at the École des Hautes-Études in Paris and acquired all the living Celtic languages by staying with communities of native speakers, including those in the Aran Islands. Alexei is an officer in the Celtic League American Branch, and a board member of IMBAS, a Celtic Reconstructionist network. He is also the author of *The Apple Branch: A Path to Celtic Ritual*, as well as many articles. He has lectured frequently on various aspects of Celtic tradition at Pagan and interfaith spiritual conferences throughout the Northeast. Together with his partner Len Rosenberg (Black Lotus) he coleads Mnemosynides/ Children of Memory, a Protean coven in New York City.

Brigit

In a glen in the east of Ireland, protected from the toil and battle of the world outside, a group of chosen women came together within a round enclosure to tend a fire lit before any of them were born.

It was, on the face of it, a simple thing, this tending of a fire. It was what women had been assigned to do for countless generations while their menfolk hunted or made war on each other. It involved little that was spectacular or likely to be remembered in stories or to enhance the individual reputation of any of those engaged in it—such things, in a warrior society, were still largely the province of men.

And yet, however discreet and unassuming this activity might have been, no one doubted its fundamental importance to human survival. Without fire, there was darkness, and people were at the mercy of nocturnal beasts of prey—and even more sinister, less easily defined presences in the night. Without fire, the frosts of winter would kill without mercy, and nobody in the community would live to see the spring. A fire in the dark night was a beacon, a reassuring sign that a place of safety and comfort existed, that there was a home one could come back to from the perils of the outside world. It was also through fire that one could operate the miraculous alchemy that turned raw into cooked, transforming the gory animal corpses the hunters brought back into something not only nourishing but pleasant to eat.

Whatever heroic exploits men performed—raids on enemy tribes, conquests of new territories, plunder of rich, alien civilizations, battles to enhance the glory of their name and their status among other warriors—they knew that the home fire the women tended gave them the only opportunity they would ever have to rest and enjoy the fruits of their endeavors. For all the adventures and brave deeds that might seize the community's attention and wake its imagination, it was the home fire that was the true focus; today, we recall this very ancient concept in our everyday speech, since *focus* in Latin means "hearth." Fire, especially in a hearth, is a symbol of continued existence, giving all activities a dependable and creative center. Because of its irreplaceable role, fire was held sacred—as was the female care that maintained it.

While it was, of course, ordinary mortal women who tended the fire, the power that sustained it was known to be something much larger, something that had stood, dependable and unchanging, for countless generations of the community's existence, regardless of who actually did the work at any given time. The power of warmth and safety that worked through the women was felt to be

eternal, unlimited by human fallibility. It was natural to think of
this power as a goddess, since it made itself known through the
work and care of women. The best way to honor and propitiate
this goddess was to ensure that the women would continue to
tend the fire, always with the same time-hallowed gestures, enact-
ing a ritual of supreme importance, without which the goddess
might remove her benefits from the human tribe.

In a patriarchal society, each woman belonged to a specific
household, headed by her father or her husband, and worked only
for that household. It was to feed the people in this household
that she prepared food; it was to clothe them that she spun wool
and flax and wove cloth; and when she kindled the fire and took
on the role of the goddess, protection was extended only to the
people gathered around her particular hearth.

Kinship was the strongest bond known to that society: it created magical channels through which energy flowed as freely and
strongly as blood within a living body, but which were closed to
anything that stood outside that relationship.

There were, nevertheless, many occasions when the entire community's need called for cooperation between several kin groups.
To defend their common territory against invaders (or to have
success in invading a foreign land themselves), warriors of many
different families would have to join together for a single purpose—
the outcome of which would depend on all of them collectively.
Their hope was that the same degree of divine protection would
apply to all of them at the same time.

Material survival, as well, might require a large number of kin
groups to participate in joint projects of forest clearance, building,
irrigation, herding, and the like. As social life grew more complex,
kings appeared as nodes of sovereignty, rallying points for different
kin groups who could then justify their working together on a
basis of equality.

Obviously this larger tribal entity would also have urgent need
of the blessings of the goddess of the hearth fire, without whom

nothing was assured of a future. Yet if it was through the rituals performed by women that such blessings were obtained, and if what women did benefited only the specific households to which they belonged, how could one ensure that the protection of the goddess would be given to the tribe as a whole?

The solution was to designate some women as belonging not to any one particular household, but to the tribe collectively. These women would be consecrated to serve the goddess for the benefit of the entire community, not just their own families. They would be absolved of other responsibilities so that they could concentrate on performing the rituals pleasing to the goddess continually, making this their sole function. In order to make sure that the power of their ritual actions wouldn't get diverted to the benefit of one specific family, they remained unmarried, and generally abstained from any sex with men (for, according to their laws, any sexual act was a kind of "marriage," implying some commitments and obligations).

While other women continued to tend the hearth fire for their individual households (and the goddess, of course, continued to be present in every one of those home fires), what the celibate priestesses did in the tribe's collective sanctuary was soon felt to be far more effective, for they served the whole community. The luck of the entire tribe came to depend on how well the priestesses pleased the goddess, and on how well the rest of the community could assist the priestesses in doing this. So, without weapons or other physical means, these women managed to have some authority over even the warriors and the kings.

INDO-EUROPEAN ROOTS

Because the Celtic peoples of that early period (whose culture, in ancient times, extended over a wide area of Europe, from Ireland and Spain all the way to what is now Turkey) left us very little in the way of written documents, we have no way of knowing for sure how widespread these sanctuaries of the hearth fire goddess were in the Celtic world, or exactly how the life of the priestesses was organized. Every tribe may have had a sanctuary of this sort, or it may have been a custom that, by the height of Celtic civilization during the Iron Age (700 B.C.E.–100 C.E.), survived in only a few places.

We do know, however, that such customs correspond to some very ancient ideas in Indo-European tradition. When, some time around 3000 B.C.E., peoples speaking related languages of the language family we call Indo-European (from which most of the languages of modern Europe are descended) first entered Europe by way of the Danube valley (while other related peoples went to Iran and India), they brought with them a large body of shared customs. These were based on a common view of what the universe was like and of the place that gods and humans had in it.

The Celts were one such Indo-European people; so were the Germans, the Greeks, and the Slavs, among others. All developed some differences in their cultures according to the specific material circumstances in which they found themselves and the contacts they had with yet other cultures, but they shared a core heritage that remained little changed for many centuries.

ROMAN FIRE PRIESTESSES

One other Indo-European people, the Romans, kept very good records, so that we know a good deal about how their society and religion developed over time. We know about the college of Vestal Virgins who tended the fire of the Romans' own hearth fire goddess, Vesta, for the benefit of the entire city of Rome. There were, at the height of the tradition, six women in the college. The Pontifex Maximus—the High Priest—of Rome would choose a group of young girls for their beauty and healthful appearance. Those who actually got to serve were chosen from among this group by casting lots, calling upon the will of the gods.

The need for the Vestals to maintain their chastity was very serious: if discovered to have broken their vows, they could be buried alive. There was simply too much at stake. Whatever great conquests the Roman armies achieved, however great the power and riches the rulers of the city managed to amass, the continued prosperity of Rome depended on Vesta's protection, which in turn depended on her fire being properly tended by women who belonged to no man, but only to Rome itself.

The shrine where the Vestals performed their ritual duties was near the Forum Romanum, in the shadow of the Palatine Hill, one of the oldest parts of the city. In keeping with its origins and function, this shrine wasn't at all made in the style of the other Roman temples. Instead, it was designed to resemble a round house, such as the ones early Italians (and Celts) had built long before Rome was a real city. The part of the shrine the fire was in was called the *atrium Vestae* ("Vesta's courtyard"), and the altar was literally the hearth of the house and, by extension, the central hearth of all Rome. As the Vestals carried on a tradition begun in the earliest days of their community, so their shrine was intended to re-create those ancient surroundings.

The fire that manifested the presence of Vesta had to be kept lit at all times. If by any chance it was inauspiciously extinguished (as happened more than once in the history of Rome), it couldn't be relit in the then-modern, practical way, by striking sparks from a flint: one had to use a *chark*, a wooden instrument that produces fire through friction. From Celtic folk practices we know that they lit their ceremonial fires by the same method. Vesta's fire was also rekindled ceremonially with a chark each year on March 1.

The Vestals tended their goddess's fire throughout the year, but there was one particular season when all Romans gave it their attention. This was the Vestalia festival, which lasted from June 7 to June 15, with the culminating ritual on June 9. Vestalia celebrated the community's ability to produce enough food to sustain itself. People baked bread. The mills where the grain had been ground into flour were decorated with garlands. Eventually it became a kind of professional holiday for millers and bakers and all other purveyors of grain products.

It was also very much a holiday for the women of the community. They were given leave to visit the most sacred parts of the shrine, where only the Vestals were usually allowed to go. What exactly they did there, we don't know. There was an area of the shrine that corresponded to the house's granary, and no doubt it was where the city's ability to feed itself was magically sustained.

Another very sacred object that was kept hidden from public view in the shrine of Vesta was the Palladium, a statue of the Greek goddess Athena. According to Roman tradition, the Palladium was brought to Italy after the Trojan War by the hero Aeneas, the mythic ancestor of the founders of Rome. The luck of the city was evidently also bound up with the proper worship and care of this divine image. Perhaps the Palladium was related to the general function of the shrine because both Vesta and Athena are virgin goddesses, and Athena is especially a protector of culture and the activities of city people.

The Vestalia was the biggest festival the Vestals took part in, but they had special duties at other times of the year as well, involving service to other deities besides Vesta. The fertility feast of the Lupercalia on February 15 was the prelude to the growing season. Ritual salt cake for ceremonial use was produced from the first fruits of the previous year's grain harvest. The Fordicidia on April 15 was the time when pregnant cows were sacrificed to Tellus, the Earth Mother of Rome; the Vestals gathered ashes from the burned remains. A few days later, on the April 21 feast of the Parilia, the Vestals sprinkled those ashes on the bonfire around which the shepherds danced. On August 24 (and again on December 15) during the Consualia, held in honor of Consus (the horse-loving grain god), the Vestals assisted the Flamen Quirinalis—the Priest of Quirinus, one of the oldest gods of Rome—in performing sacrifices. Clearly all these deities and the activities with which they were concerned needed to have some association with Vesta and her representatives: without the focus she provided, all those activities would fail.

BRIGIT: IRISH SAINT AND CELTIC GODDESS

This, then, was how a hearth fire goddess was honored in ancient Rome. Now let's take this information into the Celtic world. Even though we have no direct evidence from the Iron Age that any Celtic tribe on the Continent had any institution like that of the Vestal Virgins, we do have a striking example from Ireland at the time when the island was rapidly becoming Christian.

Toward the end of the fifth century C.E., in Ireland's eastern province of Leinster, at a holy place called Cill Dara (the Chapel of the Oak, now known in English as Kildare), there lived a community of celibate women devoted to tending a sacred fire.

By the time we hear about them, these women were Christian— they had become nuns. Yet the nature of their community had little to do with Christian precepts, and bore little resemblance to the way Christian monastic communities were starting to organize themselves elsewhere in the Celtic world. Instead, they were remarkably similar in concept to the Vestal Virgins.

Perhaps they would have been forgotten by history if it hadn't been for their leader, although most of what we know about her comes from legend rather than from contemporaneous documents. There is absolutely no doubt that she was an extraordinarily charismatic person. Her name was Brigit.[1]

---

[1]In modern Irish and Scots Gaelic the name of the goddess/saint is spelled Brìd and Brighid respectively (both are pronounced "breedj"). For the sake of convenience and simplicity I've used the medieval Irish spelling Brigit throughout, as I suspect it's one of the more familiar versions of the name.

In Welsh the goddess's name seems to have originally been Breint (like the river on Anglesey), but today, especially in relation to the cult of the saint, she is more usually called Ffraed or Ffraid, as in Llansantffraid (the Church of St. Brigit), the name given to several small towns in Wales.

That was definitely the name of a goddess. We can trace its use throughout Celtic-speaking areas on the Continent and in Great Britain, wherever the names of gods and goddesses were worshipped at holy sites and recorded through inscriptions. Beginning around the third century B.C.E., influenced by their literate trading partners in the Mediterranean, the Celts had started to write their own languages. They first used Greek letters, then Roman ones. Soon after that, when the Romans had conquered most of the Celtic world outside Ireland, writing became even more commonplace. In particular, new temples would bear written dedications to the divinities in whose honor they had been built.

The Romans liked to think that all the gods of foreign peoples were merely variant forms of the gods of their own pantheon, and always tried to establish one-to-one correspondences between them. This is called the *interpretatio Romana*. For instance, a god who was mainly worshipped by warriors would be equated with Mars, a god who was a healer and had a shining countenance would be called Apollo, a god associated with thunder would have to be Jupiter, a goddess who had the character of a queen in majesty was probably Juno, and so on. Of course, these correspondences broke down past a certain level, since the gods and goddesses of different cultures are different. Local people were often well aware of the differences and preferred to think of their deities in their own way. Luckily, the inscriptions on the shrines often tell us what those deities were called originally as well as who the Romans thought they were.

One of the goddesses the Romans thought they recognized among the Celtic deities was their own Minerva, their goddess of arts and culture and civilized life, whom they also equated with the Greek Athena. Julius Caesar, who had good opportunity to observe the Celts closely as he was conquering Gaul, took note of the worship of a Celtic goddess that he compared to the Roman goddess Minerva.

We do indeed find, at sites held sacred by the Celts both before and after the Roman conquest, records of a goddess who has this kind of interest in crafts and creativity and how they enhance the well-being of the human community. She usually has a name that contains the element "brig-", which means "to be raised up."

In what today is eastern France we find the goddess Bricta, who, together with the local god Luxouius, protected the thermal spring at Luxeuil, to which pilgrims came for healing. A little to the south and west, at Alesia, the goddess Bergusia ruled in partnership with the smith god Ucuetis. Their temple was dedicated to the art of metalworking. At Auxey (not far from where I grew up), a local landowner named Iccauos Oppianicnos in the first century C.E. wrote a dedication to the goddess Brigindo. And across the channel, in what was to become Yorkshire and Lancashire in the north of England, the goddess Brigantia was the patroness of the large and prosperous tribe called the Brigantes.

The archetypal "element that rises," in Celtic as well as in other Indo-European traditions, is fire. Fire is, of course, what made settled human existence possible. The goddess Brigit, who protects comfortable, prosperous, and creative living, has never lost her connection with fire.

It is interesting to note that she also became intimately connected with water. For the Celts, water—in opposition to fire—is the archetypal "element that descends" down to a cold, dark, chaotic underworld. Yet there is a way in which water can become "that which is raised up"—for example, as the bubbling mineral spring that Bricta watches over. Water that goes against its fundamental "descending" nature and takes on some of the properties of fire, therefore, became associated with Brigit, "who raises everything up." Most important, such thermal springs often have healing properties, which puts them firmly within the sphere of the goddess's concern for human well-being.

In a larger sense, all water that breaks free of its underworld realm by gushing up onto the surface of the land—all rivers and springs—makes itself available to human needs (whether for drinking, for irrigation, or for navigation) and comes under the goddess's patronage. So it's no surprise that the goddess's name should have been given to rivers: for example, the river Brent which joins the Thames just east of London; and the little river Breint on the island of Anglesey (the site of the last great Druid sanctuary in Britain) off the coast of North Wales.

Why, then, did the leader of a Christian community in Ireland have a native goddess's name, and why was her community engaged in some activities that had little direct basis in Christian tradition but instead reflected some well-known pre-Christian concepts?

We simply don't have enough historical evidence to answer that question with certainty, but we can make an educated guess. Very probably, the community existed before the coming of Christianity. It was dedicated to the worship of the hearth fire goddess, along lines broadly similar to the college of the Vestal Virgins in Rome. The leader of these priestesses was considered a human incarnation of the goddess herself, and so was called by her name (the Old Irish name Brigit is the exact equivalent, in linguistic terms, of the goddess name Brigindo in eastern France). The power of the goddess manifesting in her gave her an authority that could match that of any of the male political leaders of the country.

TRANSITION

In circumstances unknown to us, this high priestess of Brigit (who was herself Brigit) converted to Christianity and made her community a Christian one. She didn't, however, renounce the goddess who was present in her (How could she? That presence was obvious to everyone) and so she lost none of her authority, holding her own against male Christian leaders, and influencing the way Christian institutions developed in Ireland during her lifetime. Her community retained its most basic pre-Christian practices.

As a result, the boundary between the identities of the goddess and the saint (for so did Brigit of Cill Dara come to be considered, perhaps within her lifetime) became blurred in the consciousness of later generations. Since the woman who was the goddess had become a revered icon and indisputable authority throughout the Celtic Christian world, didn't this mean that the goddess herself had become an accepted part of Christian tradition?

It was comforting for people to feel that they didn't have to give up the goddess who had always looked after their welfare and given them the energy they needed to do their daily work. She could remain at the heart of the official religion their nations had chosen to follow. And if this was so, then the stories and rituals they had always associated with the goddess could continue to be passed down, even if they didn't specifically correspond to episodes in the life of the saint (who, after all, was the goddess). The authority of the saint protected all of the rich lore surrounding the goddess whose identity she shared.

By at least the seventh century, the saint's feast was celebrated on February 1. Learned Irish tradition also identified this with the ancient festival of Imbolc or Oímelc, which was considered to be the first day of spring. Throughout the Gaelic-speaking world, *Lá Fhéile Bríde* ("the Day of the Feast of Brigit") has become the means of expressing all the patterns and symbols relevant to the worship of Brigit the goddess, in the process of honoring Brigit the saint. Today, much of what allows us to renew our living contact with this goddess comes from the stories and rituals that have been used to celebrate this feast in Celtic communities for many centuries.

The Day of the Feast of Brigit falls on the eve of the important Christian feast of the Presentation (popularly called Candlemas in England). This holy day celebrates Jesus' being taken to the temple by his parents forty days after his birth to be blessed, in accordance with Jewish custom. (This feast is also called the Purification of the Virgin, since it marked the occasion of the *mikvah*, or ritual bath, Mary had to take after giving birth.) Over time, Brigit was connected with that celebration as well, making her hold on Christian tradition even more secure (we will return to some of these stories later).

Everything about the saint points back to the goddess who lived in her. Without the stories about the saint, we would have far less understanding of the goddess.

PRE-CHRISTIAN STORIES

What stories do we have about the goddess that clearly predate the stories about the saint?

From the materials Irish scholars compiled between the eighth and the twelfth century, we can piece together a broad picture. Brigit is the daughter of the Dagda, the "Good God" who married the goddess of the Boyne, the most sacred of the rivers of Ireland; her name means "the White Cow." Said to be the ultimate source of all of Ireland's waters, the Boyne goddess is one of the most powerful images of nurture and protection in the tradition.

The Dagda (or Eochaidh Ollathair, "Stallionlike Huge Father," to give him his proper name) is not only a giant and powerful masculine presence, but is proficient in many different skills. He plays the harp so well that he can move the year into changing its seasons. He is the "red one of great knowledge," who can see into the dimensions beyond our world and use magic and prophecy. He is a feared warrior who goes into battle with a great club with which he kills people by striking them with one end, and restores them to life by striking them with the other end. He is also a conscientious provider, possessing, by virtue of his marriage to the Boyne, a cauldron that is "never dry," a source of food that can never be exhausted. Thus Brigit inherits, on her mother's side, an unending capacity for caring and nurturing, and on her father's, a connection with the very many and diverse skills that ensure human survival and enrichment.

Brigit's brother is Aonghas ("Single Vigor"), the *Mac Óg* (the "Young Son," or "Young Boy"). He is a god of youth and beauty, of the strong growth of springtime, and of love—especially illicit and romantic love. His stronghold, which he tricked his father, the Dagda, into giving him, is Brú na Bóinne (or Newgrange, as English speakers call it today), the great Stone Age passage grave (neolithic underground burial chamber) in the valley of the Boyne.

Brigit has two other brothers, Aodh ("Fire") and Cearmhaid Milbhéal ("Honey-Mouth"), who appears to have inherited some of the same seductive qualities as has Aonghas. Cearmhaid Milbhéal was killed by Lugh (the great all-purpose god, about whom we will have more to tell later) because he was said to have committed adultery with Lugh's wife. This was later discovered to be a lie, a malicious rumor spread by a druid. The Dagda, after long and patient searching, eventually found the means to bring his son back to life.

Cearmhaid's sons (Brigit's nephews) are Mac Cuill ("Son of the Hazel"), Mac Céacht ("Son of the Plough"), and Mac Gréine ("Son of the Sun"). They are married to Éire, Banbha, and Fódla, the three goddesses who are the essence of the land of Ireland itself and whose permission must be sought by anyone who wishes to live and prosper there. When the ancestors of the modern Irish first set foot on the land, their bard did a ritual of praise to these three goddesses, who then favored him and his people over the previous inhabitants.

Brigit has two "royal" and "faithful" oxen (castrated bulls), Fea and Mean. She also owns Cirb, the rìgh-mholtraidhe or "king of the wethers" (castrated rams often used to lead a flock of sheep). Since Brigit, as we shall see, is very much concerned with cattle and sheep and their products, it is natural that she should have the "kings" of these species as her pets. It is also appropriate, in light of what we will learn of Brigit's character, that these should be hardworking but not sexually active males.

These, then, are Brigit's family and her companions. There is no record of Brigit marrying or having children herself. The only possible allusion to such a thing we have is in the story called *Cath*

Maige Tuired, which is an Irish version of the widespread Indo-European myth of the battle between the Gods Above and the Gods Below.

The Celts, like Indo-Europeans in general, divided their divine beings into two main categories: deities associated with the sky, clarity, reason, and all the ordered forms of human culture and deities that live in a dark, watery underworld below the land, who are the source of fertility but whose nature is chaotic and generally unfriendly to humans. Both sides—the rational patterns conceived by the human mind and the wild, unpredictable fertility of nature—are necessary for human survival, so neither one can eliminate the other. Since humans do need to be protected from unpredictability and disorder, however, the Gods Above have to win a victory over the Gods Below, and get them to cooperate.

In medieval Irish literature, the Gods Above are identified with the *Tuatha Dé Danann* (a people counted among the successive "invaders" of Ireland), and the Gods Below are called the *Fomhoraigh* ("Monsters from Below") or Fomorians. The Second Battle of Maigh Tuireadh is the great confrontation between them in which the Fomorians are defeated.

In the context of this battle, we are told that Brígh, a daughter of the Dagda, was married to Breas, the part-Danann, part-Fomorian who had been chosen as king of Ireland by both groups in an attempt to reconcile their differences peacefully. Breas, however, attractive in outward appearance, was inwardly very much a Fomorian, ungenerous and uncooperative. Under his reign Ireland suffered terribly, and this was what eventually led to the final great battle.

Brígh and Breas had one son, Ruadhán. Because the divine smith Goibhne could, with his magical skill, make an unlimited supply of weapons for the *Tuatha Dé Danann* (whereas the Fomorians had no such craftsmen), the Fomorians decided to send Ruadhán to murder Goibhne. They assumed that, because he was part Danann on his mother's side, the *Tuatha Dé Danann* would accept him as kin; and they were right. Ruadhán had Goibhne make him a spear, then returned to the smithy and cast it at him. Although the smith was wounded, he was able to pull out the spear and throw it back at his assailant, piercing him through. Ruadhán managed to run back to the Fomorian camp, where he died in the presence of his parents. In a paroxysm of grief, Brígh broke out in lamentation over her son's body. We are told that this was the first time that keening for the dead was ever heard in Ireland.

Brígh, although related, is not the same word as *Brigit*, and it may be that the story was not originally about the same person. However, by making her the daughter of the Dagda, the author of the story obviously meant to identify Brígh with Brigit. The *Banshenchus* (the Lore of Women, another medieval Irish text), by repeating this identification, seems to confirm it. If the story indeed refers to Brigit, it indicates that her marriage was short-lived, painful, and left no issue. It also suggests that, in relation to Brigit, the very notion of marriage is disastrous—a concept we shall see confirmed in some other stories.

Cormac Ua Cuillenáin, a brilliant Irish scholar of the late ninth century, wrote a famous glossary, the *Sanas Cormaic*, in which he explains the meanings and origins of pre-Christian terms that were in danger of becoming completely unintelligible to the thoroughly Christianized society of his day. We learn from him that Brigit is the name of three sisters with different occupations—which we can understand to mean that she is a triple goddess, with three specialized functions (something quite common in Celtic tradition). First and foremost, she is a *banfhile* or "female poet" (or a *bé n-éicsi*, a "woman of poetic art"), who was worshipped by poets because of her beauty and splendor. Her sisters were, respectively, a *bé legis* ("woman of healing") and a *bé goibneachta* ("woman of smithcraft").

While the word *bé* originally meant simply "woman," it gradually came to imply a women with somewhat exalted attributes, an object of romantic infatuation or of spiritual awe; and in modern

Irish usage it can usually be translated as "muse." The three Brigit sisters, then, are the "muses" of their three occupations: one inspires the work of poets, the second lends her energy to healing, and the third aids smiths who make both weapons and the tools of technology.

It is undoubtedly in relation to her role as muse that we are told of Brigit being the "wife" of Seanchán Toirpéist, the seventh-century poet who "rediscovered" the *Táin Bó Cualnge*, the epic telling of the exploits of the great hero Cú Chulainn. This was one of the most famous works of medieval Irish literature. According to the tale, Seanchán conjured up the spirit of Fergus mac Róich, a long-dead warrior king of Ulster and one of the characters in the epic itself, and got the story from his own ghostly lips. The presence of Brigit suggests that she had more than a casual hand in the composition.

Brigit is also a patron of law and legal counsel—an absolutely crucial component of civilized culture. We are told that she was at the origin of the laws that codified the rights and privileges of women.

In very traditional Gaelic-speaking areas, people have retained some knowledge of this lore of Brigit as goddess—not quite eclipsed by Brigit as saint—into modern times. They remember her family, and are strongly aware of her presence at the beginning of February, when she awakens the spring. In the Scottish Highlands, it is said that at the end of every autumn the Cailleach (the winter hag, the unfriendly aspect of the land goddess) traps Brigit inside Ben Nevis, the highest mountain in Scotland. Throughout the winter Brigit is forced to work as a drudge, enduring continuous abuse and humiliation. When the year returns to her feast day, however, her brother Aonghas rescues her, so that her fiery nature, which will be discussed further, can warm the land again and guide it back toward summer.

Another version of the story says that it is the Cailleach herself who grows weary of her cruelty and ugliness, so that on the dawning of Brigit's feast day she goes to a certain sacred well and washes herself in the pure water, and is transformed into Brigit.

Among the things Brigit sees to as she kindles the fire of the new spring in the land is the awakening of her prophetic adder, which hibernates through the winter. With the growing warmth of increased sunlight, the snake begins to stir. On the goddess's feast day, it peeps out to see what weather conditions are like. If winter winds still seem to predominate, it will go back to its shelter; but if it looks as if spring weather has come to stay, it will leave the mound and resume an active life. Although the adder is poisonous, all the traditions stress that on this day it is harmless and helpful. As one ritual verse from Scotland puts it:

> *Moch maduinn Brighde*
> *Thig an nimhir as an toll.*
> *Cha bhean mise ris an nimhir,*
> *Cha bhean an nimhir rium.*

(Early on Brigit's morning the adder will come out of the hole. I will not harm the adder, nor will the adder harm me.)

ABBESS, BISHOP, AND SAINT—CHRISTIAN STORIES

The themes that are developed most vividly with regard to Brigit relate to her as a saint. Her stories were first given their Christian form in the *Life of Brigit* written in Latin by the monk Cogitosus in the mid-seventh century. The *Lives of Brigit* written in Irish later in the Middle Ages included new episodes.

The child who would become Brigit of Cill Dara was the daughter of Dubhthach Donn, a chieftain from Ireland's eastern province of Leinster. Her mother, Broicseach, was one of his slaves. Female slaves (*cumhala*) were considered important property in early Ireland (so much so that one of the units of currency in trading was called a *cumhal*). These women were exploited sexually as a matter of course. The father, however, was responsible for the upkeep of any children that resulted.

In Brigit's case, her origins are important because they establish her as the result of a magical union of opposites. Her father was, in the local context of his tribe, a king, at the pinnacle of the social hierarchy. Her mother was at the other extreme, completely powerless. Since she was both the daughter of a chieftain and the daughter of a slave, Brigit's status was ambiguous. On the one hand, she could be seen as the child of a slave and could be neglected without any real consequences. On the other hand, she had royal blood and could become useful as a political pawn—she could be offered in marriage to another chieftain seeking a political alliance, for instance. By her heritage, then, Brigit embraced the whole spectrum of the community she would serve when she became a mediator of the energy of the hearth fire goddess.

The very manner of Brigit's birth indicated an opening to influences from beyond our everyday reality. Broicseach took care of her master's cattle. As she was crossing the threshold of a house while carrying a pail of milk—she had one foot outside and the other foot inside—she suddenly, right then and there, gave birth to Brigit. To be born in this "liminal" situation (quite literally, since *limen* means "threshold" in Latin), on the boundary between two states but not belonging entirely to either one of them, creates an ideal opportunity to be a bridge between two realities—between the world of humans and the world of the gods and goddesses, for instance, as would be the case with Brigit.

The pail of milk that was also on the threshold when this happened indicated the nature of what Brigit would be attracting from the divine world: nourishment, health, abundance. Brigit would indeed come to be associated very closely with milk and cattle. To make the relationship even clearer, Broicseach at once washed her newborn baby in the milk from her pail.

During her earlier years Brigit was definitely treated as a slave. She was often left alone and unfed. The powers who had presided over her birth, however, kept their attention on her. A mysterious white cow with red ears would come to care for her, and fed her milk when nobody else would. In Celtic stories, white animals with red ears are immediately recognizable as not being natural beasts but creatures from the Otherworld. The red-eared white hounds that fly in the skies with the Wild Hunt as it herds the spirits of the dead during the Samhain (Halloween) season, are one example. Another is the red-eared white cattle that belong to the fairies and come out of certain lakes to graze in meadows on moonlit nights.

In Brigit's case, however, one should remember that as a goddess her mother is the White Cow, the river Boyne being the mother of all rivers, the chief source of sustenance for the whole land of Ireland. Here we see the White Cow come to care for her child when the latter is in human form, identifying the child with the goddess.

If Brigit's affinity for milk and cows was obvious from early on, so was her fiery nature. Once her mother left the child Brigit asleep in a hut. Soon afterward people saw a blazing light in the hut, as though it were on fire. Remembering that the child had been sleeping inside, some of the other slave women broke in to try to rescue her, and they found Brigit lying peacefully inside a fierce fire that emerged from her body and rose up in a great column toward the sky. Brigit herself, of course, was completely unharmed.

From then on it was noticed that Brigit was no ordinary child. Not only did mysterious things happen around her, she had a unique, boundless generosity toward all living beings, and she always seemed able to satisfy their needs. She made sure that all domestic animals were cared for properly, and she also extended her concern to wild animals and birds. In time, she began to feed needy people liberally as well. Much of what she gave them was from her father's store of goods. Needless to say, her father, Dubhthach, was less than pleased with her complete disregard of private property.

One day Dubhthach invited some very prestigious noblemen to a feast. In traditional Celtic culture feasting was one of the most important social rituals, an occasion to discuss community and political issues among families. The lavishness and generosity of the host reflected a great deal on his standing among his own people. Dubhthach was anxious to make a good impression, and so he gave five pieces of the best pork to Brigit to boil up in a big cauldron, making sure that she understood that every single piece was needed for the feast and had to be accounted for. Brigit set about cooking the meat.

Before long a starving dog came to her, drawn by the delicious smell of the boiling pork. Unable to ignore his pleading gaze, she gave him one of the pieces. The dog devoured it, but after that he was still hungry. So Brigit gave him another piece, and then another. As it happened, one of the guests saw what she was doing and reported it to Dubhthach. Furious, he demanded that Brigit produce every one of the pieces of meat that had been entrusted to her. She showed him that all five pieces were still in the cauldron. But when the meat was served, the guests were too overcome by awe to eat it because they were aware of its supernatural origin. They were honoring Dubhthach by their reverence for his daughter. Unable to understand that, he felt humiliated.

Things rapidly got worse. Brigit freely gave away her father's property—all of the wealth Dubhthach had amassed so carefully, and that was so important to him as a sign of his power and prestige—to anyone who had need of it. She gave away food, money, jewelry, weapons. Nothing could stop her. In the end Dubhthach decided that enough was enough. Brigit was a slave's daughter, and he would treat her like one. He would sell her.

He had heard that Dunlaing, the king of all Leinster, always had need of slaves to work in his mill. So he took Brigit with him in his chariot and went off to the king's fortress to arrange the sale. When he arrived, he had to leave his sword behind him in the chariot, as was the custom, since one didn't come armed into the presence of the king; so, having no other choice, he left the weapon in Brigit's care. While he was conferring with the king, a leper came by and asked Brigit for charity. Cast out of his family and community because of his frightening disease, the leper couldn't work for a living and had nothing he could sell in exchange for food and clothing. Brigit looked at her father's sword, which was beautiful and expensive. It was the only valuable thing she had with her, so she gave it to the leper.

Dunlaing, meanwhile, had been a little puzzled by Dubhthach's eagerness to sell his daughter. After all, if she was half a slave, she was also half a princess. There were also widespread rumors about her as an exceptional person, full of beauty and glamour. Dubhthach's response was simple: "She's giving away everything I own—giving it to totally worthless, poor people." Hearing that Brigit was waiting in the chariot outside, Dunlaing suggested that they go out to see her.

When they reached the chariot, the sword was gone. This was one more instance of Brigit's outrageous behavior. Dubhthach, of course, was insane with rage. Not only was the sword a costly thing in itself, it was a crucial symbol of his status as a warrior aristocrat. Brigit calmly explained that the leper needed it more than he did. Dunlaing asked her, "Why have you been giving away all your father's property? Why did you give even his sword away?" She replied, "Because I could. And if I had access to all the resources you can command as king of all Leinster, I'd give all of that away, too."

The king was overcome with awe before Brigit, even as Dubhthach's guests had been. He no longer saw her as just an eccentric girl, but as something larger than life, a force from beyond mundane reality. Turning to Dubhthach, he said, "She is beyond my authority. And it's certainly not right to treat her as a slave." From then on Dubhthach was forced to treat her as his true daughter— as a noblewoman of his lineage.

He could no longer get rid of her by selling her as a slave, but he could draw upon the other kind of value she had: he could marry her off as a bride of royal blood. Discussing the matter with his sons, he found that they agreed that this was an excellent idea. Since Brigit was beautiful and Dubhthach's family had great prestige, there was no lack of suitors eager to win her hand. She refused all of them, however. She was adamant about avoiding marriage.

Her half brothers tried to cajole her into accepting the plans they had made for her. One of them said, "What good is that beautiful eye of yours, if it isn't on a pillow beside a husband?" This gave her an idea: when a prospective suitor would come to look at her, she would put her finger under her eye so that it popped out of its socket and dangled against her cheek. All the suitors found this sight so repulsive that they made a hasty retreat. When they left, Brigit would restore the eye to its former state. So she defied her family, and eventually they gave up on her. No one could control her, and she was free to make her own choices.

This insistence on Brigit's remaining unmarried—so crucial to the stories about both the goddess and the saint—receives an added twist in some episodes that are not part of the Irish version of the story. Some Celtic and formerly Celtic areas of the Continent have versions in which Brigit does get married, with horrifying results for her and bad consequences for everyone around her. Things return to normal only when her marriage is dissolved and her freedom fully restored. In some cases this is linked to the widespread story that she became the midwife and foster mother of Jesus (I will have more to say about that story later).

In a ballad from northern Brittany, we are told that Mary and Joseph, having arrived in Bethlehem, were knocking at every door and meeting with refusal everywhere. A man told them that his house was full of travelers, all of them lords and sons of noblemen, and that he would never give lodging to poor people like them. Finally they came to a house owned by a woman (in some versions, they appeal separately to the wife of the man who owns the house). Mary had gone into labor and begged the woman to fetch her daughters to assist her as she gave birth. The woman said that all of her daughters had gone to bed and wouldn't rise again until morning, except for Berc'hed (as Brigit is called in Breton), who was sitting by herself in the ashes of the hearth. Told to take Mary to the stables and help her, Berc'hed pointed out that she couldn't possibly do so since she had no arms. Mary nevertheless begged for her help and promised her that she would have a feast day right next to her own, sharing in her glory. And then:

> *Oa ket he ger peurachuet*
> *Ma 'devoa dorn ha bizied,*
> *Daou dornig kaer evel an deiz*
> *Evit sikour gwir vab Doue.*

(She had hardly finished speaking when she had a hand and fingers, two little hands as beautiful as the day to help God's true son.)

Why on earth was Berc'hed armless? We find the answer in several stories written on the Continent during the Middle Ages, as well as in folk tradition. These stories follow a narrative pattern usually referred to as "the Armless Maiden." In one of the medieval versions, the heroine is explicitly called Brigit, so the connection with the goddess-saint is pretty certain. Basically, the heroine is married against her will to a man who brutalizes her. The abuse comes to a climax when she is discovered to be pregnant, and the husband suspects that the child isn't his own. As she gives birth to twins, her husband cuts off her arms and, having put the two babies into a bag that he hangs from her neck, chases her away into the forest to fend for herself in that helpless state.

All of nature reacts in sympathy to Brigit's situation: the land becomes waste, crops refuse to grow, domestic animals are barren. Finally, after many adventures, she reaches a sacred fountain and is able to dip the two stumps of her arms into the healing water. As her arms are restored to her, the land itself blossoms into a long-awaited spring. Here, as everywhere in the Celtic world, we see that the return of Brigit to her freedom and full power means the return of the yearly cycle to its fertile part.

More light is shed on this general "anti-marriage" theme by a story from the Cartulary of Levroux in north central France. A cartulary is a collection of documents concerning foundations, deeds, and anything else related to property transactions, but it sometimes also contains interesting and ancient stories that are associated with them. One such is the story of Rodena and Sylvanus, which seems to have been passed down from Gallo-Roman times.

Rodena (*Roudêna*, "the Red One" in Gaulish) was being forced into a marriage she didn't want. Having run out of other methods of resistance, she disfigured herself so horribly that her suitor—who had originally been drawn to her great beauty—fled from her. Her family, however, realizing that they could no longer marry her off to anyone, and that she had no value to them any longer, threw her out. She was left to wander in the forest, alone and far from help. There Sylvanus ("Forest God" in Latin) found her. He took her to a sacred spring in which she washed her face and was restored to her former beauty. They became friends and partners then, but as celibate clerics, did not marry.

One of the projects they worked on was a castle that they had to build in one night. Sylvanus had a magic sickle that could cut down a great number of trees in a very short time. As he worked to clear a space in the forest, Rodena showed her own divine ability by carrying in all the huge building stones in her apron. Through both their efforts the castle was raised up just in time, right before the cock crowed.

Although, as written, this is an account of the miraculous deeds of Christian saints (St. Sylvanus became the patron saint of stonemasons in France), the pattern of the story is obviously more ancient. Night is the time when Otherworld beings are active (for good or ill), and cockcrow puts an end to their activities. There are many stories in European folklore that tell of castles and even

monasteries and churches built magically during the night by
beings from the Otherworld.

We see another important theme here: the goddess-saint
acquires a male helper, but he doesn't try to marry her or establish
any other kind of control over her. Their relationship is a free one
between equals. They're collaborators, "working partners," partic-
ipating in common projects but not bound to each other by any
permanent, exclusive legal ties. The goddess's energy must be given
freely, to anyone she chooses. (Unless it's given freely, it will ultimately be no good at all. The land becomes waste when Brigit's
husband, in his rage to possess her, cuts off her arms.)

The Irish version of the saint's life contains no such drastic illustrations of how unsuitable marriage was for Brigit. Yet by refusing
to marry or do anything else that was expected of her socially,
Brigit estranged herself from her family and put herself in the difficult position of a woman alone, unprotected by male kin. How
did she survive? What options did she have?

The solution was to take on one of the few roles that were
indeed reserved for celibate women in her society. In a pre-
Christian context, she could become a priestess of the hearth fire
goddess whose fire had to be tended by unattached women to
keep the community safe and prosperous. We've seen that everything in her early life had prepared her for that role, since the
main traits and powers of the goddess were spectacularly obvious in
her. In a Christian context, she could join a monastic community—
become a nun. Brigit evidently did both. The later accounts of
her life, written from a church perspective, naturally tried to play
down any pagan strangeness and eliminated any mention of a pre-
Christian religious role she might have played. They have her take
the vows of a nun, and then found her very odd (from a Christian
perspective) community. There are, however, elements in the story
that hint at what really happened. It shows how difficult it was to
portray Brigit as a "normal" church figure, no matter how hard
one tried!

We are told that Mel, the bishop of Ardagh, who is said to have come from Britain to Ireland as a missionary, was in Meath, the land of the High King of Ireland, to perform the ritual of giving the veil to any women who wished to take monastic vows. Brigit was there and, out of modesty, waited until all the other women had gone before her. When her turn came, a pillar of fire rose up from the top of her head to the ceiling of the church, and burned the bishop's veil to cinders. Three times Mel tried to place the veil on Brigit; on the third, magical time, the veil remained in place. Clearly, this was the power of the goddess reacting to any attempt at imposing different vows on someone already consecrated to her—someone known by all present to have been consecrated to her, since she had acted publicly as her priestess. Placing the veil on Brigit was a way of bringing her activities within the Christian fold, and of neutralizing the goddess's presence in her.

The goddess, however, had her revenge: losing control for a moment and going into trance, Mel also pronounced the ritual formula that made Brigit into a bishop herself. The other church-men were aghast at this: the church had never allowed women to take on that role. But the words once said couldn't be recalled. Brigit had, quite legally and officially, become a bishop. Even in later centuries, when women had far less of a chance to gain power in the church, nobody ever tried to deny that she, alone of all the women of Ireland, had been absolutely equal in status and author-ity to all the male leaders of the church.

Brigit's community was made up of twenty women who tended a sacred fire. She wanted to build a permanent shrine for them at Cill Dara, the place where a giant oak linked heaven to earth with its height. Brigit needed to obtain help and raw materials from the local noblemen. Ailill, the son of Dunlaing, king of Leinster, had a caravan of a hundred packhorses on its way to him, loaded with newly prepared boards and staves of wood for one of his own projects. Brigit sent one of her women to ask him for the wood. He refused. Immediately, all hundred horses collapsed on the ground. Even when the loads of wood were removed from them, they couldn't move. Ailill knew when he was beaten. He agreed to give the wood to Brigit. He also assigned a team of workmen to help raise the building in which the fire would be kept. To thank him, Brigit assured him that someone descended from him would continue to have power in Leinster until the end of the world.

The shrine was built, with the sacred fire at its heart. The place where the perpetual fire burned was surrounded by a hedge, and, like the *atrium Vestae* in Rome, it was forbidden to men. One man who tried to cross the hedge on a dare found that the leg he had swung over the barrier instantly shriveled to a withered stump. Other men who defied the taboo either died or went mad. A man who tried to blow out Brigit's fire became so thirsty that he couldn't stop drinking and eventually burst.

While Brigit's own community would always be composed only of women, and its most sacred precincts remained off bounds to men, she welcomed cooperation with men on other levels and encouraged the formation of a male monastic group near her own shrine. The leader of this group, Connlaedh, or Conleth, would become a close associate of Brigit for many years, working with her as an equal on joint projects rather than being bound to her by a formal mutual obligation or a hierarchical dependency.

This is the kind of relationship that is always seen as the ideal context for the Brigit energy. The energy has to be freely given to those who can make use of it freely, unencumbered by the sticky complications that can arise out of marriage and sexual intimacy.

Conleth had been trained as an artisan of precious metals, with an outstanding talent for making jewelry of rare beauty. Brigit constantly encouraged him to create beautiful objects for liturgical use. Buoyed by her inspiring suggestions, Conleth was always hard at work, so that his talent always had an outlet. We are reminded here of Brigit's role as the *bé goibneachta*, the "muse of smithcraft," and of the partnership between Bergusia and the smith god Ucuetis in their temple at Alesia on the Continent.

Nevertheless, even in the case of Conleth, Brigit eventually found herself running into the same problems she always seemed to have had when dealing with men, starting with her father, Dubhthach. These revolved around men's grasping ego, their need to maintain their sense of personal security by status and power over others. Rather than being content to feel empowered from within, the men around her trusted in their power only if it was clearly reflected in the world outside them.

For example, they might control resources that people needed. If they could exchange some of those resources for articles that were rare and hard to obtain, these articles would become symbols of their power. In time, they would come to see such symbols as the source of the power, not merely the outward sign of it. They would become very uneasy—sometimes going to murderous extremes—if the symbols were somehow hidden from sight or taken from them.

Conleth, as it turned out, was no exception. After a while he became irritated by Brigit's undiscriminating generosity. Even as she spurred him to produce work of the most cunning craftsman-ship, she didn't seem to value the end result as much as he did, since she gave it away so easily. Worse still, when he became a bishop she didn't seem to understand that he was entitled to the beautiful vestments that symbolized his high status. Those vestments of fine cloth, imported at great expense, were in the care of the women of Cill Dara; but whenever Brigit saw someone in severe need of clothing, she would give them away without a qualm. On some occasions Conleth was so upset that she restored the vestments to him magically.

Once she had nothing to give him but a tight-fitting skin gar-ment that looked like a seal's head. Some commentators have sug-gested that this was a liturgical vestment of pre-Christian origin, similar to those worn in other parts of the Indo-European world. Such vestments were meant to evoke the tightness of the birth canal, and to indicate that the one who wore it was transformed and reborn. Perhaps this was something Brigit had retained from her own pre-Christian religious practice. She may have been offering Conleth the chance to become a "true priest," someone who had been born anew to the world of the spirit and had cast aside his grasping, insecure old nature. If so, Conleth failed to understand this; he merely felt humiliated.

In the end, Conleth decided to go on a pilgrimage to Rome. Perhaps one of his primary motives in doing so was to renew his contacts with a far-off male hierarchy that would truly appreciate and affirm his own status as a bishop. Brigit tried to dissuade him from going, but he was adamant. So she prophesied, "You'll never get there, and you'll never come back either." And she was right. As he was walking to the coast to board a ship for the Continent, Conleth was surrounded by a pack of wolves and devoured. Medieval Irish scholars, who loved strange puns and far-fetched etymologies, declared that his fate had always been implicit in his name, which they explained as being a combination of "con" (meaning "of a dog or wolf") and "leth" (meaning "half" or "share"), so that he was destined to be "the wolves' portion"!

Another man with whom Brigit had a confrontation—a much less tragic one, fortunately—was Brendan the Navigator, the monastic leader from Kerry whose voyage across the ocean to fantastic islands became one of the favorite adventure stories of the Irish Middle Ages.

Once when Brendan was returning from a tour of monasteries in Britain, he stopped on a small rocky island in the Irish Sea. He climbed to the craggy heights of this island to meditate and pray. As he sat there he saw the sea below him begin churning wildly. Soon two sea monsters emerged from the waves, locked in a ferocious battle. One of the monsters appeared to be weaker and soon tried to get out of the fight, but the other one kept on attacking it. At last the weaker monster cried out, "In Brigit's name, leave me alone!" Instantly its opponent gave up and fled away. (In another version of the story, Brendan was set upon by sea monsters when he was sailing in his boat. His companions tried to control them by invoking the names of Patrick and other saints, but this had no effect at all. Finally, they remembered to invoke the name of Brigit, and at once the monsters became obedient.)

Amazed to learn that Brigit was known even to the sea monsters and had power over them (and perhaps a little peeved to realize that he had no such power himself), Brendan decided to go to Cill Dara and experience firsthand what sort of woman this was. When he arrived, Brigit did him great honor, treating him like a venerable teacher, far above herself in status. Brendan suggested that they hear each other's confessions (although what he really wanted was to talk about his encounter with the sea monsters). Brigit told him that he should be the first to speak—"because," she said, "you're a man."

As they turned to go into her cell, a bright sunbeam slanted across the air beside them. Brigit, taking off her cloak before going inside, hung it casually on the sunbeam, where it stayed as securely as on a peg. Brendan tried to do the same thing, but his cloak fell down into the mud.

When they finally got to the point where they were discussing the sea monsters, Brendan said that since the day he had taken religious vows he had never crossed seven furrows of land (or seven waves of the sea) without thinking of God. Brigit replied that, no matter what was happening around her, her consciousness was always focused on the Divine, and would never waver from that focus until the end of the world. "But you," she said, "have so many responsibilities and undertake so many projects and face so many dangers; because of them you have to keep your mind on mundane matters a great deal of the time. It's only at every seventh furrow that you remember your connection with God."

Then Brendan understood that Brigit, being so constantly at one with the Divine in her consciousness, kept no barriers between herself and everything else that is, so that her love and generosity extended to all beings at all times. Humbled, he praised her: "I

can see, now, how it is that the monsters of the deep know who
you are and honor you. And they're right to do so."

Brigit also became famous as an arbiter of disputes. Although
the goddess she represented gives energy to those who make
weapons (since a community incapable of defending itself isn't
likely to be left in peace for long), her efforts were directed at pre-
serving peace by any means possible. What the hearth fire goddess protects most specially, after all, is the safety and comfort of
life at home. To emphasize this preference for peace, no weapon
was allowed to touch the great oak tree around which Brigit's
shrine had been built.

Yet she worked in mysterious ways: once two brothers who were
about to go to war against each other went to Brigit separately,
each one asking her to bless him and give him the victory. Instead,
Brigit put a spell of confusion on both of them, so that they were
unable to recognize each other and didn't know whom to fight.
Then she offered them a blessing of prosperity in exchange for
giving up all thought of war.

Brigit was also very concerned that people be truthful and
honest in their business dealings. Once a merchant was passing
by carrying a load of salt in a sack on his back. Brigit asked him
what was in the sack. Afraid that she might ask him for a gift of
some of the salt, the merchant said it was stones. At once the salt
did indeed turn to stones, which almost crushed the merchant
with their weight. "Are you sure it's stones?" said Brigit. "It's salt,"
the merchant admitted, and the salt was restored.

For all the influence she had on the male rulers of the surrounding lands, Brigit's compassion and aid were primarily lav-
ished on the women who were in her care. She treated them as if
they had been given to her in fosterage—a custom that was
extremely important in Celtic society, and that determined much
of what people felt about family ties.

For the Celts, kinship was what held communities together. You
had obligations toward relatives, but hardly any toward strangers.

Not all kinship, however, was real blood kinship: you could extend it by contracts, as in the case of adoption or clientship (having one family become the dependents of another family). One of the most effective ways of expanding one's circle of kin was the institution of fosterage, which was practiced by virtually all Irish aristocratic families. People would arrange to have at least one of their children brought up by a different family. The foster parents would have exclusive care of their charges, would teach them and serve as role models for them, until they reached the customary age (fifteen for girls, seventeen for boys) to return to their birth families and assume adult roles. All of these arrangements served to establish more links between families, thus strengthening the sense of community.

In fosterage, since you spent far more of your formative years with your foster family than with your birth family, your emotional ties to your foster family tended to be far stronger. Your foster siblings were much closer friends than your biological siblings were. Your foster parents were the true image you had absorbed in childhood of what a mother and father should be. The Irish word for "foster mother" is *muime* (literally, "mommy"). You would never think of your birth mother in quite the same intimate terms. So, because of such strong feelings, your foster kin were really as much a part of your family as your biological parents and siblings were, even though you weren't related to them by blood.

When the monastic movement became popular in the Celtic world, in the second half of the fifth century, people tended to think of monastic communities as kin groups, bound together by ties of affinity rather than blood ties. The leader of the community was a foster parent, and all the other members were fosterlings in his or her care, receiving both material protection and spiritual instruction. This meant that anyone could be the parent or the child of anyone else, regardless of birth origin. The relationship was voluntary, and it was nonetheless real, a genuine instance of the kind of exchange of love and learning that takes place between child and parent.

Such an arrangement was particularly well suited to Brigit's boundless generosity. As the representative of the goddess of abundance and well-being, she gave those gifts to all people, disregarding the limits that the obligations of blood kinship might have placed on her. As a *muime*, she really could be a "virgin mother." Just as the fire in the goddess's shrine was lit to warm and comfort the entire nation, so could the saint become anyone's *muime*, providing a mother's attention and nurturing presence to anyone who placed herself or himself in her care. Again, it was the freedom and openness of this nurture that were Brigit's special attributes, and that drew people to her.

One illustration of this can be found in the widespread story we mentioned earlier: that Brigit had been the midwife at Jesus' birth, and had taken care of him during his early childhood. Nobody in the Middle Ages seemed to be troubled by the inconsistency of having Brigit appear at such widely separated points in space and time. Perhaps people believed that the two figures—the one in Ireland and the one in Bethlehem—had both been incarnations of the immortal goddess, and thus shared a single identity.

In any case, Brigit's relationship with Mary and her son, Jesus, was held to be intimate and unbreakable. On the feast of the Purification of the Virgin, when Jesus' parents went to the temple with him, Brigit rode before them carrying a candle to light their way. This helped explain why Brigit had her own feast on the eve of this one, and associated her with the theme of Candlemas. It also must have played a powerful role in making Jesus attractive to Celtic communities: if Jesus had been Brigit's *dalta* (foster child), he couldn't be that bad, could he? It made him an acceptable new god, and a kind of familiar foster brother to Brigit's other foster children.

Brigit the abbess was extremely concerned with the well-being of all her charges. On one occasion a girl who had joined Brigit's community broke her vow of chastity and became pregnant. This was a serious matter. Even if she wasn't likely to be put to death as a result—as she would have been in the days of the Vestal Virgins—the breaking of her oath was a great public dishonor to her family. How could she be treated well after she'd been forced to leave Cill Dara? In order to save her from humiliation, Brigit made the fetus in her womb disappear. (Later Catholic authorities were made highly uncomfortable by this episode. They tend to leave it out of their accounts of the saint's life.)

Darlughdacha, Brigit's favorite, once found herself looking admiringly at a handsome soldier. She considered this to be the beginning of breaking her vow and, on her own initiative, put hot coals in her shoes in order to distract herself from the image of the sexually attractive man in her head. The horrible pain certainly quenched any physical desire she might have had, but it also destroyed her feet. Unable to walk, she confessed to Brigit what had happened, and the saint healed her. Some have suggested that Darlughdacha was imitating the fire walk that was associated with a goddess who bore her name, and that it had been the core element of a fertility ritual. If so, she was doing it for the wrong reason, and she suffered for it.

All this emphasis on her remaining unmarried and maintaining chastity could lead us to believe that Brigit—both goddess and saint—had an aversion to sexuality in general. Nothing could be further from the truth: Brigit was entirely supportive of sexual activity in people who were called to a married life. She used her healing power to benefit those who had sexual problems. For example, a man came to Brigit complaining that his wife was sexually unresponsive, and that he was afraid they wouldn't have any children (a serious danger in a time when children were one's only source of support in old age). Brigit made the man's wife so lustfully aroused by him that she couldn't take her hands off him and couldn't bear to stay in a part of the house where he wasn't.

Nor was Brigit against pleasures of other kinds. Once when a group of clerics came to visit her and she had nothing to offer them, she turned her bathwater into a generous supply of beer. She commented, "I'd like to have a great lake of beer for the King of Kings, and to have all the saints of heaven drinking from it."

It was, however, the two staples of the Celtic home—milk and grain—that featured most prominently in the many miracles where Brigit caused food to appear out of nowhere, or increased the amount of food already there. On one occasion several holy people came to Cill Dara to ask for hospitality and, as seems to have happened pretty often, the women had nothing to give them. They tried to milk the cows but could get hardly a drop of milk out of them. Finally Brigit went out to milk the cows herself. Under the sure pressure of her hands, the milk began to flow plentifully. It soon filled several buckets that were meant to serve the guests, but it didn't stop there. The milk kept on flowing until it could have filled every vessel in Leinster. It flowed across the grounds until people could wade in it. Finally it spread across the floor of the valley as a lake, which is still called Loch an Ais, the "Lake of Milk."

There is one story where, in the process of healing, Brigit was herself hurt—that is, the healing itself came out of her hurt. She contracted a sickness of the eyes (this is significant in itself, as we shall see—remember, also, how Brigit popped her eye out of its socket to scare away her suitors) which caused her extreme pain. Bishop Mel (who had accidentally made her a bishop) suggested that she go see a physician with him. As they were on their way, Brigit fell out of the chariot and dashed her head on the stones so that it bled profusely. Two deaf-mute women were splashed with the blood and suddenly found themselves able to hear. As for Brigit, she was also healed instantaneously—both of the wound and of her original ailment. The physician who eventually examined her told her that she had no need of his services.

Let us end our survey of the innumerable stories about Brigit's generosity and helpfulness with one that emphasizes her oneness with Nature, her easy familiarity with all living beings—wild creatures as well as cattle, foxes as well as sea monsters.

A somewhat feebleminded young man was walking in the vicinity of the king of Leinster's house when he saw a fox sitting fearlessly out in the open. Too stupid to realize that wild animals run away from people, he congratulated himself on his good luck and killed it. In reality, the fox was tame, and had in fact been a favorite pet of the king's. Since a great many people had seen him kill the fox, the young man was at once apprehended and taken before the king, who, as one could well imagine, was out of his mind with rage. The king demanded that the young man give up his own life in compensation for the fox's, and threatened to make slaves of his entire family—unless he could provide another fox every bit as tame and well trained as the king's pet had been.

When Brigit heard the story, she felt pity for the poor idiot, who couldn't have known any better. Mounting her chariot, she rode across the plains of Leinster until she came upon a group of wild foxes. She called one of them to her, and it came willingly, jumping up onto her chariot and sitting in the folds of her robe as she traveled to the king's court. There, the fox began to perform all kinds of clever tricks, delighting the assembly. Realizing that the saint had intervened with a miracle, the king agreed to forgive and release the young man.

Years passed, and the holy woman died. All the stories that had been told about her became absorbed into the lore of the undying goddess that had always sustained the Celtic people's faith in the future. These stories continued to be told as part of Brigit's rituals, and still are today—especially when, every year, the winter grows old and the lengthening days awaken hopes of spring.

CORRESPONDENCES

The most basic attribute of Brigit is, of course, fire. It isn't the wild, unstoppable fire that erupts out of volcanoes or burns down forests and buildings, although Brigit has power over this kind of fire too, mostly to keep it away from humans. Imagine, instead, a cold winter day. The weather outside has been miserable. Your body is tense from resisting its onslaughts. Now you come indoors to find flames dancing in a fireplace, and relax in the sudden warmth. This is Brigit's fire.

As you become accustomed to the more comfortable atmosphere, you start to feel energized. You're able to do all kinds of things. You look around for a purpose: you can choose to feed your mind by reading a book, or you can create something useful or beautiful with your hands, or you can perform some household chore that will make your space more comfortable. All of this is made possible by the radiating warmth and cheer of the fire. As early darkness sets in outside, you can still see and be active thanks to the light of the fire—either the brightness of the hearth fire itself, or in the flames of candles (or the glowing filaments of electric bulbs). And if you have a cold or some other illness that's made worse by the winter weather, the fire will take away the chill and help you heal.

Brigit is also intimately connected to water. Again, this isn't the overwhelming water of a flash flood, or of the boundless ocean where one can get lost and drown. Hers is the water that satisfies urgent human needs—when you're thirsty, or overheated, or need to wash. Think of a large fountain in a public square or park on a hot summer day. The air becomes cooler as you approach. You can dip your hands in the cooling water or splash it over your face. A drinking fountain (perhaps a short distance away in the same park) will allow you to moisten and cool your insides as well. Both are the blessings of Brigit. She is concerned with balancing the conditions that affect you so that you can be in the best possible situation to think and act. And when you get home and step into the shower, that abundant, cleansing flow is also a sign of Brigit's presence.

Both fire and water can heal, but usually through opposite action. They can't normally be found in the same space, since they cancel each other out. But on the rare occasions when they do seem to occur together, they are a very powerful symbol of healing, and belong to Brigit. Hot springs are a good example of such a combination, and Brigit-type goddesses are always honored at such places. Water that has been held in the sunlight (especially on the dawn of a day specially marked by the sun's power, such as Bealtaine) also has the magical strength of water mixed with fire. And sparkling water—with the firelike motion in its liquid coolness— definitely evokes Brigit too.

As one of the most important embodiments of fire, the sun (which in Gaelic tradition is always seen as female) is also a form of Brigit. She is the sun of the waxing half of the year, when the days are lengthening and the sun's increasing power is a welcome part of the struggle against darkness and cold. The scorching sun of high summer was represented by entirely different imagery in Celtic myth, as Balor of the Evil Eye, whose single eye burned to ashes anything he looked at. As always, Brigit is associated with the benign, helpful aspect of any natural phenomenon.

Brigit's season begins on her feast day, Imbolc, or *Lá Fhéile Bríde* (February 1), and lasts until Bealtaine (May 1). Spring is the season when seemingly dead things come back to life as if by magic. Crocuses and daffodils pop out of the earth, springing from bulbs that have lain unseen and dormant underground all winter. Bare trees suddenly fill with running sap; buds begin to swell at the tips of branches and erupt into clouds of a living green we had almost forgotten. Birds that have vanished mysteriously during the winter months suddenly reappear in their old territories, as though returned from the Otherworld like Brigit herself. It all feels like a spontaneous triumph of life over death. When Bealtaine comes around, the wedding of the Flower Maiden brings summer, the time of fruiting and nesting, sex and reproduction, a season very different from that of the "virgin mother."

The number associated with Brigit is three—and, by extension, nine, the more "powerful" three. Three is the number of comple-

tion, of a process having gone through a full cycle of transformation. Stories, which give form and meaning to human experience,
have beginnings, middles, and endings. The phases of the moon
are also often interpreted as a three-part process (waxing, full,
waning). In an operation of logic, the three parts are thesis,
antithesis, and synthesis—the arguments for, the arguments
against, and the balanced conclusion. Three also suggests the three
basic divisions of society in Indo-European traditions: the priests
and intellectuals who guide, the warriors who protect, and the
farmers and artisans who provide. In her triple muse aspect, Brigit
inspires and empowers poets, smiths, and healers.

Nine, as three times three, carries this symbolism to a higher
level. If someone who has initiated an event, dealt with all of its
implications, and concluded it has necessarily acquired more
knowledge and experience, then how much more empowered by
such experience will that person be if he or she goes through the
whole process three times, taking it a little further every time? Also,
in cosmologies (such as the Celtic one) where there are three
worlds—the World Where We Are, the World Above Us, and the
World Below Us—doing something not just three times (which
makes it complete in this world) but three times three (making it
resonate with equal thoroughness in each one of the three worlds)
ensures that one's purpose will be accomplished not just in the
world we see, but also in the subtler realms beyond our perception.

As a result, in Celtic rituals things are often repeated nine times,
or done in groups of nine. In Scottish Gaelic tradition, for
instance, when a midwife (who, in fulfilling this function, is playing the role of Brigit) has delivered a child, she blesses the baby by
splashing it with water nine times. These splashes of water are
referred to as *tonnáin* ("little waves"), and each *tonnán* is accompanied by an invocation of protection on an area of the child's
future life: *cruth* ("shape," physical beauty), *guth* ("voice," articulateness in speech), *manrachd* ("crooning" or "singing," actually
the ability to attract love interests), *rath* ("prosperity, good for-

tune," general luck in life), *math* ("goods," material possessions), *slànachd* ("healthiness"), *ruch* ("throat/esophagus," ability to breathe properly and digest food), *sguch* ("straining," courage, endurance) and *gràsachd* ("graciousness," good behavior toward one's fellows). Human gestation takes nine months. In many Imbolg rituals the person playing the part of Brigit is supposed to do the blessing gestures over foodstuffs nine times.

By the same reasoning, the triple goddess can also be seen as a ninefold goddess. In the Welsh medieval poem *Preiddeu Annwn* ("The Spoils of the Otherworld"), for instance, we're told of a magic cauldron with a pearl-studded rim that is fanned by the breath of nine maidens. These nine maidens are a further tripling of the three goddesses (or three aspects of Brigit) who provide energy to the three main types of human activity.

Brigit's triple nature also, as we've seen, associates her with the three primordial colors: white, red, and black. White and red appear on the aspects of her that freely give energy to humans. Black is the color of the Cailleach, who, as a necessary part of the cycle, withholds energy for the space of a season so that rest can point the way to renewal. The colors also correspond to Brigit's "triple muse" aspects.

- As the *banfhile* or *bé éicse*, inspiring poets and learned people, Brigit can be seen as white.

- As the *bé goibneachta*, who assists smiths, giving them the means to make weapons for the defense of the community against invaders (and tools of technology to protect people against all the other dangers that threaten human survival), she can be seen as red.

- As the *bé leigis* or "muse of healing," she deals with renewal after the "death" of illness, part of the larger process in which life and death are rooted in each other and cannot exist without each other, as two sides of a single reality that is always changing. Although the Cailleach tends to be seen as hostile to humans, and somewhat apart from Brigit in her positive aspects, her role in making all things submit to the transient rule of death is a necessary forerunner of resurrection and renewal. So we're justified in ascribing the color black to Brigit's third role. Even as the harsh-faced Cailleach, she can't completely conceal her generous nature, and the negative experience of illness turns out to have a gift inside it.

Brigit's sacred bird is the oystercatcher. With its bold black-and-white plumage and long, bright red bill, the oystercatcher displays the three primordial colors. Any creature in nature that is tricolored in this fashion is, in Celtic tradition, thought to have an intimate connection with the goddess. The oystercatcher also lives on the shore, on the border between the very different realms of sea and land, an in-between place that has the magic qualities of all things that are neither nor. Accordingly, it is capable of attracting to itself experiences that are usually shut out of the too definite categories of our everyday life—new things, out of the Otherworld. The oystercatcher's loud, piping cries are the voice of something from beyond our reality, an oracle of the gods.

In Gaelic Scotland it is called the Brighid-eun, the "Brigit-bird," and regarded as her messenger. If it seems to be trying to attract our attention, it is speaking for the goddess. It is good for us to follow where the oystercatcher leads. There are folktales about children lost on the seashore and in danger of being drowned by the rising tide, until Brigit sends the oystercatcher to guide them to safety.

Also most conspicuously associated with Brigit is, as we have seen, the snake. Indo-European tradition has an ambivalent view of snakes. This is related to the ambivalent nature of the Gods Below, who are often portrayed as snakes or as having snakelike features. On the one hand, the Gods Below lack all of the cultural restraints that make human life easier, such as respect for the law and customs, and openness to sharing. They are treacherous and stingy, and appear to have no values at all. On the other hand, they are the source of all the fertility in nature, the abundance and diversity we see there, and without that, humans could never survive.

Snakes—who appear to live in the earth—are likewise seen as both dangerous and beneficial. In myth, the frightening, destructive side of nature is often shown as a gigantic serpent, which has to be killed or tamed (or transformed into a beautiful woman) by a culture hero or culture-protecting god (such as Lugh). But snakes are also symbols of healing, shedding their old skin and revealing a new skin underneath. Snake poison, used in proper dosage, is a cure. Although classed with the "creeping things" themselves, snakes eat the rodents that damage the crops—so they help the harvest even as they represent the Gods Below who try to hinder it.

Despite her associations with the fiery intellect, the World Above, Brigit is very much at home in all three realms. She is never to be separated from the complexity of physical nature. We've seen her, as Brigh, try hard to end the conflict between the two groups of gods, going so far as to marry one of the Gods Below herself (even if the marriage—like any marriage in her case—is disastrous and short-lived). Nevertheless, she makes the best of the connection. She mediates the energies of raw nature to humans, so that their bad effects are neutralized and their good effects are amplified. The poisonous adder, in her presence, becomes a harmless sign of Brigit's power at the beginning of spring. The snake energy rises in the land, not to frighten or destroy, but to empower living things for growth.

In Ireland, famous for its lack of snakes, the hedgehog is Brigit's animal, awakening with her in the spring. Its behavior as it comes out of the ground on her feast day is used for weather divination. Throughout Celtic and formerly Celtic areas in Europe, different communities have designated different animals as the official "sleepers" whose behavior on the first day of spring is a sign of what can be expected in the weeks to come. This is usually a large rodent, such as the marmot or the German hamster; but it can be anything that hibernates. Immigrants in Pennsylvania transferred their traditions about an animal of this kind to the American woodchuck or groundhog, giving us Groundhog Day.

Brigit, as goddess of human culture and skill, is most closely associated with domestic animals, especially cattle. Brigit is herself the daughter of a cow, the White Cow who is the goddess of the river Boyne. Cattle were the measure of wealth, important status symbols in ancient Celtic society. But the usefulness of cattle was perfectly real. Without the many things they contributed to material culture—milk, meat, leather, horn—the Celtic world would have been very much worse off. Of all these products, milk is the one that stands out, in Celtic tradition, as an absolutely basic staple, one of the two staffs of life (the other being grain).

Newborn babies need milk long before they can use any other food, so milk has become the archetype of nourishment itself. With a mother's milk also comes a mother's love, so that nourishment is tied to nurture in the larger sense. Cows also provide so much more milk—more nourishment—than nursing human mothers! How powerful a symbol of all-round nurture the cow becomes! She is, in fact, regarded as an idealized mother. Although cows in the Celtic world never quite got the same sacred, protected status they enjoy in India, they were thought about much the same way. And Brigit, the source of all nourishment (and the nurturing *muime*, the primal caretaker), is naturally to be found among cows.

Because cows, of all living beings, are among the most helpful to humans, they are most likely to become the targets of the Gods Below. Those entities would very much like to be rid of the unwanted rational order imposed on them by humans and human culture. So cows are in danger from all kinds of malignant spells aimed at making them ill or drying up their milk. People in Gaelic communities traditionally protect their herds with talismans of red yarn—the color of both striving and magic, and a sign of Brigit in her most potent aspect.

Brigit also looks after sheep. We've seen that Cirb, the mythological wether which is king of all the sheep, is one of her pets. Imbolc, her own feast day, is also called Oímelc, which literally means "sheep's milk," since originally it was meant to coincide with the first flow of milk in the udders of ewes, as they came close to lambing.

Brigit's sacred flower is the dandelion. One of its names in Irish is *bearnán Bríde*, "little notched one of Brigit," because of the shape of its leaves. Its many bright yellow petals radiate outward like a little sun, a symbol of Brigit's sunny energy. If its stem is broken, it leaks out a milky sap, another connection with Brigit, the ultimate divine source of all milk.

In traditional societies, the dandelion is highly valued as a medicinal herb. Its leaves make a respectable salad, as well as working as a potent diuretic and purifying the blood. Herbalists know that a preparation from dandelion root can give relief from liver and gall bladder problems. And makers of textiles have learned that they can get a purple dye out of it as well. The very fact that the dandelion is so common and grows so readily near houses is taken as a sign of Brigit's generosity. She wants the benefits of her wonder plant to be available as widely as possible. When the little golden suns begin to appear everywhere during the latter part of Brigit's season, it means that her gifts have come to fruition.

Another flower commonly associated with Brigit is the snowdrop, because in most of Europe it's the only flower that's likely to be in bloom by Brigit's feast day. The small, jewellike petals—pure white, the first of Brigit's three colors—unfolding even under the assault of snow and sleet, are a powerful image of rebirth, of life forcing its way into the light even under death's rule.

No tree is specifically Brigit's tree (the oak tree around which Cill Dara was built is more an attribute of the thunder god, one of her collaborators), but she has a special affinity for the apple tree, since its fruit exhibits her three colors: red skin, white flesh, and black seeds.

The kitchen is, of course, one of the places in the house where Brigit is most obviously present. All the activities that result in feeding people are directly blessed by her. The aroma of food cooking is a vivid reminder of the bounty she provides. We might think of kitchen smells as Brigit's "incense!" Brigit likes all foods that are nourishing and filling. She's a bit like the mother who hovers over her children, urging them to "eat, eat!"

Foods that are a product of the two staples—grain and milk— are especially dear to her. During Imbolc rituals the goddess (or her representative) blesses samples specifically of grain and dairy foods so that both kinds of nourishment will increase in the household during the coming year. Cream, custard, yogurt, butter, and related foods are all an expression of her nature, as are the grainier and richer types of bread. Perhaps the taste experience most evocative of Brigit is that of a thick slice of country brown bread with a generous spread of butter on it.

In many Celtic and formerly Celtic communities, one of the ritual foods for the season of Imbolg is a round bannock, or pancake, that is blessed as a representation of the household's food supply. The roundness of the cake is a symbol of the sun, whose strength, increased by energy from Brigit, will lend its own warmth and light to the growing crops. Sun and grain are thus united in a single image, since both of them are Brigit's gift.

ATTUNEMENT

RITUAL OBJECTS AND THEIR USES

In Celtic folklore, we can find seasonal customs for honoring Brigit. These customs involve the use of several traditional ritual objects. The most prominent among them is the *crosóg Bríde*, commonly known as the "Brigit's cross." This is made in a variety of ways in different parts of Ireland. The one most often seen (and sold as a souvenir to tourists) is made out of rush stems plaited and bound together into the shape of a swastika: four branches emerging at right angles to a four-sided center, giving the impression of motion toward the right-hand side (sunwise).

Today, because the swastika was blasphemously used as a Nazi symbol, most Westerners view it with distaste. But in the ancient world it was widespread as a symbol of good fortune. Because it moves in the same direction as the sun as it gathers strength in spring, the swastika represents increase, the assurance that your energy will continue to grow, and that you will be better off in the future than you are now. And this, of course, is the promise of Brigit, and an image of the energy she gives, especially during her own season of the year.

While the swastika-shaped *crosóg* is probably the most ancient and symbolically apt form of that ritual tool, there are many other kinds that have been in traditional use. The only common denominator between them is that they're made of rushes or sedge or vine stems plaited or woven together, and that they have a radiating shape somewhat like a cross, although they can occasionally be triskeles, three-limbed instead of four-limbed. Some *crosóga* are very elaborate in structure, featuring large crosses composed of smaller crosses in complicated designs.

In Celtic ritual the *crosóg* is the implement that conveys Brigit's blessing. The person who acts on Brigit's behalf turns the *crosóg* sunwise—usually nine times—over the people or objects that are to be blessed with increase during the coming year. A pile of bannocks is blessed in this way to ensure that the most basic food— bread—will never be lacking in the household. After the ceremony the *crosóg* is hung up on a wall to remain as a sign of Brigit's protection throughout the year.

Another one of the goddess's ritual objects is the *crios Bríde*, or "Brigit's girdle." This is a hoop of woven rope or straw, about four feet in diameter (wide enough for an adult to pass through it),

usually with a smaller cross-shaped appendage marking each of
the circle's four quarters. It can be further decorated in a variety of
ways, with brightly colored ribbons or rags. The *crios Bríde* is a
symbol of the birth canal. By passing through it, we become the
goddess's children, without the need for a biological connection.
We acknowledge her as our *muime*, and accept the protection and
healing she's always ready to give us. During the Brigit's Day ritual
as it is done in the west of Ireland the people holding the *crios*
announce:

> *Crios Bríde mo chrios*
> *Crios na gceithre gcros!*
> *Éirigh suas, a bhean an tí,*
> *Agus gabh trí huaire amach!*
> *An té a rachas trí mo chrios,*
> *Go mba seacht bhfearr a bheidh sé bliain ó inniu!*

(My girdle is Brigit's girdle, the girdle of the four crosses! Get
up, lady of the house, and go out three times! May whoever
goes through my girdle be seven times better a year from
today!)

This is the signal for all the members of the household to go
through the *crios:* the men stepping into it sideways, starting with
their left foot , and the women having it brought down over their
heads, so that they step out of it. Doing this three times promotes
the healing of the illnesses one may have contracted over the
winter and strengthens the body against other sickness in the year
to come.

The same group of young people who carry the *crios Bríde* from
house to house on Brigit's day also have with them the *brídeog*
("little Brigit"), which is a representation of the goddess herself.
This usually looks something like a "corn doll"—an image about
the size of a child's doll made out of the straw from the grain of
the preceding harvest, as an embodiment of the living spirit of the
crops being passed on from one year to the next. The two tradi-

tions are probably related, since one of Brigit's functions is to maintain the abundance of grain in the community. The *brídeog* is generally made of straw (rarely of cloth) shaped roughly like a doll, but with no clearly human features. It is then carefully and lavishly decorated with ribbons, lace, interesting-looking stones, and any other baubles that might be at hand, often arranged in complicated loops and layers.

As the ritual party goes through the village, entering each house in turn, the women carry the *brídeog* while the men carry the *crios Bríde*. After being given some food or drink or a small amount of money (much as in trick-or-treating), the men invite all the people present to go through the *crios Bríde* while the women convey a blessing through the *brídeog*. Often the people of the house will add to the decorations on the *brídeog*, tying on a ribbon or string or piece of yarn that will, by its nearness to the effigy of the goddess, make certain that the blessing will remain with them.

In Scotland, each household will invite a *brídeog* to stay overnight. After the goddess has been brought in with formulas of welcome, her image is laid down in a specially prepared "bed" among the ashes of the hearth—the most appropriate place for the hearth fire goddess. During the night, when the people are asleep, Brigit will rise up from her bed and—if she's satisfied with what she sees around her (no signs of waste or neglect)—will strike the ashes with her staff. In the morning the mark of the disturbed ashes should be visible next to the *brídeog*, indicating that the house has indeed been found worthy of her blessing.

A talisman created every year during the Imbolc ritual and used throughout the following months is the *brat Bríde*, or "Brigit's mantle." Very many sayings and poems in both Irish and Scottish Gaelic refer to coming under Brigit's mantle as a symbol of receiving her protection. Here the *brat* is a strip of cloth (any shape, size, or color) that has been ritually charged with Brigit's energy. Sometimes the cloth is placed on the windowsill so that it can be touched by the first rays of the sun as it rises on the morning of

Brigit's day. It can also simply be placed there for the length of the Imbolc ceremony, or it can even be tied to the *crios Bríde* just before people go through it. The *brat Bríde* then becomes a talisman of healing, and can be applied to any ailing part of the body to provide energy and comfort.

PRAYERS AND CHARMS

Because Brigit has never ceased to be a major spiritual force in traditional Celtic communities, a huge number of prayers and charms invoking her have been passed down to the present day. Since most people for the past thousand years have thought of Brigit primarily as a Christian saint (while continuing to give her the attributes of the goddess), many of these prayers are explicitly and conventionally Christian in their imagery and terminology. Others use language that comes from much older sources in Celtic tradition. Most of these prayers come from Gaelic Scotland, where they were recorded by the scholar Alexander Carmichael during the nineteenth century and published in his collection *Carmina Gadelica*.

The main prayer used to call for Brigit's help is called the *Sloinntireachd Brìde* (Genealogy of Brigit). It is addressed, of course, to the saint, and refers to her father as Dùghall Donn rather than Dubhthach Donn, as he is called in the Irish sources:

> *Lasair dhealrach òir, muime chòrr Chrìosda,*
> *Brìde nighinn Dùghaill Duinn*
> *Mhic Aoidh, mhic Airt, mhic Cuinn,*
> *Mhic Crearair, mhic Cis, mhic Carmaig, mhic Carruin.*
> *Gach là agus gach oidhche*
> *Nì mi sloinntireachd air Brìde:*
> *Cha mharbhar mi, cha spuillear mi,*
> *Cha charcar mi, cha chiùrrar mi,*
> *Cha mhu dh'fhàgas Criosd an dearmad mi.*
> *Cha loisg teine, grian no gealach mi,*
> *Cha bhath luin, lì no sala mi,*

Cha reub saighid sithich no sibhrich mi,
Is mi fo chomaraig mo Naomh Muire
Is i mo chaomh-mhuime Brìde.

(Brilliant flame of gold, eminent foster mother of Christ, Brigit, daughter of Dùghall Donn, son of Aodh, son of Art, son of Conn, son of Crearar, son of Cis, son of Carmag, son of Carruin. Every day and every night I shall recite the genealogy of Brigit: I shall not be killed, I shall not be robbed, I shall not be imprisoned, I shall not be tortured, Christ shall not leave me forgotten. No fire, sun, or moon shall burn me, no lake, water, or sea shall drown me, no arrow of fairy or specter shall pierce me, as I am under the protection of my Holy Mary, and Brigit is my dear foster mother.)

Despite all the obvious Christian references, this prayer has deep roots in pre-Christian Celtic tradition. First, there's the very use of a genealogy as a means of praising someone. Reverence for ancestors and fascination with tracing things back to their origins (ultimately, in the Otherworld) is a practice much more characteristic of pre-Christian societies. Second, the prayer calls on Brigit's authority as goddess of fire and water. She is asked to restrain the destructive aspects of these primal elements so that only their benefits will remain. Most important, the speaker recognizes Brigit as a *muime*, the most intimate and trusted caretaker one can have.

Another spell gives a sense of the range of things Brigit protects against:

Seun romh shaighead,
Seun romh chlaidheamh,
Seun romh shleagha,
Seun romh bhrùdh 's romh bhàthadh.

Seun romh athain,
Seun romh nathair,
Seun romh bheithir,
Seun romh bheud air bhlàraibh.

Seun romh shìodhach,
Seun romh shaoghlach,
Seun romh bhìodhbhach,
Seun romh bhaoghal bàsach.

(A charm against an arrow, a charm against a sword, a charm
against a spear, a charm against crushing and drowning.
A charm against fire, a charm against a serpent, a charm
against a wild beast, a charm against harm on battlefields.
A charm against an Otherworld being, a charm against a
being of this world, a charm against an enemy, a charm
against mortal danger.)

The *crosóg* is also the visible sign of Brigit's relationship with you.
People who worship Brigit in the context of a traditional Celtic
ritual cycle will receive *crosóga* on her feast day, and then hang them
up in their homes to invoke her protection. Often the *crosóga* are
actually made by the participants during the ceremony. Whether or
not you have the opportunity to take part in such a group ritual,
you might want to make your *crosóga* with your own hands. Don't
worry if the result doesn't match the classic shape found in picture
books on Ireland: the traditional appearance of the *crosóg* varies a
great deal from community to community. The important thing is
that it should adequately represent to you the goddess's power of
increasing energy, like that of the sun in springtime.

A *crosóg* is usually hung over the main doorway, where the main
comings and goings between the home and the outside world
occur. *Crosóga* are also often placed at the four quarter points of
the house. You should have one wherever you keep food (so that
the supply of food will never fail), and one in the main place
where you do work (as a reminder of Brigit's unfailing inspiration
and support).

Brigit doesn't need elaborate altars for her worship. Her shrine,
you must remember, is your home. Once invited into that home
space, she makes it into her own sacred territory, the domain that

she will protect and enhance. Whatever your home contains becomes the raw material for her work.

Nevertheless, you may want to establish certain areas where you can connect with her energy and let it infuse your own creative work with the goddess's power. Beyond that, if you engage in any of the crafts Brigit blesses, you might want to consecrate your work area.

In preparation for Brigit's feast day, clean your work area thoroughly. Discard anything that is no longer serviceable. Clean and maintain any tools. Restock or replace whatever is necessary. Then formally renew the consecration on the actual day of Oímelc.

Brigit manifests her presence in fire, so lighting a fire is one of the most obvious ways of invoking her. Today most people don't keep a hearth fire burning all the time, which means that they don't have that constant reminder of Brigit's presence and function in their home. Lighting a candle to her whenever you need to call her to mind, however, is a perfectly adequate way of using fire to relate to her ritually. Whenever you do so, take the time to appreciate the glowing warmth of the flame, the sense of quickening and comfort it brings to your body, and how it awakens your mind as you let in the light.

Some people specially dedicated to Brigit keep a perpetual fire burning in her honor, like the saint's original one at Cill Dara. You may want to do this as well, but before you make that decision, think it over carefully. Engaging yourself to show your faithfulness to the goddess by tending her fire without cease is a serious commitment. The goddess will hold you to it. You will pay a price for any negligence. If the fire goes out by accident or for any other reason, relight it mindfully, with proper ceremony. If you have a compelling reason to extinguish it for a period of time, do it consciously, in a way that makes it clear to you that it will be kindled again soon, and that there will be no break in the continuity of your devotion. Be mindful of the flame even when it has been put out. Brigit is generous and forgiving, but she insists on the keeping of promises, and she rewards seriousness of purpose.

Brigit's power, as discussed, also shows itself through water, and traditional rituals to her naturally make use of that element as well. One Imbolc ritual that involves washing the head, hands, and feet (and which may have given the feast its name: *imb-fholc*, "washing, bathing") is equally appropriate to do every day at rising. Here's what it is:

Take a basin of water and consecrate it as *tobar Bríde*, "Brigit's well." You now recognize the water in it as a sacrament of Brigit's power to cleanse, comfort, and inspire. Dip your hands into it. Take a moment to appreciate its coolness and the way it flows easily around your fingers. Notice the way it yearns to go back down toward the earth, taking with it anything it happens to be carrying. Understand that whatever you wash off during this ceremony will truly be removed from you and returned to the welcoming land. Then perform this threefold ablution:

As you splash the water over your face and the crown of your head, dedicate all your thoughts over the coming day to Brigit. Cleanse away the nagging feelings of envy and anger that poison your relationships with other people. Release obsessive fears about the future that draw your energy away into useless worrying. Pay special attention to your eyes, which are the organ of your body that Brigit is particularly attuned to. Pray that you may see all people and things as clearly as possible, appreciating them for what they are rather than projecting your own fears and prejudices on them. Think of the water clearing away the dirt of those emotional and intellectual obstructions so that the light of Brigit's inspiration can shine in and show you all things in their true shape. Your thoughts will be ennobled because you are striving for truth.

Next, wash your hands, taking the time to wash each hand thoroughly with the other. Your hands represent your actions, the changes you make in the world around you. Dedicate all your actions over the coming day to Brigit. You know that what you do can harm the world as well as help it. The water of Brigit now cleanses your intentions, so that, to the best of your ability, you will avoid selfish decisions that cause harm to others. Submit all your actions to the judgment of Brigit as it manifests in your mind, which you've just purified. Brigit loves you as her foster child, and she also loves all creatures. When your actions lead to greater peace and harmony between them, you're doing her will.

Finally, sprinkle some water on both your feet. Working together with your declared intentions are your old habits. Your feet are used to treading certain paths, and may walk those paths even without your conscious assent. Some of your acquired habits may be harmless or even beneficial, but others may be self-destructive, or lead to shoddy destinations you should have outgrown. Brigit's cleansing water on your feet keeps you mindful of where you're going. Make yourself aware of your long-term goals, and don't let yourself be turned aside by a craving for satisfactions that aren't worthy of you. Accepting Brigit—the goddess of creative energy at its highest and purest—as your guide, you are led onto the right paths, never straying from your purpose.

After completing the ritual, pour the water out onto a patch of ground, and watch the water seep away into the soil. All those things that you've gotten rid of because they got in the way of your true intent are now given back to the goddess, who can transform them into energy that will be useful elsewhere.

The main prayer used in devotion to Brigit is the *Sloinntireachd Brìde*, which was quoted in full earlier. This should be recited every morning upon waking. Some people who have tried to distance themselves from Christianity might feel uneasy about the explicitly Christian references in some of the verses. Even so, many Celtic Pagans recite the *Sloinntireachd* exactly as it's been passed down to them, leaving in all the Christian allusions, simply out of respect for authentic Celtic tradition, which has absorbed a great deal of Christian elements over the last fifteen hundred years while nevertheless retaining its identity. Try to follow their example; but if it makes you too uncomfortable, simply leave out those specific verses. Don't try to put ersatz "Pagan" innovations in their place; keep the focus on Brigit.

Ideally, you should learn to recite the *Sloinntireachd* in Gaelic. By doing so you will bring into play the kind of focus and discipline that is necessary for gaining any form of real knowledge, or for applying creative energy to get a worthwhile result. This is the sort of effort that Brigit approves of particularly. If, after making an honest attempt, you feel this is beyond you, you can resort to a translation. Here is a short English adaptation of my own, which my group has been using for years in Imbolc celebrations:

> *I call upon Brigit the daughter of the Dagda, the daughter of*
> *Dubthach Donn.*
> *Whoever learns the story of Brigit and teaches it to others,*
> *No fire of sun or stars or moon—or any lightning from on*
> *high—will harm them. Nor need they fear the waters of lake,*
> *river, or sea—or anything that comes out of the deep.*
> *I do not fear these things,*
> *For Brigit is my foster mother.*

The *Sloinntireachd* can be recited again for protection at bedtime, or you can simply use the short affirmation: *Le Brighid fo brat* ("with Brigit under her mantle"). Think of Brigit's healing *brat* laid gently over your body and your mind, focusing the attention of your caring *muime*. Knowing that you are held in the consciousness of someone both powerful and loving, you can safely abandon your own consciousness to sleep.

A LUNAR CYCLE WITH BRIGIT

Brigit's triune nature makes her an ideal deity to meditate on within the framework of a lunar cycle. Divide the lunation into three nine-day periods, with one intercalary day after each one. Each of these nine-day periods will be dedicated to one of Brigit's three primary aspects. The in-between days can be used to take stock of what one has learned in the preceding nine days. If the meditation is a collective undertaking, those are also the appropriate days to come together for group rituals. Each of the nine-day periods will also be divided into a triad of three-day periods, each focusing on a different phase in one's relationship with the goddess.

The first nine-day period is dedicated to the white aspect of Brigit, the *banfhile*, the "female poet." Every evening, light a white candle, wash mindfully in a basin of water, and recite the *Sloinntireachd*. Then spend some time focusing on the candle flame as you meditate on the image of Brigit as inspirer of poets and writers.

For the first three days, as the sickle of the newly waxing moon gradually becomes visible in the sky, concentrate on the whiteness of Brigit as you see her in your mind's eye. White represents clarity, reason, the intellect, articulateness, purity of intention. What else does the image of white Brigit suggest to you? If she is energy given to thought and word, what part of your life needs her now? What kind of nourishment do your mind and spirit crave? During the middle three days, address the goddess directly. Ask her the questions that arose during your previous meditation. Open yourself fully to her answers. The goddess will plant an idea in you, together with the energy to bring it to fruition. You will then spend the last three days putting that idea into an intelligible form—perhaps a poem, or a song, or an essay. It should be an expression of your finest, most generous work, worthy of white Brigit's energy.

The next day should be spent in praise of Brigit. If this is a group endeavor, people should come together to sing songs to the goddess, recite poems and tell stories about her, and share the insights they've gained over the preceding nine days.

The second nine-day period will focus on Brigit in her red aspect: the *bé goibneachta*, the "muse of smiths," who provides the energy to make the weapons and tools that maintain our well-being. Our ritual format will remain the same, but we will now be lighting a red candle, and building up an image of red Brigit as we meditate on the candle flame.

As the moon swells close to fullness during the first three days, fill your imagination with the bright scarlet flame of Brigit as you now see her. Red is the color of the impassioned will, the energy that is centered in us and makes it possible for us to strive against obstacles. It affirms our selfhood, it gives us the ambition to shape our selves in the most complete and satisfying way we can imagine. Red is also the color of transformation, of the neither-nor period that marks the change from day to night and back again.

We cannot survive without making changes in the living world of which we are a part, and we cannot grow without being changed ourselves. Think about the interplay between yourself and others, between yourself and your society and the material world that sustains it. What is it that your self needs, that motivates your will to act? How can that be nurtured, without compromising the ideals of fairness and harmony that white Brigit has taught you? During the middle three nights, while the moon is splendid in its roundness, address red Brigit directly with the questions that have been raised by your meditation.

Her advice to you will be practical. It may impel you to actually make something with your hands, it may plant in you the kernel of a long-term project that will benefit you and your family, or it may simply shed light on how to make your work habits more efficient and less stressful. Ask, also, how to deal with the conflicts that are getting in your way. Once you have a clear sense of what you must do, open yourself to a generous outpouring of the red energy that sustains the will in its struggles. Spend the remaining three-day period applying that energy to working on the project Brigit has pointed out to you.

On the day after, again, review your experience of the preceding nine days. If you come together in a group ritual, continue in your collective praise of Brigit and the sharing of your insights, but also use the red energy you've all been filled with to make something concrete (however simple) in ritual context. This will give you the satisfaction of feeling the effectiveness of your creative ability, and knowing that you are a worthy vessel for Brigit's energy.

During the last nine-day period, as the moon wanes and is eventually swallowed up by the darkness, you will be lighting a black candle to commune with Brigit as the *bé leighis*, the "muse of healing," who watches over us as physical beings, as bodies rather than intellects. Because the hidden processes that keep our bodies alive and functioning properly are often poorly understood (and sometimes deliberately ignored) by us, this is likely to be the most difficult of the three meditations.

Black represents chaos, irrationality, unconsciousness, the unexpected—everything that is unquestionably real, but beyond what can be known by our thinking selves. It means letting go—in sleep, or in death. It is the period of rest that is necessary to counterbalance activity. As we gaze at the reality of black Brigit, she confronts us with our limitations. Our physical natures place restrictions on what the white energy of knowledge and the red energy of ambition can accomplish in us. As we get older, the state of our health can seriously impair our ability to control the shape of our lives.

During the first three days, look honestly at what limits you. Examine the pains, the weariness, the boundaries to your endurance. Where do you need healing? This is what you tell Brigit during the middle three-day period. She may give you practical advice on how to get help for your problems, since she's an herbalist, the guardian of all medicinal plants. But, as all good physicians know, the key to healing is rest. For the last three days, as the last light of the waning moon finally dissipates into the night, open yourself up to the goddess's black energy of renewal. Let go of pain and fear and unrealistic demands on yourself so that the peace of the mysterious darkness can foster a new beginning in you, as what can't be helped is washed away and what is still strong is given greater strength.

And on the thirtieth and last day, as the moon is new again, give thanks to Brigit for all her gifts. For it is only after being cleansed by black Brigit's energy that we find ourselves again ready—and readier than we were before—to appreciate white Brigit's purity and certainty, which is directed at our spirit, our higher selves.

Retreats and Gatherings

As you must certainly have realized by now, Brigit isn't the sort of deity who has to be sought out in some remote wilderness area, in special circumstances very different from your everyday life. She can be found in such wild places as well, to be sure, since she generously gives her energy everywhere (which is why the monsters of the deep know her name). But she relates most effectively with human beings in their own homes, the main place where their needs have to be met. If you want to organize a weekend gathering or longer retreat to honor and explore the energy of Brigit as a group, all the resources for it could be found in someone's house. The rhythm and material of Brigit's interactions with humans is simply the rhythm and material of human life.

Perhaps the best way to perfect the attunement of city people to Brigit is to hold a retreat on a small, family-run, working farm, where the Brigit-ruled processes that transform natural resources into human nourishment can be experienced firsthand.

With Brigit's affinity for cows, a dairy farm would be a good choice. Mindful of the sacredness of the activity and of the example of Brigit whose expert hands got her cows to produce the Lake of Milk, your group could observe and participate in the work that takes the milk from the cows' bodies and then transforms it into not only the rich-textured beverage that gets sold in cartons but many other products such as skim milk, cream, butter, yogurt, and cheese. Learn the techniques to make them and apply them with a full awareness of Brigit's blessing in the gift of the food.

Another project might involve a retreat at a farm when some edible crop plant is ripe for harvesting. Learn as much as you can about the plant as it is when alive and growing: the kind of soil it needs, how much water, other requirements for bringing it to maturity. Then participate in the harvesting of it while showing respect to the spirit of the plant, which is going to nourish your physical body, and thanking Brigit for the energy that sustained its growth to this point. The culmination of your ritual will be a celebration of the joint gifts of Brigit and Lugh as some of the fruit of the harvest is cooked (with the utmost mindfulness of the process) and consumed.

Even simpler and more rewarding is to time the retreat with the ripening of a berry crop—cultivated or wild. Picking the berries will make it very clear to you how much the fruit is a product of the land, with its distinctive soil, its weather, its other life-forms. After the harvest, work together to make the fruit into preserves— keeping in mind constantly how this kind of transformation is one of the ways Brigit feeds people while also enriching their range of experience. Sing songs and tell stories in praise of Brigit as you're doing the work. It will be easy for each member of the group to take home an individual jar of the jam, by which to remember the power of Brigit through the following year.

A BRIGIT MEDITATION

Here is a meditation I like to do whenever I need to remind myself of Brigit's all-surrounding protective presence. You may want to read it onto a tape, then play it back to yourself as you meditate. Read it slowly, pausing often, in a soft and gentle voice. Then play it back as a guided meditation (or at bedtime, as a form of dream incubation):

Imagine yourself outdoors at the end of a bleak winter day. The last of the light is seeping out of the heavily overcast sky. It's cold, a harsh wind is blowing, and you're in open country, with no shelter from trees or buildings. Soon a freezing rain comes down on you as well. The wind drives the little ice crystals into your skin like bullets, compounding your feeling of helplessness and misery. And as night falls, the path you're following fades into invisibility, so you become afraid of losing your way. It seems as if you're a tiny, weak spark of consciousness wandering without direction in a vast, dark universe.

Then you become aware of movement around you, of presences surrounding you in the night. You hear the thump of heavy steps, and an occasional snort. You sense large bodies passing on either side of you. You have come into the midst of a large herd of cattle. The long-suffering animals are moving steadily on, as badly treated by the weather as you are. Lonely and lost yourself, you welcome their company. You move closer to them, trying to warm yourself by the heat of their bodies. Now that you have other living beings around you, you feel less frightened.

Soon you notice that the cows are being led by a tall woman wrapped in a dark hooded cloak. Even after you've made your way to her side you can't see much of her face, but she nods to acknowledge your presence and make you welcome. As the herd trudges on, you observe that the woman is keeping track of every individual cow: she sometimes walks to the back of the herd to encourage cows who are slowing because of exhaustion; and at other times she goes after animals that are straying from the path that only she, now, can clearly see. As she whispers in their ears they appear to gain new energy, and move forward with a bolder step. You feel her affection for the cows, and the cows' trust in her, and you're quite as content to follow her guidance as the cows are. She alone seems to know exactly where she's going, and in the freezing night you have no better choice than to follow her.

Eventually, after what seems like hours of weary plodding through the lashing rain, you find that the path has turned into a road going through the middle of a village. There are houses on either side of you, and every once in a while one or two cows leave the herd as they recognize the barns that are their homes. The woman lays a hand briefly on the flank of each cow as it separates from the herd, and speaks a blessing over it. Before long all the cows have found their own homes, and you alone are left at the woman's side.

She beckons you to a low and narrow doorway, which appears to be where she lives. Since you have nowhere else to go, and the night is very dark and cold and wet, you gratefully accept her hospitality. You go through the door into a space that at first seems just as dark and cold as the outside is, though it at least offers the shelter of a roof.

But when the woman has followed you in she makes a gesture at the fireplace, and great, bright flames suddenly spring up from the logs and twigs of apple wood that had been piled up there. The blessed warmth from it is so comforting that it brings tears to your eyes, and the fragrance of the burning apple wood is bewitching, reminding you of beautiful spring days full of apple blossoms and helping you forget the nasty weather outside. You sit down as close to the fire as you can, and the dancing flames melt the ice crystals that had been clinging to your hair.

When you look up at your hostess again, you realize that she is far taller than you remembered, far taller than a mortal woman could be: she towers above you in a room that itself seems to be higher than the house looked from the outside. And as she opens up her dark cloak, you see that underneath it she is wearing a garment of the most brilliant scarlet, a color that seems as hot and living as the flames in the hearth themselves are. The redness of it jolts you awake, it banishes the terrible weariness from your limbs as an energy like fire courses through them. Enlivened by that energy, you feel courageous and hopeful.

Then the red garment itself splits open, and underneath it is a shining white garment, as pure as snow or moonlight, but many, many times brighter. The whiteness of it is so per-

fectly even and unblemished that it gives a sense of the
utmost peace and harmony. Gazing upon it, you feel that the
worries and conflicts in your life are much less important
than you had thought, that there's a space in your deep self
that is always sheltered from such fears and from which you
can look out at existence with clear-minded detachment. And
that peace makes you free to let your thoughts soar, to find
your way to the level of the gods and their wisdom.

Brigit (for you can name her now) brings you food for
your body: a bowl of milk and a round flat cake. You partake
of the food with reverence, giving thanks to the goddess who
is the source of all such nourishment. As you eat and drink,
she takes a *crosóg* and moves it sunwise nine times over your
head. Direct each one of the nine blessings to an area of your
life where you feel it is most needed.

Now, if you wish, you may make your own appeals to
Brigit. Tell her about the obstacles on your path, for she's
always a compassionate listener. Ask for the advice of her
white nature, her red nature, and her black nature. Each of
these energies has something to give you, something you
need.

You notice that the house of Brigit is full of riches. There
are plentiful supplies of food here, of course, but also all
kinds of tools and gadgets, some of which you can recognize,
some of which look strange. The fire sheds light on elegantly
beautiful ornaments, and you see corridors leading off into
other rooms, and even stairways to upper storys, where you
can glimpse shelves lined with books. You realize that the
house goes on and on, that there's no end to what you can
find here. Someday you will explore more of it.

Now the comfort of the hearth fire and the food are
making you sleepy. You're aware of the cold, wild weather in
the night outside, but here you're absolutely safe. As you lie
down on the pallet Brigit has made for you close to the fire,
the goddess takes her dark cloak off and covers you with it.
You hear her speak her blessing of protection over you, and

then you can give yourself over to the comfort of sleep, knowing that nothing can harm you in her presence.

There's no need to find your way back to the mundane world from this meditation, because the house of Brigit is in reality your own home, as the goddess sees it and as she wishes it to become for you. She wants to guide you to a greater awareness of her presence in it, so that the blessing of her energy can flow to you more freely.

COMING CLOSER

Since everything you can possibly do makes use of Brigit's energy in some way, virtually everything in the world of form can remind you of her influence. Her concern is that you may live a fuller and more satisfying life, on every level. So she participates in your every activity.

Engaging in those activities mindfully, realizing at every stage how and where Brigit is offering her energy to you, will make you more intimate with the goddess than you could ever be with the help of ritual paraphernalia in a specially designated sacred space. Look at all the ways in which you nourish yourself, in which you create a secure physical environment for yourself, as well as a secure social and intellectual environment so that your self won't feel stifled or misunderstood. For all this, Brigit is your source of energy, and your guide. She wants you to achieve those goals as efficiently and fairly as possible, avoiding waste, as well as harm to others, who are also her foster children. So, in all you do, try to see with the goddess's eyes, and to judge with the goddess's wisdom.

Even as mundane an activity as shopping can be an opportunity to commune with Brigit. Be mindful of what you're buying, and of its relation to your true needs. For each item, ask yourself: What is my reason for buying it? What particular need in me will it satisfy? Is it a real need, or an illusory one? Will it actually nourish me (on whatever level I need to be nourished), or will it only provide a semblance of nourishment, and leave me hungry, all my deep needs unmet? Brigit provides only genuine nourishment, and frowns on those who deceitfully try to replace it with something else. She also rewards fairness, and hates greed and hoarding. So, ask yourself again: Who else will profit by my buying this? Am I rewarding destructive and wasteful practices, or the exploitation of one group of people by another? In many cases, the choices will be ambiguous and difficult, and your final decision won't leave you entirely satisfied. But following Brigit's guidance in such matters and thinking deeply about decisions that most people make without thinking at all will enrich your understanding of your inescapable links with the world around you, and will teach you that all spirituality begins with such an understanding.

For the lesson Brigit most wants you to learn is that of her own generosity. Whether you need inspiration to solve an intellectual problem, or endurance to perform a routine task, or strength to apply a special effort to some work, it is Brigit's freely given energy you're drawing on. She is your *muime*, your caring foster mother, whose help and support will come to you all the more easily as you learn to trust and honor her. In her very generosity, however, she doesn't want her own gifts to be hoarded; and she hopes that you will see the wisdom of passing the energy on, to other places where it's needed.

By being her devoted foster child, you learn to be like her, and your chief concern comes to be the great game of balancing what seem to be opposites—giving and taking, nature and culture, yourself and others, indulgence and discipline, activity and rest. As you glimpse ways of achieving that balance, you will also see that this is where you will find healing, and happiness.

Resources

The main sources of the traditions surrounding Brigit the saint are Cogitosus's seventh-century Latin "Life of Brigit" and the later Irish-language *"Bethud Brigte."* They can be found in *Lives of Irish Saints*, edited and translated by Charles Plummer (Oxford University Press, 1922).

Descriptions of the customs associated with Brigit's feast of Imbolc can be found in Kevin Danaher's *The Year in Ireland* (Dublin, 1972), F. Marian McNeill's *The Silver Bough* (Edinburgh, 1956), Trefor M. Owen's *Welsh Folk Customs* (Cardiff, 1959), and my *The Apple Branch: A Path to Celtic Ritual* (Cork, 1998). Seamas O Cathain's *The Festival of Brigit* (Dublin, 1995) traces some of these customs back to their earliest roots. Mara Freeman's *Kindling the Celtic Spirit* (San Francisco, 2001) offers some modern approaches to celebrating the feast, as well as giving instructions on how to make a *crosóg*.

The many Celtic healing goddesses (among whom Brigit had her beginnings) are well described in Miranda Green's *Celtic Goddesses: Warriors, Virgins, and Mothers* (New York, 1996). Mary Condren provides an interesting feminist perspective on the traditions of Brigit in *The Serpent and the Goddess* (San Francisco, 1989).

The invocations to Brigit quoted here (and several more) were collected by Alexander Carmichael in *Ortha nan Gaidheal/Carmina Gadelica* (Edinburgh, 1900).

For information on the Vestal Virgins and their role in Roman religion, see H. H. Scullard's *Festivals and Ceremonies of the Roman Republic* (London, 1981).

Ord Brighideach is a modern order of Brigit devotees, some of whom tend a perpetual fire. Their Website (members.aol.com/gmkkh/brighid/ob.htm) provides information on the order as well as resources relating to the goddess/saint.

Noirin Ni Riain sings a traditional Irish hymn to Brigit *(Gabhaim molta Brighde)* as "Ode to Bridget" on her album *Celtic Soul* (Living Music 01048-81506-2). The Breton ballad of armless Berc'hed can be heard sung by Iffig Troadeg on the album *E skeud tosenn Vre* (Arfolk CD 425).

PART III

BELTAINE

Maureen Reddington-Wilde has for many years been a consecrated priestess of Aphrodite. She is an ordained minister of the Church of the Sacred Earth: A Union of Pagan Congregations (COSE, pronounced Cozy), and belongs to Daitales, a Hellenic Reconstructionist congregation within COSE. She contributed the historical research to HMEPA, the reconstructed Athenian calendar online. Among her ministerial interfaith activities, she serves on the steering committee of the Massachusetts Religious Coalition for the Freedom to Marry. The RCFM is a broad-based interfaith coalition that promotes the legalization of gay marriages. Maureen helps to create Aphrodite shrines and temple space at Pagan gatherings throughout the Northeast, and promotes safer sex education and practices as well as worship.

Aphrodite

ΑΘΡΟΔΙΤΗ, Aphrodite, Sea-Born, Cypriot, Heavenly One, Common One, Golden One, Dark One, Warlike, Prostitute, Protector of Marriages, Nurse, Grave Digger, Fair-Sailing One, Laughter-Loving. By all these names and many more, and by whatever name you wish to be called, we honor you.

May your Graces, the fair Kharities[1]—The Bright Shining One, She Who Brings Flowers, She Who Rejoices the Heart—and all the many others who serve you help us to learn your ways.

---

[1]Throughout I have used the Greek names; their Latinized versions are given in the Glossary.

APRODITE'S STORIES: MYTHS

Myths cannot be understood in isolation. Each story is but a single snapshot, one perspective, one revelation out of the many possible, for the Gods are far greater than human comprehension. Deeper understanding comes from placing the myths, even contradictory ones, in context with each other. We should start by placing them in the context of the culture in which the first revelation of the myths appeared. They should be placed in the context of the rituals of that culture. And then, as practicing Pagans, we can deepen our spirituality by placing these ancient myths in the context of our own culture, our own rituals, our own lives.

I am a dedicated priestess of Aphrodite. She is best known as the Greek Goddess of love, but, like all the Gods, Her reality is much more complex and ambiguous. Her self-revelation is never complete.

Love and Beauty are indeed among Her chief characteristics. Hers is also the strength to be the Gold One and the Black One, symbolic colors of the high heavens and the dark earth. She inspires not only humans, but all the wild animals and the beasts of prey, to mate. Aphrodite is the Lover and is also She Who Dances Upon Graves. She is needed to keep the cycle of life turning. Her capabilities are not limited by our concepts.

I am a reconstructionist, drawn to worship the classical Deities of Greece. Reconstructionists try to replicate authentic historical ways of worship, so I began by reading many books. However, academic writers prefer simple definitions. In their striving for tidiness, they overlook a lot of reality and history. They restrict the Gods to specific, limited functions. They oversimplify Sacred reality, which is always more complicated than we humans think.

In this chapter, I will present many aspects of Aphrodite, many stories and symbols and associations. Always remember that there are many more: those that I have not yet discovered, and those that She has not yet revealed. May our understanding of Her, and of all other Gods, always remain open to new insights.

Books are a resource for learning, however flawed. Our challenge as readers is to first learn how to question authority, how to critically assess the evidence given and the conclusions drawn. Here are some basic questions to keep in mind while reading any book, no matter how renowned the author:

- Does the writer clearly distinguish between evidence, reasoning, personal interpretations, and just plain presumptions?

- Do other, equally respected, writers present different evidence or draw different conclusions? Check the books' dates— perhaps there were new archaeological discoveries in between various publications.

- How do your own assumptions color your interpretations? What evidence would cause you to change your own preconceptions?

With these critical thinking skills, your learning can advance beyond superficial knowledge. The most important step is to draw your own conclusions.

EPITHETS: NAMING APHRODITE'S ASPECTS

All of the Greek Deities, maybe all living Deities, are complex in nature. Knowing this, Their worshippers call and praise Them with many epithets. Scholars tend to interpret these epithets as defining or even limiting the functions of a Deity. When confronted with epithets that appear to be contradictory, they speculate that perhaps these originally applied to separate Deities that were later conflated.

The ancient epithets, preserved in the original sources, suggest a richer understanding. To get a sense of Aphrodite's complexity, try to hold all Her epithets in mind at once. The prayer that opens this chapter contains only a few of the epithets by which the Greeks knew and praised the Goddess Aphrodite. There are more. There will be more yet, as her new worshippers deepen our knowledge through practice and experience.

When we call on Aphrodite in ritual, we can use only so many epithets in one invocation. Obviously, we will select some of these to remind Her and ourselves of particular aspects or associations we hope will be in the forefront of how She presents Herself. But She comes only in Her totality and how She chooses to present Herself is entirely up to Her.

Aphrodite lives. Our ancient Pagan Deities live, and They waken. As we go on, experience further enriches our knowledge. The stories of their lives, and their dealings with humankind, are not limited to those told in ancient times. New myths are waiting to be revealed. New epithets need to be called.

Today, there is an exuberant Pagan renaissance in progress. At many Pagan gatherings, we share friendship, celebration, laughter, and learning. One of these gatherings, which I attend regularly, is called Panthea. When I was remembering my times at Panthea, a new epithet came to me: Aphrodite Panthea. Speaking this new name, and feeling it resonate in my body, I still understood that calling Her Aphrodite Panthea can never limit Her to this singular aspect or negate the many other ways She has made Herself known.

Aphrodite Panthea is a very powerful way of naming a moment I had with Her. If the name for this one moment brings such a visceral response, how would it work with many names for many past experiences, each reinforcing the others? Perhaps each name or epithet brings us a bit closer to the unnameable heart of Her mystery.

To add to the complexity, although Greek Deities have primary spheres of powers, They are not limited to those. Their many overlapping powers are reflected in Their shared epithets. Both Aphrodite and Hera are known as Golden One. Both Aphrodite and Artemis are known as Mistress of the Animals. Both Aphrodite and Demeter are known as Black One. And some identifying epithets, such as foam-born, are unique to Aphrodite.

In his book, *Greek Religion*, Walter Burkert describes how the Deities accumulate epithets. Some are formulaic (for example, ancient and traditional epithets, such as "foam-born"), some are spontaneous, and some relate to specific rites or festivals. Different types of epithets serve different functions in worship.

In Classical times, Greeks began their invocations with a litany of names and epithets, ending, like the opening prayer of this chapter, with "and whatever name you wish to be called."

- ❦ The very traditional "formulaic" names let all present know exactly who is being invoked, which particular aspect of the Deity is the focus of this rite. They also connect us with Her worshippers of other times and places, giving us a sense of solidarity and continuity over the span of centuries.

- ❦ Other names or epithets may recall the memories and experiences that this particular group shares. These evoke a more heartfelt connection with the Deity.

- ❦ Spontaneous names or epithets are those that arise in the moment, that express what we are feeling right now. If a new epithet resonates strongly and deeply in the hearts of those present, it will be remembered and become one of the second type of epithets.

By offering to call the Deity "by whatever name you wish to be called," we acknowledge that we cannot limit the identity and powers of the Deity. We defer to Her desires, and we open ourselves to Her ongoing revelations. From a reconstructionist perspective, we also do it because this is the way the rituals have always been done. In this manner, we maintain our connections with other rituals and worshippers throughout the ages.

And so I invoke Her in ritual by formulaic names that everyone can recognize. And by specific names that some will recognize, and

by Her ancient names in Attic, the language of Classical Athens,
that She Herself will recognize. Together, Goddess and worshippers,
we all bring our memories of sharing ritual into the present ritual
moment. These memories are a well from which we draw.

APHRODITE'S BIRTH

There are two very different myths of Aphrodite's birth, coming
from the epic poets Homer and Hesiod. Homer probably lived
sometime during the eighth century B.C.E.[2] and not later than
ca. 700 B.C.E. His *Iliad* and *Odyssey* relate the stories of the Trojan
War and the wanderings of Odysseus.

Hesiod lived around 700 B.C.E. He was a shepherd tending his
flocks when the muses called him to write poetry, and provided
his revelations. Hesiod's *Theogony* ("Birth of the Gods") tells the
Greek creation myth, including the origins of the Gods.

In Hesiod's telling, first there was Chaos, undifferentiated
potential, then Gaia (Earth) emerged. She gave birth to Ouranos
(Heaven), and then, with him, to a number of creatures including
the Titans (elder Deities). The Titans for the most part represented
the raw forces of nature. They in turn bore children.

The children of two of the Titans, Kronos and Rhea, were
Demeter, Hades, Hera, Hestia, Poseidon, and Zeus. Zeus led a
revolt against his parents and then divided the universe with his
brothers. Zeus took the heavens, Hades the underworld, and Poseidon the sea.

Zeus established a court on Mount Olympos. He and the other
Deities who resided there became known as the Olympians. They
represented human cultural ideals, so the establishment of Zeus's
rule on Olympos can be understood as the foundation of civilization. The Olympians are certainly the Deities at the center of Greek
civic rituals.

[2]B.C.E./C.E.—Before the Common Era/Common Era. These terms reckon dating by the
common civic calendar without recognizing the supremacy of the Christian god.

The advent of this new order of Deities did not cause the demise or disappearance of Gaia, Ouranos, and other elder Gods. Those who did not join the new Olympic hierarchy still continue to be recognized and worshipped.

As Homer tells it, Aphrodite is conventionally born of two parents, Zeus and Dione, a Goddess who has very little surviving mythology. Both Zeus and Dione were worshipped at Dodona in northwestern Greece, where there was also a temple to Aphrodite.

Homer's perspective on Aphrodite's character is somewhat limited. He depicts Her during the siege of Troy as a Goddess whose capabilities are limited to love and desire. She is ineffectual in battle and must seek the protection of her parents.

Hesiod tells a very different birth myth. In his *Theogony*, the Titan sky God Ouranos would not let his children into the light. Eventually, with their mother's assistance, and at her instigation, they rebelled. While Ouranos lay atop Gaia, their son Kronos cut off his testicles and threw them into the sea. As the waves carried them away, a white foam grew around them. Presently, the beautiful foam-born Aphrodite arose near the coast of Cythera. This is the version made familiar by Botticelli's well-known painting *The Birth of Venus*.

The waves bore Her to Cyprus, where She stepped ashore. Aphrodite is still honored today in Cyprus, which promotes itself as Her birthplace and entices couples to hold their weddings there.

According to Hesiod, Aphrodite is one of the forces driving the world out of its original timeless chaos and darkness. At the first moment of the separation of Earth and Sky, of Gaia and Ouranos, Aphrodite, the embodiment of both desire and union, appears. Placing her as one of the earliest Deities acknowledges that lust, love, and desire, all of which are Her powers, are primary forces driving the growth and development of life from the beginning of time, long before the evolution of humankind or human culture.

The widespread use of the epithets Sea-Born and Cypriot attest to the prevalence of Hesiod's myth within Greek culture. The pow-

erful foam-born Aphrodite is honored from the poetry of Sappho
to the mystical rituals of Orpheus. In the mystery traditions of
ancient Greece, seekers confront Persephone and Aphrodite in the
Underworld as part of their initiation.

By observing how people actually used the myths in worship
and other cultural practice, we can understand which of the myths
were important, or irrelevant, to them. The version of Aphrodite's
birth and nature recounted by Hesiod is the one most often
referred to in formal art and ritual. However, the lessons to be
learned from Homer were so important that his version was told
and retold in ritual recitations of his poetry for centuries.

Having two quite different accounts of the origins of a major Deity
may seem strange to us. However, in Greek religions, contradictory or diverging myths such as those regarding Aphrodite are
commonplace.

An important key to understanding Greek religions is that they
were pragmatic, not dogmatic. In a pragmatic system, practice is
what matters, while dogmatic systems emphasize belief. So, in
Greece there was no common religious calendar. Each city and village established its own cycle of regular public religious festivals
and sacrifices, according to its own local needs. People performed
private rituals as they deemed necessary.

Art competitions were a common and very popular type of
public gathering in Greece. The art itself was an offering to the
Gods. Plays, ritual reenactments of myth, were produced at these
competitions. So were recitations of Homer's epic poetry. Theater
and poetry transmitted the great mythic stories, providing a widespread religious education. People came together in a communal
gathering to share the emotional experience of the dramatic presentations. Beliefs were private matters, left to individual choice.
There was no dogma, just artistically presented lessons to ponder.

There was also no centralized priesthood. Some priestly positions were held for a year, some for longer terms, some for life.

Some positions were appointed by lottery, some by election, some by heredity. Every citizen was qualified for the priesthood. Every priestess, every priest, had authority only over his or her own rituals, his or her own sanctuaries.

Just as in classical practice, no matter how many years I have spent dedicated to Aphrodite in my own priesthood, I can only offer my experience and advice to others. If the way I lead my rituals and manage my temple space is different from the way others lead theirs, Aphrodite should be quite used to the contradictions of our mortal perceptions by now.

THE JUDGMENT OF PARIS

This myth explains what precipitated the Trojan War, one of the defining events of Greek and Roman mythic history. Paris, son of King Priam and Queen Hekabe of Troy, is commanded by Zeus to decide which of three Goddesses is the most beautiful. Each offers him a bribe. Athena promises that She will give him victory in all his future battles. Hera promises him an Asian empire. Aphrodite begins by opening Her robe to display Her own beauty, then promises him the most beautiful of mortal women for his own wife.

Paris chooses Aphrodite. His trophy bride is Helen, who is already married to Menelaus, king of Sparta. When Helen flees with Paris, Menelaus and his allies pursue her. Thus begins the Trojan War, which ends in the utter destruction of Troy.

On a literal level, Paris is simply choosing among the three competing Goddesses in a beauty contest, although the unanticipated outcome of his choice is tragic. Metaphorically understood, however, Paris represents all mortals. As the Greeks understood, mortals have only limited capacity to accept gifts from Deities. We cannot exercise all talents or follow all opportunities at once, and so must choose.

Paris's choice was actually between the different guiding values that the contesting Goddesses' bribes represented: Love (Aphrodite),

Victory (Athena), and Royalty (Hera). Such choices existed long before Paris. They still exist. Any choice we make will have consequences, anticipated and unanticipated, and sometimes tragic.

Some of the illustrations of the Judgment of Paris found in classical art show three identical figures being led by Hermes, the messenger God, to Paris for his judgment. Now they are simply the Kharites (the Fates), not individual Goddesses at all. When three specific Goddesses are present, Paris is making a choice between specific gifts. When the Kharites are shown, he faces the dilemma of all choices.

APHRODITE'S HISTORY

Birth myths are one approach to the study of a Deity. Another is to trace the history of how humans have understood and related to Her. We don't know for certain when or where Aphrodite first revealed Herself to humankind, or how human perceptions of Her changed over time and space. Among some ancient cultures that had some contact with Greece, we encounter Goddesses—for example, Astarte, Inanna, Ishtar, and Venus—that seem very like Aphrodite. Are they Her ancestresses? Her twin sisters? Herself in some different ethnic garb? We have some informed guesses, some speculations, but no definitive proofs. Learning more about Her counterparts, and their connections, might deepen our understanding of Aphrodite Herself.

Why might these Goddesses be so similar? Perhaps Aphrodite is the same Goddess as these others, known by other names in other languages, just as a man named John in this country would be called Sean in Ireland or Ivan in Russia. Some details might be different because the same divine revelation was received and interpreted differently in different cultures and different time periods. Or it might be that they are different, but similar, Deities, with somewhat overlapping functions. I haven't had any personal revelation to support either theory.

By examining the relationships between the peoples concerned, we might come to understand a little bit more about the connections between their Deities. The problem with this is that our knowledge even of Rome is sketchy. The further back in time we go, the less we know for sure. Surviving records from those ancient times are few and fragmentary, and not always completely reliable.

HISTORIOGRAPHY

Historiography, the study of historical methodology, is about weighing evidence from a variety of sources, including ancient texts. Throughout much of the history of classical studies, scholars tended to take these texts at face value. So a scholar writing in the first century B.C.E. about events in the fifth century B.C.E. was considered an authoritative source, being much closer in time to the actual events than we are.

Recent scholarship is more skeptical of the ancient historians. We're learning that Aristotle and Herodotos were just as adept as the authors of the Bible (or any modern-day Pagan) at spinning tales of ancient religious practices without much supporting evidence. We now look for archaeological or other corroboration before we simply accept their word.

For example, we have archaeological evidence indicating that there probably was a Trojan War. One of the strata excavated at Troy looks as if the city had been intentionally and utterly sacked. But this took place around 1200 B.C.E. Homer lived and wrote some five hundred years later. He was not an eyewitness, nor did he have access to the kind of extensive written records we have for more recent events. Moreover, we have no archaeological confirmation at all for the specific people Homer mentions, such as Hekabe, Helen, or Paris, let alone for the interventions of various Deities that he describes. So Troy is both a historical event and an important component of the Greek myth of origins.

Since we have no contemporary records from the time of Troy, we cannot know whether Aphrodite had yet emerged as a Goddess by then. We also don't know whether those who fought there worshipped Her by any name at all.

Remember, though, that inaccuracy doesn't equal dishonesty or even baseless speculation. It could just mean that the ancient authors were writing with a different purpose.

Some of them may simply have been repeating long-standing oral traditions of their cultures. Others were myth spinners, writing from inspiration or revelation rather than from objective fact, telling tales to illustrate and convey important cultural values or insights about Deity, information far more important for our own attempts to rebuild this religion than historical details would be. Certainly, their interpretations were shaped by culture, gender, region, and class, as those of all writers are.

On the other hand, lack of supporting evidence does not prove that information from ancient sources is wrong. Archaeologists are still exploring and discovering, sometimes using ancient texts as a guide. For example, scholars didn't even believe that there ever was a historical city of Troy until archaeologist Heinrich Schliemann unearthed the remains of the city in the late 1800s. Up until 1915, leading scholars also denied that Sumer ever existed. More sadly, some discoveries will never be made, because war, vandalism, and industrial development have destroyed the sites.

Remember that, although descriptions by Homer of rituals and sacrifices are not necessarily factual sources about religion in the Bronze Age, they are an invaluable insight into the religious thought of the Archaic Age, when Homer lived and worshipped.

Before going further into specifics, I want to present an overview of the times and places that concern us. This will take some time, but it will help you understand how the pieces fit together. Please be patient.

HELLENIC TIME LINE

A brief outline of ancient Hellenic history can provide a context for understanding developments in worship.

⚘ **Bronze Age** (3300–1050 B.C.E.) First palaces on Crete, 2200. One of the archaeological layers at Troy, dated to this era, contains a sacked city, possibly the historical basis for the myth of the Trojan war.

⚘ **Dark Age** (1050–776 B.C.E.) From the collapse of Mycenean and Achaean civilizations, which existed in pre-classical Greece, till the first Olympic Games.

⚘ **Archaic Age** (776–479 B.C.E.) From the first Olympic Games and the earliest recorded dates of Greek history, till the end of the Persian invasions. Corinth emerges as the premier Hellenic city, 730. Draco writes the earliest Athenian legal code, 620. Traditional date for the founding of the Roman Republic, 509. First Persian invasion of mainland Greece defeated by the Athenians at the battle of Marathon, 490.

⚘ **Classical Age** (479–336 B.C.E.) From the end of the Persian invasions till the ascension of Alexander the Great. Radical democratic reforms in Athens, 462.

⚘ **Hellenistic Age** (336–30 B.C.E.) The period from the ascension of Alexander the Great till the Roman conquest of the Greek world. Foundation of Alexandria in Egypt, 331.

READING THE MAP *(pages 172–73)*

An understanding of geographical relationships gives us a clearer picture of the emergence of Aphrodite and Her worship in the Mediterranean. Different communities seem to have encountered or emphasized different aspects of the Goddess. This map shows the location of some of Aphrodite's most important sanctuaries. Of course, there were many more.

Phoenicia was on the eastern coast of the Mediterranean, largely modern-day Lebanon. Cyprus (A) is the largest island near Phoenicia. The Phoenicians, being renowned seafarers, always had some amount of contact with and settlements on Cyprus. Achaean Greeks, Homer's protagonists, established settlements there in the

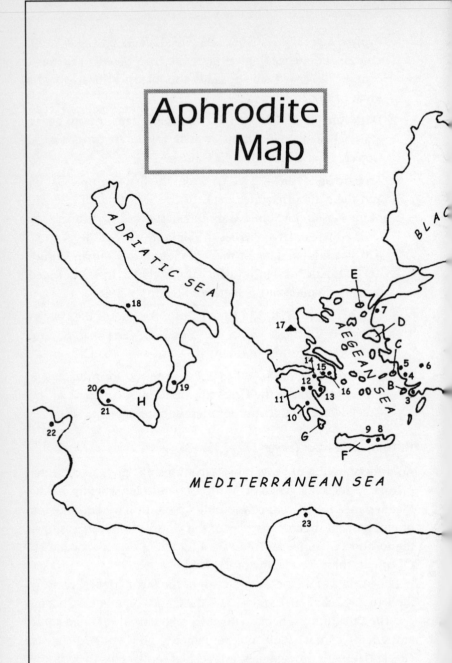

Aphrodite
Map

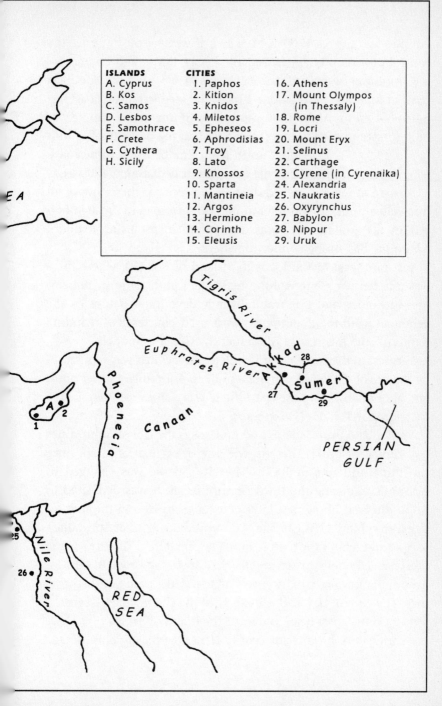

ISLANDS
A. Cyprus
B. Kos
C. Samos
D. Lesbos
E. Samothrace
F. Crete
G. Cythera
H. Sicily

CITIES
1. Paphos
2. Kition
3. Knidos
4. Miletos
5. Epheseos
6. Aphrodisias
7. Troy
8. Lato
9. Knossos
10. Sparta
11. Mantineia
12. Argos
13. Hermione
14. Corinth
15. Eleusis
16. Athens
17. Mount Olympos (in Thessaly)
18. Rome
19. Locri
20. Mount Eryx
21. Selinus
22. Carthage
23. Cyrene (in Cyrenaika)
24. Alexandria
25. Naukratis
26. Oxyrynchus
27. Babylon
28. Nippur
29. Uruk

late Bronze Age, ca.1200 B.C.E. Later, it was variously under the
control of Syria, Phoenicia, Assyria, Persia, Egypt, and Rome.

Continuing westward, the Achaeans also settled the southern
coast of Anatolia, modern-day Turkey, the Mediterranean coast just
north of Cyprus. At the southwestern tip of Anatolia, a temple was
built for Aphrodite Euploia (Fair-Sailing) at the port city of Knidos
(3) in 394 B.C.E. Extending north from Knidos is the Ionic coast,
where many Greek settlements were established around 1000 B.C.E.

Austere Athenians looked down upon Ionia as the center of all
things luxurious, soft, and feminine. For a woman to "scratch herself in the Ionian way" was a euphemism for using a dildo.
Aphrodite has strong connections here.

Just northeast of Knidos is the island of Kos (B), where there
was a noted temple to Aphrodite. In the fourth century, the temples at Knidos and Kos featured nude devotional statues by the
Athenian sculptor Prakhiteles, who used courtesans, including
Kambuse, the mistress of Alexander the Great, as models.

Farther up the Ionic coast is Miletos (4), which was reputed to
be the site of the world's largest temple to Aphrodite. Farther north
and about halfway up the coast, there was a shrine at Ephesos (5)
to Aphrodite Hetaira (Courtesan).

Well inland from Miletos and Ephesus is the city of Aphrodisias
(6), capital of Lydia. There is evidence of occupation there since
the third millennium B.C.E. The city's name was changed to
Aphrodisias during the third century B.C.E. It was dedicated to
Aphrodite and home of a large cult center to Her. In the mid-to-
late fifth century C.E., Christians destroyed the icons at Aphrodite's
temple and rebuilt the temple into a larger church. The city's name
was changed briefly to Stavrapolis, the City of the Cross. But the local population preferred to use Caria, also the name of the province. The current-day Turkish village at the site is called Geyre.

Just off the coast near Ephesos is the island of Samos (C). There
is a shrine to Aphrodite adjacent to Hera's temple at Ephesos. One

of Aphrodite's epithets is Presiding over Marriage. Hera has the ultimate power of presiding over marriages, so it is not surprising to find Aphrodite included in Hera's temple.

Samos was also a large center of the hetairai, or courtesans. In some instances this profession is seen as religious, sometimes secular. North of Samos is the island of Lesbos (D), home of Sappho, who wrote great poetry to Aphrodite early in the sixth century.

At the northern end of the coast, up above Lesbos, stood the city of Troy (7). Near Troy is Mount Ida, not to be confused with another Mount Ida on Crete. The Judgment of Paris took place here. In an early hymn, Aphrodite is described moving through the wooded slopes of Ida with a retinue of wolves, bears, lions, and panthers, Mistress of the Animals. Here, also, She sought out the herdsman Ankhises and begot their child, the Trojan hero Aineias, who later became the mythic founder of Rome.

Northwest from Troy is the island of Samothrace (E). There is some evidence that Aphrodite was worshipped here. However, since it was the practice on this island to keep the names of the Deities secret, speculations about Their identities by authors from Herodotos onward are suspect.

Back down the coast, southwest of Knidos is the island of Crete (F). There at Lato (8) is a joint temple to Aphrodite and Ares, God of war. At Knossos (9), another Cretan city, one priest served them both. The child of Aphrodite and Ares is Harmonia. Also on Crete, at Kato Syme, there is a joint temple to Aphrodite and Hermes. The child of this union is the transgendered Hermaphroditos.

The island of Cythera (G) lies northwest of Crete, just at the southern tip of mainland Greece, near the Peloponnesos peninsula. According to Pausanias, the Phoenicians brought the worship of Aphrodite to this island. Hesiod wrote that Cythera is where Aphrodite first arose from the foam.

At the southern tip of Peloponnesos is Lakonia, ruled by the city of Sparta (10). At both the cities of Argos (12) in Argolis at the eastern tip of the Peloponnesos and Mantinea (11) in Arkadia in the center, there are temples jointly dedicated to both Aphrodite and Ares. In Cyprus, Crete, Cythera, Sparta, and throughout the Peloponnesos, Aphrodite was honored as a Goddess of war.

Northward again, Aphrodite Pelagia (of the Sea), was honored at Hermione (13) on the southeastern coast of Argolis and across the Aegean sea from Miletos (4).

Corinth (14) is on the isthmus connecting the Peloponnese with central Greece, with ports on both the eastern and western coast. While Poseidon, God of the Ocean, is the patron Deity of Corinth, the city is also particularly noted for its devotion to Aphrodite Pandemos (Belonging to all the People). It is claimed that all of the prostitutes of the city were Her priestesses. The prostitutes were one of the civic groups who publicly honored Aphrodite for Her help in defeating the Persian invasion of 480 B.C.E. After his second victory in the Olympic Games, Xenophon of Corinth dedicated fifty slaves to serve as sacred prostitutes at Aphrodite's temple. In the Attic language both *aphrodisiazo* and *korinthiazomai* are verbs for sexual intercourse. "Going to Corinth" was a metaphor throughout antiquity for having a good sexual time.

Northeast of Corinth is Attica in the easternmost part of central Greece, the region ruled by Athens (16). Aphrodite had a temple at the bay of Eleusis (15) on the southern coast, as well as on the eastern coast at Athens. At the Acropolis in Athens, there is an enclosure for "Her in the Gardens." There was also a separate shrine to Aphrodite Hetaira (Courtesan).

While it is likely that the cult[3] of Aphrodite Pandemos was first established in Athens during the Archaic Age, it was vigorously and successfully promoted in the classical period by Solon the Lawmaker. In 594–593 B.C.E. Solon was Archon of Athens, the

---

[3]The word is used here in its scholarly sense, meaning "a pattern of worship," rather than in its modern pejorative sense, meaning "any religion being described by someone who dislikes it."

annually elected chief ruler. He is noted for introducing many legal reforms, including a much more humane legal code than the original one established by Draco. He also established many houses of prostitution for the common good. With the profits from these houses, he built a temple to Aphrodite Pandemos. Late in the third century B.C.E., an Aphrodisia festival for Aphrodite Pandemos was started in Athens and a new cult arose in Attica to Aphrodite Hegemone (Leader of the People).

At the time of this writing, the remains of another temple have just been discovered at modern Marcopoulo, about nine miles southeast of central Athens. Most temples of Aphrodite, like most Greek temples, are simple square buildings where sacred objects are stored to be used for rituals. Typically, only priestesses, priests, and other attendants dedicated to each temple are allowed inside. Worship takes place outside in the sacred precinct. However, this temple complex functioned as a sacred brothel and has many rooms including baths and massage rooms.

Continuing up the eastern coast from Attica, in the northern region of Greece lies Thessaly, across the Aegean Sea from Lesbos and Troy. From here comes the epithet of Aphrodite Anosia (the Unholy). According to Pausanias, there are grave memorials in Corinth and Thessaly to a noted and extremely beautiful hetaira, Lais. Apparently, she traveled from Corinth to Thessaly. Feeling threatened, a gang of wives lured her into the temple of Aphrodite and murdered her. In the aftermath of this incident, the people of Thessaly began honoring Aphrodite Anosia to help make amends.

To the southeast of Thessaly, on the Egyptian coast of the Mediterranean, Greeks settled in Naukratis (25) in the Nile Delta, where Aphrodite Ourania was worshipped. They also established a large colony at Cyrene (23) on the coast of modern-day Libya. The Cyrenaic school of philosophy, in the fourth century, promoted a rather extreme version of hedonism based on the concept that reality exists only in the present moment, so immediate pleasure becomes the highest goal in life. While this philosophy is not directly connected to Aphrodite, Her priestesses might assist students of this school.

To the west, the early Achaeans had an active trade with Sicily. In the eighth-century migration, Greeks established some colonies up both coasts of the Adriatic Sea, in southern Italy, Sicily, and southern France, and even some as far as the southern coast of Spain, on both sides of the Pillars of Herakles, which defines the Strait of Gibraltar.

At Locri (19) in Italy, Aphrodite's priestesses practiced sacred prostitution comparable to that at Corinth. Also at Locri, we find ritual portrayals of Aphrodite and Persephone strongly juxtaposed in the underworld. Ritual objects were widely exported from here, and later reproduced in other locations such as Selinus (21) on the western tip of Sicily and at Oxyrhynchus (26) on the Nile.

By the fifth century, the eastern half of Sicily was largely settled by Greek colonies, and the western half mostly by Phoenicians. There was a temple of Aphrodite at Mount Eryx (20) in Sicily. This was the inspiration for the temple to Venus Erycina built in Rome (18) in 217 B.C.E. The Sicilian town of Selinus (21) was founded in the seventh century and flourished until the fifth century when it was destroyed by Carthage (22). There were strong cult connections between the Gaggera sanctuary at Selinus and mainland Locri. In 241 B.C.E., Sicily became a Roman province.

The diffusion and diversity of Aphrodite's worship attest to Her power and appeal. When we place Her on the map, we notice that Her worship is above all seaborne and urban. Most of Her major temples thrived in port cities. As much as She presides over war, seafaring, fertility, and gardens, Her primacy over love thrives within the communities of cities and civilization. Aphrodite's worship continues most strongly as one of urban delights.

Aphrodite's Sisters

In cultural rather than mythic terms, Aphrodite may be the younger sister of several Goddesses from nations that flourished in the Middle East before the rise of Greece. She may also be the elder sister of the Roman Goddess Venus. By exploring these cultural connections, we can gain more perspective on Aphrodite.

We can trace a strong connection in place and time between Aphrodite and Astarte. There is an equally strong linguistic connection between Astarte and Ishtar. Yet, the relationship of Ishtar and Inanna, even though their names are used almost interchangeably in Sumerian and Akkadian myth, may be as tenuous as that between Aphrodite and Venus. Understanding the historical uncertainty of whether or not Aphrodite and Venus are one and the same also helps to frame the question of whether or not Astarte, Ishtar, and Inanna are names of the same Goddess.

Venus

Many people believe that the Greek and Roman mythologies are interchangeable, that they are the same religion, just using different languages.

Even the Romans themselves said that the Deities they worshipped were the same as the Greek ones. The Romans' politically motivated assertions of religious similarities, however, are rather suspect. In the Imperial period, the Romans attempted to impose their religious system on other nations as a means of cultural co-optation. For example, Caesar claimed that Mercury was the predominant God of the Gaulish Celts, followed by Apollo, Mars, Jupiter, and Minerva, and that the Celts had almost the same idea of these Deities as the Romans did, only different names. The conquered Celts did not necessarily agree.

The assimilation of Greek and Roman Deities, however, started much earlier in the development of Roman religious and cultural identity, and involved some actual borrowing of Greek religious concepts. Originally the Romans honored *numina*, or spirits or divine beings of natural or abstract powers. Through contact with Greek colonies in Italy, the Romans adopted the Greek concept of anthropomorphized Deities.

Whether or not the Greek and Roman Deities are the same, their religious institutional structures are quite different from each other, particularly in terms of governance. Roman priesthoods were highly regimented and arranged in a strict hierarchy with government officials at the top. From Caesar onward, the post of Pontifex Maximus—High Priest, "head of the pontiffs"—was held by the emperor. This is in strong contrast with the decentralized Athenian structure, where citizens voted on the conduct of public festivals. (Modern Pagans who reconstruct either Hellenism or the Religio Romana treat the two as separate religions.)

The Roman Goddess Venus was originally seen as the power of fertility of vegetable gardens, fruit, and flowers. There is no evidence that those early myths bore any Greek influence. So the original Venus was probably not the same Goddess as Aphrodite. Very early in the process of Roman development, however, the Italian Venus was syncretized with Aphrodite and anthropomorphized. The myths of Aphrodite were applied to Venus.

There is always the chance that the Romans had begun by separately worshipping the Goddess the Greeks knew as Aphrodite, then later combined Her with their Venus. If They are different beings, it is still left to divine revelation which one, or if both of Them, would respond to invocations after the Romans grafted Aphrodite's characteristics onto Venus's name.

CANAANITE GODDESSES

In the earliest references, records from the second millenium B.C.E., written in hieroglyphics and in cuneiform scripts, Canaan was a large territory including the lands we now know as Israel, Jordan, and Syria. Among the Goddesses the Canaanites worshipped were three, Ashtart, Anath, and Asherah, that were associated with fertility, love, and war. These Goddesses were not particularly distinguishable from each other: their common energies raise questions. Are these different names, used like Greek epithets, for what was perceived as the same Goddess? Were they originally separate Deities? Once again, neither history nor divine revelation has provided an answer for me.

ASTARTE

The next important question is how the Phoenicians understood the relationship between Anath, Asherah, Ashtart, and Aphrodite.

The Phoenicians, renowned seafarers whose homeland was in what is today Lebanon, established an empire not of conquest but of trade, with colonies and trading links across the Mediterranean. They developed an alphabet, which was later adopted by the Greeks—and many others—and which we still refer to as the "phonetic" alphabet.

They worshipped Ashtart, whom we know better by the Greek spelling of her name: Astarte. The Phoenicians were strongly bilingual and frequently translated their own names into Greek equivalents when dealing with the Greeks. At some unknown point in time before 333 B.C.E., they translated Astarte to Aphrodite Ourania (Heavenly).

The Greek historian Herodotos, writing in the fifth century, had been quite liberal in assigning the label of Aphrodite Ourania to many Goddesses foreign to Greece. So the Phoenicians may have simply observed an identity between Astarte and Aphrodite, then adopted the Greek name, perhaps from Herodotos. Or their understanding of their own Goddess may have taken on strong Greek influences, as the Roman concepts of Venus did, so the name change represented a real shift in perception. Or, perhaps, the Phoenician and Greek Goddesses developed in tandem.

Early on, the Phoenicians established settlements on Cyprus, and maintained a continuous presence there. Kition, which had been a Mycenean city, became Phoenician in about 800 B.C.E. The Mycenean temple at Kition was replaced with one dedicated to Astarte at that time.

In 333 B.C.E. the Phoenician merchant community from Kition requested and received permission from the Athenian assembly to build a temple in Athens dedicated to their own Goddess, Aphrodite Ourania, just as the Egyptians had been given permission to build one for Isis.

We can find earlier and stronger links between the Greek and Phoenician Goddesses. The identity of Aphrodite emerged on Cyprus, where there was long-standing contact between the two civilizations, at some point between the Bronze Age and the dawn of the Archaic Age. From the *Iliad* onward, Aphrodite's most commonly used epithet is Kupris (Cypriot). Hesiod describes Her as rising from the sea foam near Cythera and coming ashore at Cyprus. In Homer's *Odyssey*, Paphos in Cyprus is identified as Aphrodite's home.

The Temple at Paphos, which dates back to the twelfth century B.C.E., was regarded by the Greeks as the center and origin of Aphrodite's cult. Although we have no definitive proof, it's possible that this temple has been dedicated to Aphrodite since its founding. By then, Achaean Greeks, who might have already known Aphrodite, were settling on Cyprus. There is also a second sanctuary to Aphrodite at Paphos, dating from the Archaic Age. Votive offerings found there include many with Phoenician features. All this suggests that Astarte and Aphrodite may spring from the same roots.

INANNA AND ISHTAR

At the dawn of history, the city states of Sumer and Akkad were competing with each other for supremacy. Akkad, where Ishtar was worshipped, controlled the middle region of ancient Mesopotamia, comprising the northern part of later Babylon, largely current-day Iraq. The supremacy of the Akkadian dynasty lasted from about 2350 to 2150 B.C.E., when it collapsed under barbarian invasions, and the Sumerians regained primacy. The first writings in Akkadian appear in about 2000 B.C.E., after the fall of the dominant empire. Akkadian remained the common Semitic language until it was supplanted by Aramaic around 500 B.C.E.

History, the written record of human activity, begins at Sumer, where Inanna was worshipped as Queen of Heaven. Sumer was located in the southern region of Mesopotamia. The Sumerians, a non-Semitic-speaking people, migrated into the Persian Gulf area sometime before 3000 B.C.E. The earliest known writings are Sumerian cuneiforms that date back to about 2050. The final remnants of Sumerian civilization lasted until about 1700.

The Sumerian language continued as a sacred language used by the Semitic temple scribes long after that. The temple scribes at Nippur seem to have made a concerted effort to collect all of Sumerian literature, much to the benefit of modern knowledge after archaeological excavations at Nippur.

Inanna is born directly from the union of Earth and the Starry Heavens, during the time of the coming of light, right after the birth of Nanna (Moon) and Utu (Sun). She presides over fertility, love, and war. This echoes Hesiod's version of Aphrodite's attributes and Her birth at the beginning of the separation of light and darkness.

The poetry that relates Inanna's myth was discovered and translated by Samuel Noah Kramer, the great scholar of Sumerian culture, the man who coined the phrase "history begins at Sumer." Kramer worked from cuneiform clay tablets, some of which were worn into illegibility in spots or even missing chunks. Later, working in close collaboration with Kramer, poet and storyteller Diane Wolkstein built a more complete and more poetic version from these fragments. This poetry, believed to have been written by a princess and priestess of Sumer, is the oldest recorded liturgical poetry in Western history, and contains themes that are still salient in contemporary Paganism.

Phoenician and Akkadian are Semitic languages. Ashtart is the Canaanite and Phoenician spelling of the Akkadian Ishtar. Astarte is the Greek spelling of the Phoenician Ashtart. Still, the relationship between them is not as clear as the shared name might imply.

Akkadian mythology is difficult to distinguish from Sumerian mythology. Sumerian civilization was a thousand years old before the Sumerians invented writing. There was much contact and conflict with Akkad before there were written records. The Sumerians developed writing first and wrote down their myths. When Akkadians eventually wrote down theirs, they may have been heavily influenced by the Sumerians. The myths are quite similar. The Akkadian Ishtar is almost identical to Inanna.

So, even though Inanna and Ishtar are linked when They enter the written record, we don't know how that linkage came about. Was Inanna-Ishtar always seen as the same being, as Astarte and Aphrodite may have been? Was the identity and mythology of one grafted onto the other as Aphrodite's were to Venus? Was She (were They) part of indigenous Semitic Akkadian religion, or brought in by the Sumerians?

COURTESANS

In addition to their shared historical roots, Venus, Aphrodite, Ashtart, Ishtar, and Inanna also have a strong ritual connection through sacred prostitution. In that practice, worshippers would achieve communion with the Goddess through the physical body of Her priestess.

It may be surprising that these ancient priestesses did not necessarily have to be women. Transgendered priestesses, transvestites, or transsexuals served in ancient temples. In modern times, too, Aphrodite's priestesses include anyone who chooses to live as a woman, regardless of her birth.

Not all priestesses of the erotic Goddesses served as prostitutes, nor were all prostitutes priestesses. Outside of the temples, however, these distinctions are not always clear. There are two broad classes of prostitution: the common street-walking variety (*pornai*) and the professionally trained courtesans (*hetairai*). Either could be a priestess. In Corinth, *all* the prostitutes were considered to be Aphrodite's priestesses.

Any pious Greek would have viewed his or her personal skills as being gifts from the Deities, and so any *porne* or *hetaira* would have been seen as having a special relationship with Aphrodite, even if that relationship wasn't specifically one of being Her priestess. Sacred slave prostitutes *(hierodoulai hetairai)* at temples were called literally just that.

In Athens, although male prostitutes had a very low social status, female hetairai had a relatively high one. It was the most socially liberated and educated role for women. Athenian social life was highly segregated along gender lines. The wife and female servants of a household stayed in their own designated rooms and did not participate in the larger social life of the males.

Hetairai, on the other hand, were frequently invited guests at male social functions. In addition to providing entertainment through music, dance, and sex, they were expected to be able to converse intelligently about current events and politics. Hetairai were not citizens, and so a male citizen would not marry one, but they could achieve very prominent roles as mistresses. While the details are not clear, it's possible that they could even own property, which citizen class women could not do.

Uruk: The Deepest Root?

If Venus is Aphrodite who is Ashtart who is Ishtar who is Inanna, if they are all different names, and variant perceptions, of the same Sacred being, then the earliest known temple to Her is at the city of Uruk on the Euphrates River, about 160 miles south-southeast of modern Baghdad. Uruk, known as Erech in the biblical book of Genesis, was one of the oldest cities, founded before 3000 B.C.E.

The Great Temple of Uruk was dedicated to Inanna and Her father An (in Akkadian, Anu), Heavenly Sky, Father of the Gods. The Greeks saw Aphrodite as arriving from the East. If indeed all of these similar Goddesses are one, then the progression of Her worship has been one of continuous direct movement westward from Uruk.

APHRODITE'S RELATIONSHIPS

From the day humans are born, they are formed and defined by their relationships. If you want to know somebody better, observe with whom, and how, that person interacts. The Gods are shown in humanlike relationship to other Deities. They are parents, spouses, children, friends, allies, and rivals. As we understand these relationships, we come to know more about the Deities.

THE KHARITES

The Kharites, the Graces, are Aphrodite's close companions and handmaidens, who help Her adorn Herself with all Her seductions. Known by different names and in different numbers in various times and places, They finally came to be known as three: Aglaia, the brilliant; Thalia, who brings the flowers; and Euphrosune, who rejoices the heart. In the springtime They dance with the nymphs, presiding over budding plants and ripening fruit. They are also seen as rays of sunshine, and are frequently in the company of Apollon. As well as being in the retinue of these Deities, They were worshipped in sanctuaries of Their own.

FLORA

The Roman Goddess Flora is very similar in concept to the original Roman perception of Venus: the spirit of fertility in vegetable gardens, fruit and flowers. Venus, in turn, was conflated by the Romans with Aphrodite.

Flora was worshipped throughout Italy at a very early date by Latins and non-Latins alike. A month roughly equivalent to the Roman month of April was dedicated to Her. Flowery spring also seems a good time to celebrate Aphrodite's seductive powers.

During the empire, Flora's festival, the Floralia, which ran from approximately April 28 through May 3 in our modern calendar, became a major celebration of flowers and springtime. The prostitutes of Rome came to identify the Floralia as their feast, revealing another parallel with Aphrodite.

The festival also resembles the later development of merry May Day in England, with its emphasis on sexuality, blossoming flowers, and the health of the crop to come. These May Day traditions are echoed today in the Wiccan May celebration called Beltaine (bright fire). In Old Irish (the language used from about the fifth to eleventh century C.E.), Beltaine refers to both the first day of May and the entire month.

Although it may be very tempting to imagine that Beltaine is derived from the Floralia, historically the Roman and Celtic celebrations were probably quite different. Celtic society was more oriented to herding than to farming at that time. The Coligny Calendar, the earliest surviving Celtic calendar from Gaul, dates to about the second century C.E. It clearly divides the year into light and dark halves. Beltaine marks the start of the light half of the year, and has strong associations with bonfires and the health of dairy cattle. There is no early evidence linking it particularly to flowers, crops, or sexuality.

Since the Celts did not leave a written record, there is precious little evidence about any ritual details. With the immense amount of contact the Romans had with the Celts throughout Italy, Gaul, and Britain, it is conceivable that similarities may have existed or developed between the Floralia and Beltaine.

Beltaine may also have mutated over the course of a thousand or so years. The earliest written evidence of gathering May flowers doesn't appear in England until about 1500 C.E. By 1550, May Day as we know it now, with its maypole and sexual license, was in full bloom in England. It became the custom for courting couples to spend the night together in the woods and to return home bearing green branches (May Bushes) at dawn. Around the same time, we find the first written reference to raucous celebrations in Ireland.

Even if they were originally very different festivals, however, today's Beltaine celebrations definitely carry on the spirit of the Floralia.

ADONIS

Adonis probably has the longest-standing ritual connection with Aphrodite. His name, Adonis, is a Greek variation of the Semitic title Adon (Lord). Like Aphrodite's, His cult worship began at Cyprus. He is also sometimes seen as the companion of Astarte.

As is common, there are variations of the myths regarding His birth, death, and return. The story begins with His father, Kinuras, sometimes said to be the son of Apollon. Kinuras came to Cyprus and is the legendary founder of the city of Paphos, and of the worship of Aphrodite.

One of Kinuras's daughters, Smurna, was said to be more beautiful than Aphrodite. This hubris enraged the Goddess, who tricked the father and daughter into having sex in the dark of the night during the time of the corn festival. Eventually, Kinuras brought a light to one of Their trysts and recognized His daughter. Upon discovering that She was pregnant, He tried to kill Her. But the Deities protected Her by turning Her into a myrrh tree. Adonis was born by bursting forth from the tree.

Aphrodite was smitten by the child's beauty and sent Him to Persephone to be raised in safekeeping. As He grew, Persephone also loved Him and did not want to return Him to Aphrodite. This dispute was finally settled by an agreement that He would spend a third of the year with each Goddess and have one third to Himself. He chose to spend His own third with Aphrodite as well.

Eventually Adonis died in a hunting accident. By some accounts He was killed by Ares, one of Aphrodite's jealous lovers. After Adonis's death, Aphrodite became furious that He would now spend the whole year with Persephone, Lady of the Underworld.

And so another agreement was reached whereby Adonis would return to Aphrodite for half the year.

Adonis's powers broadly cover love, beauty, fertility, vegetation, and rebirth. In addition to Adonis's cult origins at Cyprus, there are also later Greek reports that He had early worship at Byblos on the coast of Phoenicia. His informal but highly popular festivals, Adonia, were celebrated throughout the Greek world, including at Lesbos and Athens. Sappho and her circle of young girls were celebrating Adonia around 600 B.C.E. In Athens, Adonia became a women's nighttime festival, celebrated in the homes and on the rooftops. These were notably popular among the hetairai, and presumably wives as well. The Adonia tended to be quite emotional and bawdy rituals mourning the death of Adonis.

Adonia was also celebrated in Egypt, after Alexander the Great founded the city of Alexandria there. During the Hellenistic Age (336–30 B.C.E.), the Greeks came to associate Aphrodite and Adonis with the Egyptian Isis and Osiris, based upon the death of Osiris and the power of Isis to bring him back to life.

EROS

Another of Aphrodite's close companions is Eros (literally Love/Desire). One of the myths of His birth places Him even before Aphrodite. According to Hesiod's *Theogony*, out of the Chaos came Gaia and then Eros, before even Gaia gave birth to Ouranos. As one of the oldest, He has power over Gods and mortals.

Other myths place Him as the companion and sometimes the son of Aphrodite and Ares. Another says He is the child of Iris (the Rainbow) and Zephuros (the West Wind). Eros had an ancient cult of His own at Thespiae near Thebes. He was also worshipped together with Aphrodite at a sacred precinct on the Acropolis in Athens.

Eros was sometimes worshipped in the plural, Erotes, inspiring all sexual desires, heterosexual or homosexual. His influence covers not only desire and attraction, but marriage as well. Artwork on Athenian vases from the fifth century B.C.E. show brides being adorned by Aphrodite, Eros, and occasionally other companions of Aphrodite.

Pan

The God Pan is not associated with Aphrodite in classical mythology, but because of Their mutual interests in fertility and lust, modern Pagans tend to honor Them together in ritual. Pan's fertility powers are expressed through lust alone, without Aphrodite's civilizing traits of love and marriage. Like Eros, Pan is often worshipped in the plural, as Panes. The powers of desire are manifold.

Pan's origins are in the rugged mountains of Arkadia in the middle of the Peloponnesos. A patron of shepherds, flocks, and herds, Pan is fond of wild places, although over time His worship spread beyond Arkadia and even into the city of Athens.

Ares

Aphrodite and Ares, the God of War, were jointly worshipped at a number of locations. While Aphrodite does have Her warlike attributes, armed images of Her are rare among Greeks. Her relationship with Ares is seen more as a complementary or polar relationship. One child attributed to them is Eros. Another is the Goddess Harmonia. Desire and music are born from the joining of love and war.

Hermes

Aphrodite and Hermes were also worshipped as a couple. Hermes is honored by statues with an erect phallus, and frequently just by the phallus itself. Their child, Hermaphroditos is born male. He is raised by nymphs on Mount Ida and grows up as a wild hunter. At the age of fifteen while he was bathing naked in a lake, Salmakis, the nymph who ruled the lake, grabbed him for her own. As He resists her advances, she prays that they never be separated. Her wish is granted. They become fused into one body, neither male nor female. And so the union of female sexuality and male sexuality comes of age as a transgendered being. This myth is the origin of the word *hermaphrodite*.

Hephaistos

In some myths, Hephaistos, who presides over fire, blacksmithing, and industry, is depicted as Aphrodite's husband. He has other wives in other myths. According to Homer, He is married to Kharis (Grace), one of the Kharites. And although He had children with a number of different mothers, none is attributed to Him and Aphrodite. In Athens, He shared a festival with Athena, recognizing Their powers over technology.

However, Aphrodite and Hephaistos do share a strong link in the magical traditions. Hephaistos is commonly seen as practicing His craft within volcanoes, particularly Mount Etna. Magical practitioners saw volcanoes as portals to the underworld. At volcanic sites, including Mount Etna, Aphrodite has a place in the underworld alongside Persephone. Here, Hephaistos's name is used synonymously with the destructive fire through which one must descend to reach the life-giving and regenerative Goddesses.

Finally, please remember that Aphrodite has established relationships with other Deities. If you do eventually dedicate yourself to Her, you will also be acquiring a bunch of "in-laws." By doing any prolonged work with Her, or any other Hellenic Deity, you will inevitably be exposed to the energies of the other Deities in the cultural pantheon. The historical mythologies and dramas frequently point out the hazards of favoring one Deity while ignoring another. As your connection with Aphrodite develops, I recommend that you also perform at least one ritual during the year giving offerings to all of the Olympian Deities.

Aphrodite's Pleasures

When contemporary Pagans talk about "correspondences," we mean things that are commonly associated with a particular Goddess or God. This could be colors, scents, flowers, animals, foods, rhythmic patterns—anything that we believe that Goddess or God enjoys.

I'll be giving some of Aphrodite's traditional correspondences in this section. If you want to attract Her attention, or attune your life more closely with Her energies, it's a good idea to surround yourself with these things that both please the Goddess and quietly remind you of Her.

In general, anything connected to Aphrodite and Her worship should be as luxurious as you can contrive. References to Her worship thoughout antiquity always come back to this theme. Even the Aphrodisia in Athens became noted for its luxuriousness. Modern-day worshippers concur. You just cannot overdo the luxury when honoring Her. When creating altar space and rituals for Her, build in things to touch all the senses, as richly as possible.

Animals

Aphrodite is associated with numerous animals. These are shown accompanying Her in Greek art.

The he goat is often found near Her. Aphrodite Hetaira often rides a he goat in ancient pictures. In one story, a female goat that was about to be sacrificed to Aphrodite is transformed into a male just before the moment of sacrifice. This was taken as a sign that the Goddess preferred he goats. The goat, as well as a variety of predatory animals, accompany Her when She is shown as Mistress of the Animals.

Aphrodite is also closely associated with doves, and accepted doves as sacrifices. In art, She is designated by an accompanying dove, or by supplicants presenting Her with doves. Sappho describes Aphrodite as arriving in a chariot drawn by doves. The dove is also associated with Astarte and Adonis.

In art too she is shown sailing through heaven on a swan, a bird befitting the sea-born queen. Another animal associated with Her and the sea is the dolphin. The use of the dolphin is also a pun, since Aphrodite, as we have seen, is known as the foam-born (Aphro-genes), and a dolphin was also called a "foamer" (*aphrestes*).

GARMENTS

Aphrodite was originally depicted naked. Then from the first half of the seventh century onward, She is shown wearing flowing and colorful robes, necklaces, and a high crown.

Around 340 B.C.E. the Athenian sculptor Prakhiteles created the most renowned statue of Her in the ancient world for Her sanctuary at Knidos. He showed Her naked in the bath with arms raised. Prakhiteles's pose of Aphrodite harks back to Canaanite images centuries earlier of Asherah as a nude woman with upraised arms. Coincidentally, Asherah's fertility aspects are represented by Her standing under a tree accompanied by young male goats. After Prakhiteles's work, Aphrodite was once again depicted in art as naked or seminaked.

Today, we can honor Aphrodite with ritual nudity or with the most luxuriant and sensual of ritual garb. If you choose to worship skyclad, consider adorning yourself or each other with sweet-smelling oils, jewelry, body painting, and similar luxuries.

If you prefer ritual garb, this could range from a traditional Greek peplos (two long rectangles of fabric hanging from the shoulders, belted at the waist, and open up the sides) to an evocative harem look or an elaborate Persian princess design. In Greek art, when Aphrodite was depicted in robes, they were always more Eastern and exotic-looking than Greek, not surprising considering Her apparent Eastern origins.

Fabrics for both altar decorations and ritual garb should of course be as sensuous and flowing as possible. Silks, velvets, lamés, sheer fabrics, and furs are all in order. Use rich colors ranging from pastel aquas and lavenders that evoke the seaside to royal blues, greens, purple, and gold that represent Her majesty. For a more contemporary look, fishnets and heels wouldn't be out of place.

These clothing suggestions are appropriate regardless of gender. I have not come across any specific reference to vestments for Greek priests of Aphrodite. However, all of the references I have found for males serving Ashtart, Ishtar, or Inanna record that they wore either female garb or a mixture of male and female, and always in a variety of bright colors and sensual textures. It's a reasonable extrapolation that Aphrodite's priests would dress similarly. There are also early depictions of a bearded Aphrodite as well as an even earlier bearded Ishtar, although details of the cult worship of these transgendered aspects of the Goddesses are lost.

TREES AND PLANTS

Aphrodite is also associated with a number of trees, plants, and spices, including apple trees, pomegranates, roses, myrtle, and cinnamon. Although Her sacred gardens in Cyprus no longer stand, one can just look at the luscious plants that grow on this warm southern island and realize that all the sweet-smelling fruit trees, flowers, herbs, and spices are in the domain of Her seductive fertility.

FRAGRANCE

Aphrodite loves fragrance. Exotic and luscious fragrances will help call Her forth. They will also remind you of Her presence. Her altar at the temple at Paphos was not used for blood sacrifices, but for offerings of prayer and incense only.

Frankincense is first mentioned as an offering to Aphrodite by Sappho. Throwing a handful of frankincense on a fire became a common and affordable sacrifice to Her. She responds to other pleasant fragrances as well. I've used sandalwood, vanilla, roses, and lavender. Any perfume that works best on your body and makes you feel seductive will please Aphrodite.

FOOD AND DRINK

Overlapping with fragrances are sensual foods, spices, and drinks. Cinnamon, vanilla and nutmeg, strawberries, chocolate and honey, and many more foods are not only good offerings to Her, but are considered aphrodisiacs.

The actual effects of aphrodisiacs have long been debated. Modern scientists, including the U.S. Food and Drug Administration, generally dismiss aphrodisiacs as placebos at best. However, there is a very telling statement on the FDA's Web site: "Chilies, curries, and other spicy foods have been viewed as aphrodisiacs because their physiological effects—a raised heart rate and sometimes sweating—are similar to the physical reactions experienced during sex."

Consider this statement in light of psychological studies that show that people can change their moods by changing their physiology first. If you set yourself to smiling you are likely to become happy, if you set yourself to frowning you are likely to become upset. If you induce physical symptoms that are associated with sexual arousal . . .

Chocolate is the one aphrodisiac that has been scrutinized in the laboratory. Studies show that it contains phenylethylamine, or PEA, a psychostimulating chemical that is found in the bloodstream at higher levels in people who are "in love." Chocolate also stimulates endorphin secretion, which promotes an opiatelike effect on the body. So scientists have finally confirmed what we ritual practitioners have known all along—chocolate is good!

Even though chocolate was unknown in the ancient Mediterranean, everyone who uses it as an offering for Aphrodite today reports that She receives it quite favorably. Dark chocolate seems to be the best. As with any sacred offering, use the best quality you can afford.

The overall sensuous appreciation of food in ritual also adds tremendously to its aphrodisiac qualities. Dipping strawberries into chocolate or whipped cream and feeding each other in ritual inevitably and rapidly becomes a deeply sensuous experience that you can invite Aphrodite to share.

Wine, champagne, and liqueurs also work quite well for libations and ritual consumption. "Aphrodite and Dionusos go along together" was an ancient proverb about the coexistence of love and wine. Alcohol helps people relax and release some inhibitions. Be careful, however, because alcohol is also a depressant. Too much is counterproductive.

Champagne has long been associated with romance. Recent studies confirm the common wisdom that champagne affects people much more quickly than wine. The very high carbon dioxide content, about 250 million bubbles per glass, speeds the flow of alcohol into the bloodstream. So a small amount of champagne will give an immediate rush of physiological changes. Rich liqueurs such as Chambord are also ideal for Aphrodite rituals. Their heavy fruity aromas and tastes are best enjoyed by sipping from small snifters.

For people who do not drink alcohol, there are a number of other beverages that will help awaken the senses and sensuality. Exotic fruit juices, sparkling cider, and heavily honeyed black tea with a dash of cinnamon are all very appropriate for Aphrodite. In areas with immigrant Indian populations, you can find pomegranate juice at Indian grocery stores. Daiquiris, with or without alcohol, are also superb and festive.

MUSIC AND DANCE

For music, let yourself be guided by Aphrodite's daughter Harmonia and by the Muses, particularly Euterpe, the muse of lyric poetry and instrument playing, and Terpsikhore, the muse of choral song and dance.

While it would be exquisite to do ritual accompanied by music in the appropriate ancient modes, the musical structures and scales used in ancient Greece are quite different from our modern ones. We do have ample historical information on how to compose music in the old ways, but it would take a very concerted effort for modern musicians to become fluent with them. I certainly hope some will, so that eventually the Hellenic reconstructionist movement can build a body of music of our own. But for now and for most people, we will have to find our inspiration from more modern sources.

Musical selection will of course vary tremendously depending on your taste and the intended tone of the ritual. Classical selections can range from the reflective impressionism of Debussy's *La Mer* ("The Sea") to the hard driving rhythms of Ravel's *Bolero*. Belly dance music has a wide range of melodic and rhythmic moods. Bump-and-grind striptease music is sexy and funny. Compilation recordings of rock and roll stripper favorites, or sound tracks to movies such as *The Full Monty* and *Striptease*, are also great for high-energy rituals. I find Kay Gardner's music particularly wonderful for ritual use. Her recordings *A Garden Path* and *Garden of Ecstasy* can usually be found filed under New Age. If you are adding movement or dance to your ritual, that too can range from a simple grapevine step, which is so characteristic of Greek folk dances, to full folk dances, belly dances, or even an outright striptease as appropriate. More elaborate choreography is always usable for dramatic presentations. One study from the early twentieth century compared illustrations of dance from ancient Greek vases to positions of contemporary ballet and extrapolated a ballet flavored reconstruction of ancient dance.

STONES AND GEMS

Ancient Greeks didn't usually associate any particular stones or gems with Deities. However, there are some that I have come to favor for jewelry or altar decorations that honor Aphrodite.

The soft colors of rose quartz and mother-of-pearl evoke Her sensual nature. Opals are fitting not only because of their luxury but because they particularly benefit from regular contact with body oils to keep their luster and quality. Garnets and rubies evoke Her more dominant and regal aspects. Aquamarines and pearls reflect Her connection with the ocean.

Seashells and sea glass do likewise. Sea glass, found along the shoreline, consists of broken pieces of glass worn into smooth curves by the tides and the sands. Sharp shards of human waste, transformed into polished things of beauty by the sea itself, seem fitting objects to place on Her altar. And since the time of Botticelli, the scallop shell is the quintessential token of Her emergence from the sea.

DATES AND SEASONS

The Greeks did not universally associate any particular time of the year with specific Deities. Each city had its own cycle of major civic festivals. We have detailed records only for Athens, where the public Aphrodisia celebration was held during the month of Hekatombaion, the first month of the Athenian year. Hekatombaion began with the first new moon after the summer solstice, so it fell approximately during our month of July. The Athenian celebration of Aphrodisia was established rather late by Antigonos Gonatas (320–239 B.C.E.), a philosopher who later became king of Macedonia.

Athenians also honored the "birthdays" of a few Deities on one day each month. The fourth day of each month was celebrated for Aphrodite and Eros (along with Hermes and Herakles). Athenian months began when the new moon crescent became visible; their days ran from sunset to sunset. The Athenian civic calendar was rarely if ever in sync with the actual phases of the moon, so it would be appropriate to honor Aphrodite's birthday either on the fourth day following the new moon or on the fourth day of the calendar month.

Remember that the Hellenic custom was for every locality to determine its own festival times. So whatever time of day, month, or year works best for you to honor Aphrodite is the right time. Beltaine, May 1, is a perfectly good time for modern Pagans to invoke Aphrodite. She might even be insulted if you left Her out of Beltaine's exuberant festivities. June, being a customary month for weddings, would be a good time to call on Aphrodite too, as the one who enlivens marriage.

Remember, the historical associations of particular scents, foods, colors, and so on with Aphrodite are just starting points. Throughout the ages, new associations have always been made. There is no reason for us to stop making them now.

When an Athenian vase painter first depicted Aphrodite riding a swan through the heavens, She had already been worshipped for centuries, without the bird. But the Muses spoke through the artist. The art then spoke to the people. It speaks to us now. Yes, that image fits Her.

If an image speaks to you and your heart says yes, this is She, then so it is. There have been newly emergent artistic representations through the centuries. Prakhiteles's *Aphrodite at the Bath*, Botticelli's *Birth of Venus*, each in turn shaped people's images for generations to come. The next great image is waiting to emerge.

And so it is with all of the things that please the Goddess and invite Her presence: incense, food, music or anything that touches the senses and reminds us of Her.

ATTUNEMENT: APHRODITE'S WORSHIP

Today, we can read only those ancient texts that survived. We don't know whether these particular stories were representative or even particularly important in their own time, compared with others that were lost. We know even less about what the ancients experienced in ritual, for words are the smallest part of the living experience, and only some of the scripted words were preserved, at

that. We do the best we can with what we have. As we encounter
Aphrodite or other Deities in ritual, if we keep open hearts and
minds, our experience will deepen our understanding.

Scholarship can support and inform ritual experience, but even
the best scholarship can never replace it.

Contemporary Pagans create ritual in a variety of ways. Many
use the "generic" Wiccan-style Circle format. Some have more specific structures and techniques passed down by their own elders.
Still others strive to re-create historically attested ritual practices.

Many modern Pagans invoke Deities that they feel relate to the
purpose of their ritual, creating an eclectic mix. Others concentrate on one ethnic pantheon.

People who worship Deities from a specific culture using historical ritual practices, called reconstructionists, seek a deep devotion
to specific Deities by learning and practicing the Deities' own
ancient rituals and traditions. The intention of reconstructionism is
to maintain as much continuity of structure and practice as is possible based on surviving historical evidence while also welcoming
personal inspiration and addressing contemporary cultural needs.

Norse ethnic Paganism, under a variety of names, may have an
unbroken tradition, rather than a reconstruction. Still, it has
gained much greater visibility and vitality in recent decades. Celtic
reconstructionism is at least a century old.

Hellenic reconstructionism is a more recent development, nurtured by the Internet. We strive to gain as much understanding of
the historical religious practices of ancient Greece as we can and to
bring these elements into our rituals today. Most Hellenic reconstructionists emphasize public civic rituals or household rites.
Others work with the mystery traditions, the esoteric aspects of
Hellenic worship.

Reconstructionists do careful research, attempting to create rituals that come as close as possible to the way the Deities used to
know them, hoping thereby to welcome those Deities back into
our world. We believe that calling a Deity by the names he or she

used to know during centuries of rituals and using what we can of the old ritual structures help to bring more and more memories into the current ritual.

If you wish to pursue a strongly reconstructionist path, consider learning the Attic language, or at least enough to be able to pronounce the words and spell them in Greek and be able look them up in a Greek lexicon. If you use Attic epithets in ritual, notice whether your associations and experiences are similar or different when you use the same epithet translated into English.

Working with old practices and names also creates a feeling of solidarity of purpose with other people across the ages. I like to think that a fifth-century Athenian would be able to recognize the rituals I help create. Of course there will be some differences, but differences would have been expected by travelers throughout the Hellenic world.

Many historical details are lost, or not yet discovered, so we have to fill in the gaps with our best judgment and personal revelations. Even people working from the same historical information come up with different interpretations. Also, some known details are deliberately changed to better fit the sensibilities of our current culture. For instance, we prefer gender equality; the ancients did not.

In the rituals that follow, I use the reconstructionist model that I and my group have developed. Please do adapt it to fit your own needs. Any, all, or none of the historical elements could be combined with part or all of the generic Wiccan-style structure. Either could just help inspire your own creative adaptations. When I note specific differences between Wiccan and reconstructionist practices, this is merely for clarification. I don't mean to imply any basic incompatibility between the two approaches.

My own personal working style has developed and evolved over time. Originally I began doing solitary rituals with little formal structure. When I began attending Pagan festivals, I deliberately adopted a generic Wiccan-style structure for the rites I presented there because this format was familiar and comfortable for most people.

I was still using Wiccan ritual structure for public rituals when I first dedicated myself to Aphrodite as Her priestess. I simply stayed within the Hellenic pantheon if my ritual called for other Deities besides Aphrodite. Over time, my dedication to Aphrodite has led me to learn the Attic language to use for both research and liturgy. I have also gradually come to understand how reconstructionist approaches strengthen the experience of ritual.

People who have never seen a Hellenic ritual before are deeply moved when they have the chance to participate in a torchlight procession and to hear a hymn to Aphrodite recited in the sounds and cadences known to Her. Even if they don't understand a word of Greek, they remember more the experience of hearing the Attic version than the translation that follows.

HOME ALTARS

All you really need for a home altar or shrine is a candle and holder, and some representation of Aphrodite: a statue, painting, photo, seashell, or anything that reminds you of Her. You may want a bowl for offerings of honey or libations of wine or cream, an incense burner, or a vase for flowers, depending on what types of offerings you would like to give.

If the altar is inside, bring the offerings outside after a period of time and respectfully place them on the earth or in water. For an outside garden shrine, offerings can be placed directly on or poured over the altar stone.

Also for an outside shrine, set a basin nearby that can be filled with clean water in preparation for ritual. The basin is needed because before any Hellenic sacrifice or offering, from the smallest home gathering to the largest public ritual, the participants should ritually wash their hands. My partner and I have planned a garden shrine, set in a rose arbor, to be built as our garden progresses. We have already acquired a scallop shell be used for the washing basin.

Even for rituals at mealtime or for private meditation, ritual washing is important. It shows respect for the Deity and helps establish an appropriate ritual frame of mind. For most purposes, a simple sprinkling of water over the hands will suffice. People taking leadership roles in larger rituals or participants in initiatory rites might want to take a full and luxurious bath.

Keeping in mind Aphrodite's key theme of luxury, add additional decorations to suit your tastes. My own altar includes traditional icons of many seashells and two small baked clay statues of Aphrodite standing in a scallop shell with her arms upraised.

I also use much more modern images, including a rotating selection of cards from Annie Sprinkle's Post-Modern Pin-Up Pleasure Activist Playing Cards, an autographed photo of the actress Alexandra Tydings in her role as Aphrodite from the *Xena* and *Hercules* television series, and a Grecian Goddess Barbie.

When you first set up a Hellenic altar, and at the beginning of every ritual, cast some barley or other grain upon it. Do this first, even before lighting a ritual candle. Casting barley marks the beginning of the ritual and marks the space as sacred. Barley was one of the major grain crops of ancient Greece. It is appropriate for you to use barley because it is traditional, or you can use a major grain crop of the region where you live. Or try it both ways, paying attention to any difference in the feeling of the ritual.

DAILY RITUALS

Daily rituals in a Hellenic household center on mealtimes. Originally, these rituals took place at the cooking hearth, the center of every home. If you have a woodstove or a fireplace, and have a live fire in it, that's the most traditional place to make offerings.

For modern usage, a candle at the dining table and a small bowl to receive offerings will do.

Begin each mealtime ritually by washing your hands and lighting the candle. Call to the Goddess Hestia, who rules over the hearth of every home, to bring the sacred flame, the center of family life, and to bless all who live there and all present company. At the start of each meal, a small portion of food is offered first to Hestia. At the end of each meal, a small libation of drink is poured to Agathos Daimon, the Good Spirit of the house, frequently represented as a small snake. Call to Agathos Daimon to protect the household and to bless all who live there and all present company.

In addition, you may hold symposia, special dinner parties, in honor of Aphrodite, or other Hellenic Deities. Groups that gather to study the Greek language or religion might want to begin each study session or ritual with a shared dinner. After making the first mealtime offering to Hestia, pour libations to Aphrodite and any other Deities that will actively be involved in your study or ritual after the meal. For fancy meals, offer libations to the honored Deities at the start of each course. If you are offering more than one libation to the same Deity, you may use different epithets with each one.

If you are embarking on a specific period of dedication to Aphrodite, such as the month-long cycle of weekly rituals suggested below, then you may wish to supplement this with daily offerings to Aphrodite and the Graces. Simply offer Them libations at each meal after Hestia's offering. When dining out, I have poured libations into an extra cup, saucer, or whatever was suitable and handy. Just use due respect if you need to improvise while away from home.

To elaborate a little more, you might create a daily cycle through the mealtimes. At breakfast, pour offerings to the Graces and ask Them to help you learn the ways of Their Mistress. At lunch, pour offerings to Aphrodite. You may wish to use different epithets each day or each week. Ask Her to teach you Her ways. At dinner, pour offerings to Aphrodite and the Graces, giving Them thanks for what you have learned that day. And then, before going to bed each evening, place a fresh offering on the altar.

As part of personal devotion to Aphrodite, you may choose to also create a bedtime ritual that sets aside a time of quiet meditation and reflection at the end of each day. Such a ritual would engage as many senses as possible, but in a relaxing manner. Elements could include a candlelight bath with scented soaps, bath oils, or powders; soft music; hair brushing; and use of silk or other luxurious bedclothes and/or sheets. As you meditate and later sleep and dream, listen for the Muses. Listen for the Graces. Listen for Her. In the morning, record your dreams in your journal.

INVOCATIONS

For ritual libations and invocations, here are a few basic Attic words and pronunciations you may wish to use. Note that the reconstructed pronunciation of Attic Greek is different from that of modern Greek.

Accents on words in Attic are pitch-based rather than stress-based. For the words below, the accent will either be a rising pitch on one syllable, and then falling back to normal on the next syllable, or the pitch will rise and fall all over the course of pronouncing one long syllable.

A phonetic spelling of the pronunciation of *Aphrodite* would be ap'-raw-dee-taih. The *ph* is not pronounced *f* but *p* with a little aspiration or breathing after it. The letter *r* is always trilled a little bit. The musical pitch rises on the third syllable. The final *e* in this word is the Greek letter *eta* pronounced *ai* as in the word *air*. The final *h* shown in the phonetic spelling is just a reminder that this is not a sharp *e* or *ay* sound. The last two syllables are each pronounced for a longer duration of time than the first two.

Hestia is hes-teé-a. Here, *e* is the letter *epsilon*, a short sound as in *pet*. Raise the pitch on the second syllable. The last syllable is longer than the first two.

The verb *khairo* (khaí-raw) is used as a general greeting and means "hello," "good-bye," "be well," or "welcome." The singular form of the greeting is *khaire* (khaí-re). The musical pitch rises and falls on the first syllable. The plural form is khairete *(khaí-re-te)*. Raise the pitch on the first syllable. The *r* trills in each word. Each *e* is an *epsilon*. The first syllable is longer in duration than the final one or two.

The vocative *O* when calling to a person or a Deity is pronounced *aw*. The pitch rises and falls over this long duration syllable. *Ie* (ee-aíh) is an exclamation of joy used in processional hymns. The pitch rises on the second syllable. The first syllable is longer in duration than the second.

So when pouring welcoming and final libations to Hestia, the phrase would be *"Khaîre, Hestía."* When pouring a libation to Aphrodite, welcoming Her into the ritual, or thanking Her at the end, the Attic phrase would be *"Khaîre, Aphrodíte."* If you invoke other Deities into the ritual in English, you can also welcome Them and thank Them individually with *"Khaîre."* Or after naming Them individually in English, you can welcome Them and thank Them as a group with *"Khaírete."* *"Ié Aphrodite"* is suitable for processional chants or to use for a call and response during the ritual.

BASIC OUTLINE FOR HELLENIC GROUP RITUAL

Preparation. Before the ritual, participants wash and dress in fine clothing. Donning your own special ritual garb, jewelry, or scents helps to transform your consciousness. For Aphrodite, this ritual garb should be beautiful, sensuous, and a bit exotic. No Hellene would ever attend a public ritual without wearing a wreath of leaves or flowers. If time allows, making a fresh crown for yourself serves as a wonderful ritual preparation. However, I do keep one made of artificial flowers for when I'm traveling, or very rushed.

Procession. The formal ritual begins with a group procession to the place of the ritual. For nighttime rituals, the processional should be by candlelight or torchlight if possible. If space is limited, or for solitary rites, you may wish to substitute a simple circular procession right around the room or around the outdoor altar. If you're used to generic Wiccan ritual practice, you'll want to move in a sunwise (clockwise) direction, but we don't know whether this mattered to the Greeks.

For a group ritual, one person should carry a basket of barley or other grain, another a pitcher of water. These two people should be at the front of the procession. Behind them, one or more people should be carrying the libation and any other offerings. Other items needed for the ritual can either be carried by people in the procession or placed at the ritual site in advance.

Solitary worshippers should carry the libation and any offerings, or some portion of them if all cannot be easily held. Everything else should be set at the ritual site ahead of time.

The procession should be accompanied by music and/or chanting. Here is a very simple processional chant with the notes forming a tetrachord common in ancient Greek music. It is a variation of the Ionic rhythm, which dates back to Sappho for its earliest known use.

I- é   Aph- ro- dí- te   Aph- ro- dí- te   come to us

Hand Washing. Just outside of the ritual space, the water bearer pours the water into a basin. Then people in turn, beginning with the one carrying the barley, temporarily hand off whatever they are carrying and wash their hands.

Casting Barley. The grain carrier then holds the basket so each person, beginning with the presiding priestess or priest, can take a small handful of barley or other grain and gently cast it upon the altar. People with leading roles in the ritual take their places by the altar. Others gather around in front of it.

Note that in a purely reconstructionist ritual there is no Circle Casting or calling of directions. The first three steps here mark the participants' intentional approach and entry into ritual space. Casting the barley cleanses and charges the altar and by extension all of the ritual space. Because there is no equivalent of the magical barrier of the circle, participants are free to enter and leave the space, respectfully, quietly, and with minimum disruption.

Mixing the Libations. Traditionally, wine was always mixed with water. If you wish to follow this custom, use Mavrodaphne. This is a very sweet Greek wine which tastes good when mixed. Pour equal parts of Mavrodaphne and spring water into a punch bowl. Have ladles and small cups handy for serving. One person should serve and refill libation cups as needed for ritual leaders and participants. For large rituals, several bowls and servers can help speed things up. One bottle of wine and an equal portion of water for every fourteen people is usually sufficient. If you're using an undiluted beverage, a punch bowl still works well.

Honoring Hestia. The first cup should be filled for the person honoring Hestia. This person lights the central flame on the altar, calling for Hestia's presence and blessings, then pours a libation to Her. In all public rituals, Hestia receives the first and the last libation. Her flame is as central to the life of the city as it is to the home.

Hymn. This is a good point for the presentation of poetry or music. Traditionally, a new hymn was written for each ritual performance. Standard tunes were used over and over, but fresh lyric poetry was written for each rite. This creative effort is part of the offering to the Deity, and also serves as an invocation.

(Note: Hellenic Deities are normally invoked, or called into the ritual space, rather than into the person of the officiating priestess or priest. However, I do call Aphrodite directly into my body as well as into the ritual space, because I have made a lifelong dedication to serve as Her priestess and have given my body to Her. Also because of my commitment, I never un-invoke Her at the end of ritual. Her presence is more heightened for me during ritual, but it never completely goes away. For other people, the appropriateness of direct invocation would depend on the specific nature of their relationship with their Deity.)

Libations. As each libation is poured, the celebrant calls to the Deity or Deities being honored, pours out some or all of the wine, and then consumes whatever remains in the cup. If alcohol is being used, people who do not drink it can still participate in the libations by pouring all of their cup out. If the ritual is taking place indoors, use a large bowl to receive the libations. If it is outdoors, they can be poured directly on the ground.

After a person has finished pouring his or her libation, he or she calls out "*Khaîre*" or "*Khaírete*," and everyone else responds with the same word. For example, the libation to Hestia would begin with "*Khaîre, o Hestía.*" The celebrant would then say more about why She was being called, pour out the libation, drink any remainder, and then finish by calling "*Khaîre!*" To which everyone responds "*Khaîre!*"

Usually the presiding priestess or priest will pour a libation to the primary Deity being honored in the ritual, followed by any others that might be included. However, if the Graces are being honored along with Aphrodite, it is appropriate to pour libations to Them first, since They help prepare the way for Aphrodite to arrive. At weddings, Artemis always receives the first libation after Hestia. Different ritual leaders may take turns pouring libations if more than one Deity is being honored.

For groups larger than about five people, participants other than the leaders should participate in only one libation. This participatory libation follows the leaders' libations to individual Deities.

General Activity. After the honored Deity or Deities have been called and welcomed, the group engages in various planned activities such as group singing or dancing, or a dramatic reenactment of a myth. Contests in honor of a Deity can be held in just about any area of activity including poetry, drama, song, dance, athletics, beauty . . . the Greeks liked to turn just about anything into a contest. For short rituals, this step may be omitted. For weekend celebrations, activities, particularly contests, can span several days.

Prayer. In Hellenic religion, there is no prayer without sacrifice, and no sacrifice without prayer. There is a traditional four-part structure to prayer, which can be as short as four sentences or as elaborate as needed.

- First, call the Deity by multiple names to be present.
- Second, state your relationship with the Deity and/or things you have done in the past (a record of previous offerings, completed vows, and good works). This establishes why He or She should pay attention to you now.
- Third, make the request of what blessing or action you would like the Deity to provide.
- Fourth, promise what you will do in return if your request is met.

Here is a short, simple prayer that fits the format: "*Khaire, o Aphrodite*, welcome Aphrodite, Beautiful Goddess, by whatever name you wish to be called. I am your priestess who has served you these many years. Send your gifts to your daughter. Your joys I will teach to the people. *Khaire!*"

In a group ritual, the prayer can be preceded by a group chant or call and response. Chanting begins the call to the Deity, building up energy that can help gain the Deity's attention and help the participants to feel the Deity's presence. To build energy, you might take a simple chant such as the processional hymn above.

The leading priestess or priest should lead the chant with arms raised up high, palms open. Begin slowly. With each repetition, gradually increase the tempo and volume until the group is calling out *"Ie Aphrodite"* over and over, loud and fast. When the chanting energy has reached its peak, clap loudly. Open your arms wide, look upward, and recite the prayer aloud.

Sacrifice. For a simple ritual, the earlier offering of libations is an adequate sacrifice. Optionally, additional offerings can be made at this point. In a typical ancient civic ritual, this would have included an animal sacrifice, with a portion of the animal being offered to the Deity.

Very few modern Americans raise animals or have the skill or desire to slaughter them. Therefore, animal sacrifice is no longer appropriate ritual practice for us. Still, if meat is going to be eaten during the feast after the ritual, a portion of the meat and fat should be offered at this point. You can burn it directly on the campfire or in the grill if you are cooking outdoors. Cook the feast separately.

Fortunately for vegetarians, there is also a historical tradition of offering cakes in the shape of animals. Some historic festivals even required bloodless sacrifices only. For Aphrodite, offering cakes in the shape of, or decorated with, he goats or doves is thoroughly appropriate. For the sacrifice, set aside a portion of the cake for the Deity or Deities being honored. This portion is not to be consumed by people.

If you like, leaders and/or participants may take a small ritual taste of their portion of the food after the Deity's sacrifice has been made. The focus of the ritual, however, is on honoring the Deities. The humans' community feast comes later.

Offerings that you make to Aphrodite need not be limited to drink, food, and flowers. If you intend to maintain an altar or shrine to Her in your home, you might offer statues or other adornments. You can also make very personal offerings such as a lock of hair to symbolize your dedication. Or you might place some small personal item on the altar to be charged with the ritual's energies, so you can wear or carry it as a personal talisman.

Thanksgiving. If the ritual included any type of competition, this would be a good time to give the victory prize(s). Victors should give thanks to their personal Deity, the one who gave them talent and inspiration. Ritual leaders offer thanks to all of the Deities and participants in the ritual.

Final Libation to Hestia. The final libation is poured to Hestia, the hearth Goddess, with thanks to Her. Proclaim that the ritual is finished. Invite all the participants to feast and enjoy each other's company after the ritual. If the feast will not be in the vicinity of the altar, extinguish the altar flame. If the flame will be in sight, you may choose to let it continue burning throughout the feast. The leading priestess or priest and other officiants begin the recession out of the altar area to the feast.

Feast. Have fun and enjoy the good company. This is informal and not part of the official ritual, but eating together builds community. Even a very brief sharing of snacks and drinks after a short ritual is beneficial. Your feast will include any remaining libations and food from the sacrifice, plus whatever else people bring to share.

SOLITARY AND INFORMAL RITUALS

Solitary rituals need not be as formal or structured as group rituals, because it's easier for a lone individual to focus than it is to blend the energies of a group. A group of people who have worked together over time, who are used to each other and to Hellenic practices, can comfortably and effectively create an improvisational rite.

The critical elements from a Hellenic perspective are making an offering to the Deity and saying a prayer. If you are using an altar, cast barley and light a candle to start. Give thanks when you are finished. Everything else is ornamentation.

However, using traditional ritual patterns, such as the one given above, helps us maintain a continuity of energy with the Deity and with other worshippers through the ages. It's also an important aid to developing ritual focus and skills. Initially, the step-by-step structure helps to build your focus and intent. With continuing repetition, the steps quickly bring back body memories of previous rituals, helping you move into the state of awareness that is appropriate for interacting with a Deity. The repetition of ancient practices can also help bring back the Deity's awareness more quickly as well.

Experiment a bit to find which structural elements or styles seem important to you. However simple or elaborate your structures are, continue to repeat them over time to build your ritual fluency.

APHRODITE'S JOURNEY WEST: A MONTH OF RITUALS

Embarking on a series of four weekly rituals over the course of a month is one good way to become more deeply acquainted with a Deity. In preparation, learn as much as you can about Her. Consider what aspect of Her energies you would like to focus on. Think about which personal preparations before the ritual will be conducive to bringing your energy into sync with those you will be calling forth in the ritual. Consider ritual baths, perfumes or oils, jewelry, special clothing or none at all. Gather what you intend to use.

In Athens, the fourth day of the new crescent moon was designated as Aphrodite's birthday. This is a good time to start the series. The cycle ends with Her birthday as the moon begins to wax again.

Choose a day of the week when you will perform your rituals. For three days before the rite, contemplate your choices and prepare what you'll need. For three days afterward, absorb and reflect on your experience and what you learned.

Such a series of rituals might follow the progression of Aphrodite's worship as it expanded out of Cyprus as discussed below. The specific focus of each week's ritual will affect your choices of which epithets you will use to call Her, what types of offerings you will give Her, what you wish to ask of Her, and what you will promise to give in return. Those choices are left for you to decide.

Week One, during the waxing moon, begins with Her birth on Cyprus and emergence from the water.

Week Two, during the full moon, is Her journey west. She was received very differently in different locations. Choose one location whose energies you would like to increase in your life. Some possibilities are Corinth (sex), Lesbos (love), or Sparta (the warrior).

Week Three, during the waning moon, call on some of Her companions. Again, choose one set that reflects additional aspects you would like to learn about. Focus on Aphrodite and a choice of the Graces, Adonis, Eros or the Erotes, Ares and/or Harmonia, Hephaistos, or Hermes and/or Hermaphroditos.

Week Four, during the dark moon, ends in Sicily/southern Italy with Aphrodite and optionally Persephone in the underworld. What place does love have in the ritual transition to death and/or immortality? From here, you also have the option of emerging into a new life together with Her in the modern world. Consider whether you wish to pursue an ongoing working relationship with Aphrodite beyond this introductory series. If you do, you can ask for this in a ritual to conclude the series.

WEEKEND RETREAT

A weekend retreat is a great opportunity for an individual or a group to experience a prolonged in-depth immersion.

You can organize such weekend outings as camping events on private secluded land or at a small rented retreat center with lodging accommodations. You can also plan a personal or group schedule of focused ritual work to undertake while attending a larger Pagan festival. I have successfully used all three of these options. You can of course also do it at your own home, but traveling to another location creates a clear focus and removes you from potential distractions. A weekend retreat can include all the possible rituals and activities mentioned above and more.

Consider in advance: Would you like the focus of the weekend to be exploratory, celebratory, meditative, initiatory, or some combination?

1. An exploratory event would introduce various aspects of Aphrodite to those who are new to Her worship. It might also introduce people to Hellenic ritual forms in general.

2. A celebratory event would be for mostly experienced practitioners who gather to honor the Goddess, and deepen their own ritual practice and their connection with Her.

3. A meditative event would support those who want to enter into deep meditation or do a vision quest to seek guidance from the Goddess. This might be in preparation for an expected major life change, such as starting or ending a committed relationship, a coming birth or death, or a commitment to Her priesthood.

4. An initiatory event would mark and facilitate one or more person's dedication to establishing a permanent committed relationship with Aphrodite, to serve as Her priestess or priest.

Time during the weekend can be divided between meditative and/or physical preparation, primary ritual(s), and other related activities. A primary ritual may be held on each day, or at the culmination of the weekend's events. Even during a group retreat, allow some open time for solo reflection, journal keeping, and so on.

The weekend itself should also be treated as a ritual. Mark the beginning of the sacred space and time. Employ a series of steps gradually building the energy to one or more climaxes. Close with a quiet ritual that allows people to reflect and give thanks, then return to ordinary, secular space and activities.

Group exploratory or celebratory weekends are ideal times for planned competitions. Competitions in the arts can also build up a body of poems, songs, dramas, or dances that can be used as resources for future rituals. There is a historic method of judging such competitions that leaves the final results in the hands of the Deities. Each judge, and that can be every participant, writes his or her choice for victor on a pot shard called an *ostrakon* (equal-sized pieces of terra-cotta flowerpots work well). All of the *ostraka* are placed in one pot. Five are drawn. The person whose name is drawn three times is the victor. If three *ostraka* for one person are not drawn immediately, continue drawing one additional *ostrakon* at a time until a vote of three is achieved.

Allow time for sensual play and pleasure. Bring beautiful foods to share. Bathe and massage each other. Body painting and henna tattoos are an option. Just remember that all touching must be consensual. If some of you want to engage in intimate touch, take care to do it safely.

Another possibility is to spend part of the time creating ritual objects, either for the altar or shrine or for personal adornment. For example, you might make head wreathes together. Use twisted loops of floral wire, and floral tape to attach real or artificial flowers and leaves. You might make small clay statues or flower arrangements for the altar.

For creating the ultimate modern altar accessory, Barbie rituals are great. Use a poseable doll of the brand and gender of your choice. With an assortment of arts and crafts supplies, glues, and fine-tipped permanent markers, you can transform the doll into an archetypal image of your personal vision of Aphrodite For a more ambitious project, if you own the land, you can work together to build and landscape a permanent worship space. Or you can decorate a spare room or attic space as a temple.

If people are traveling from different places, they can bring water, flowers, or stones from home to use as offerings. If the event is planned well in advance, people can gather water or stones from any special places they visit during the year. Likewise, water or stones can be brought back from the gathering to help bring the energy of the event into people's lives.

LIVING WITH APHRODITE: APPLICATIONS

We reach this point with any Deity that we sincerely seek. First, we learn all we can. Then we connect with the Deity in worship. Eventually we are changed by the knowledge and the sacred contact. If the change is real, it necessarily makes a difference in our daily lives.

Aphrodite's energies manifest powerfully through sex, but are not limited to that mode of manifestation. Sensuality goes far beyond the sexual. Aphrodite's devotees do not necessarily need to be sexually active themselves. While She is most commonly associated with youth and fertility, in Her temple at Sikuon an old woman served as custodian of the temple and a virgin served as water carrier. There are a number of ways you can help bring Aphrodite's energies into the world through your personal life.

Start by making sure that you fully appreciate your own beauty and sexuality so that you may best reflect the gifts She has given you. Work on developing a fun and creative sex life, with yourself and/or any partner(s). No matter how good a sex life you have, it can always get better or more creative. Have good sex. Have safe sex. Have fun sex. Have lots of sex. Have some more sex.

Learn about safer sex practices. If you are having any sex with other people outside of a long-term mutually monogamous relationship, it is your responsibility to educate yourself and act safely at all times. Members of committed intimate networks often establish a "condom compact," an agreement not to have unprotected sex outside the group. Even if you are not sexually active with others, or if you are in a long-term monogamous relationship, you can still help others understand and practice safer sex.

IN THE PAGAN COMMUNITY, HELP BRING APHRODITE TO OTHERS

- ❧ If you have a garden, build a shrine to Aphrodite with a statue and altar. It will help bring awareness of the Goddess to all who see it.

- ❧ Offer workshops and rituals at local community gatherings and regional festivals. If you don't yet feel ready to teach, convene a discussion group for people to share their interests and beginning steps, to discuss ideas of how to form study groups.

- ❧ Start an ongoing study group or ritual group. In ancient Athens, there were numerous small religious groups dedicated to a specific Deity. These groups would either meet privately for study or plan and host public rituals.

- ❧ If you go to Pagan festivals, help provide safer sex information and supplies. Work with the event coordinators to make sure these are made available where they'll be easily found by all who want them.

IN THE LARGER COMMUNITY, WORK FOR BASIC CIVIL RIGHTS AND PROTECTIONS ON A VOLUNTEER OR PROFESSIONAL BASIS

- ❧ Help to repeal sex laws regarding consenting adults.

- ❧ Help people who are recovering from nonconsensual or abusive relationships. Help at a women's shelter or rape crisis center.

- ❧ Help to win marriage rights for people regardless of gender or number.

- ❧ Help to secure all women's rights to reproductive freedom and privacy and physical safety when seeking medical help.

Educate yourself about these important issues. Write letters to the editor of your local paper in support of sexual and reproductive freedom, explaining that they are aspects of freedom of religion, which is central to American democracy. Call and write your elected representatives to inform them of your opinions. Work for and vote for candidates who support these rights. Work against and vote against candidates who support sectarian agendas that erode our freedom of religion. Encourage others to vote.

If you do work for any of these causes, be up front that you are doing so because of your religious convictions that our society needs both social justice and freedom of religion.

Democracy (Demokratia) and Justice (Dike) are not just civic philosophies, they are also Goddesses. Honor them!

REFLECTIONS

There are a number of concrete ways you can record your ritual and meditative experiences to aid you in future reflection or to inspire others.

Ongoing reflections of Aphrodite, or any other Hellenic Deity, can be recorded in an epithets journal. You will come across a variety of epithets in your reading, but there is no definitive listing of all of the known historical epithets. You may hear other epithets at rituals you attend, or they may come to you in dream or inspiration. Each one reveals another aspect of the Goddess. Some will affect you more intensely than others. You can meditate upon these epithets or even do rituals to that specific aspect of the Goddess for further exploration.

Enter each ephithet and give it at least a page of its own. Write down the associations that come up after learning a new epithet or using one in ritual or meditation. If these associations change or grow over time, go back and add revisions. Be sure to date each entry and revision so that you can see any patterns of development over time. Don't limit yourself to words. You can sketch pictures or symbols that come to you, or even paste in photocopies of illustrations, postcards, or other images that relate to some aspect of Aphrodite.

If you call on the Graces, the Muses, or any other Deities for assistance in learning the ways of Aphrodite, also keep a record of your associations with Them and any insights that might come from Them. If you syncretize worship of Aphrodite, Venus, Astarte, Ishtar, Inanna, and/or other Deities, record different experiences associated with each of these names. Record, also, your significant ritual experiences and your dreams.

You can also record your experiences through art, poetry, or music. These forms are easier to share with others than a personal journal might be. Some of our most poignant imagery of Aphrodite comes from the surviving poem fragments of Sappho. Her reflections have inspired worshippers for the last twenty-six hundred years. Her poetry is another good reason for learning the language; no translation can approach the rhythms and form of the originals.

Body modification is another artistic way of record keeping. Abstract in form, yet decidedly concrete in nature, body piercings or tattoos can be done to mark any initiatory experiences or major growth points in your relationship with Aphrodite. The markings will be a constant reminder of your commitment to Her and of Her physical presence in your life, and can incorporate very personal and historical symbolism.

Tattoos are mentioned in Greek literature and there is a vase in the National Museum in Athens that shows a woman with a fawn, presumably tattooed, upon her arm. Dancers who are called fawns and wear fawn skins perform in celebrations of Artemis, Dionusos, and other Deities. Other Dionusian dancers are called foxes, with fox skins, and it is recorded that some of these people had fox tattoos. Body modifications indicate long-term dedications.

While they would not form a permanent record, temporary henna tattoos could be applied for short-term ritual use for a weekend or week-long intensive ritual dedication, or as part of mystery rituals to give participants a symbol to reflect upon.

Other artistic reflections can of course be expressed through drawings, paintings, or sculpture in clay or harder materials. The next great inspirational image of Aphrodite is waiting to emerge. Perhaps through you.

A final thought: personal devotion to Aphrodite, or any other Deity, can range from the very casual to the formally dedicated. An old friend and I have a running joke between us that we've both made the mistake of saying yes to our Deities once too often. There comes a point when you can't say no to Them anymore, and then you wind up becoming a priestess. We, of course, are very glad that we've become priestesses to our own Goddesses. The scallop shell tattoo I received immediately after my dedication ritual to Aphrodite is a permanent reminder of my commitment to serve Her. I feel my connection to Her deep in my soul. I am secure in my place as Her spiritual daughter. That feeling is always made deeper and stronger after every ritual for Her.

Khaire, o Aphrodite.
Eleibometha soi.

We have poured libations to You.

Leipsometha soi.

We will pour libations to You.

Leibometha soi.

We do pour libations to You.

Kharin ekhomen soi.

We give You thanks.

Khaire!

Glossary

Greek names transliterated with their Latinized versions.

Aineias (Aeneas)   Hermaphroditos (Hermaphroditus)
Ankhises (Anchises)   Herodotos (Herodotus)
Apollon (Apollo)   Kharites (Charites)
Dionusos (Dionysus)   Kronos (Cronus)
Gaia (also Ge) (Gaea)   Ouranos (Uranus)
Hekabe (Hecuba)   Prakhiteles (Praxiteles)
Hekate (Hecate)   Terpsikhore (Terpsichore)
Hephaistos (Hephaestus)   Zephuros (Zephyrus)
Herakles (Hercules)

The names of two major authors have not been transliterated because their works are widely published today under the contemporary spellings, and unlike Herodotos, the transliterated forms would not be as immediately recognizable:

Hesiodos (Hesiod)   Homeros (Homer)

Commonly known place names have been left in their current rather than transliterated form to avoid creating undue geographical confusion. Cythera is not as popularly known as Cyprus, but since the two are frequently mentioned together regarding Aphrodite, the spellings were kept consistent:

Arkadia (Arcadia)   Krete (Crete)
Athenai (Athens)   Kupros (Cyprus)
Cyrenaika (Cyrene)   Peloponnesos (Peloponnese)
Kinuras (Cingras)   Phoinike (Phoenicia)
Kithera (Cythera)   Salmakis (Salmacis)
Knidos (Cnidos)   Sikuon (Sicyon)
Korinth (Corinth)   Smurna (Smyrna)
Kos (Cos)   Sparte (Sparta)

Olympos has been partially transliterated. The Latin *-us* ending has been changed to the Greek *-os*, but the Latin *y* has not been changed to the Greek *u* for spelling consistency with the commonly used English words derived from it, *olympic* and *olympian*.

RESOURCES

BOOKS

Adkins, Lesley, and Roy A. Adkins. *Handbook to Life in Ancient Greece.* New York: Oxford University Press, 1997.
   A good introduction to a wide variety of aspects of Greek culture, including religion.

Beard, Mary, and John North. *Pagan Priests.* London: Duckworth, 1990.
   A study of the activities of the priesthood in Rome, Greece, Egypt, and Babylon. From a practitioner's point of view, the information is very limited, but still this is actually an extensive compilation of the very scant surviving historical information.

Burkert, Walter. *Greek Religion.* Cambridge: Harvard University Press, 1985.
   A solid introduction to Greek religion. One of the first choices of a reference book used by Hellenic reconstructionists to gain a broad understanding of classical practices.

Califia, Pat. *Public Sex: The Culture of Radical Sex.* San Francisco: Cleis Press, 1994.
   A collection of essays previously published by the author addressing a great variety of our society's repressions of sexual freedom.

Campbell, Drew. *Old Stones, New Temples: Ancient Greek Paganism Reborn.* Philadelphia: Xlibris.com, 2000.
   A primer for beginning Hellenic reconstructionism.

Conner, Randy P. *Blossom of Bone: Reclaiming the Connections Between Homoeroticism and the Sacred.* New York: HarperCollins, 1993.
   A thoroughly researched study on aspects of male and transgendered sexuality in numerous cultures.

Conner, Randy P., David Hatfield Sparks, and Mariya Sparks. *Cassell's Encyclopedia of Queer Myth, Symbol, and Spirit.* London: Cassell, 1997.
   A well-researched reference book. As with Conner's *Blossom of Bone,* the authors are pretty good about noting when they are making presumptions based on limited evidence.

Downing, Christine. *The Goddess.* New York: Crossroad, 1984.
   Chapters on several Greek Goddesses, including one on Aphrodite. Explores what each Goddess means to a contemporary woman.

Friedrich, Paul. *The Meaning of Aphrodite.* Chicago: University of Chicago Press, 1978.
  Explores the history of Aphrodite and Her relationship with other Goddesses.

Greenberg, Martin H., and Bruce D. Arthurs, eds. *Olympus.* New York: DAW Books, 1998.
  An entertaining paperback anthology of modern fiction about the Olympic Deities in the modern world.

Kaldera, Raven. *Hermaphrodeities: The Transgender Spirituality Workbook.* Philadelphia: XLibris.com, 2002.
  A spiritual workbook including sections on Aphrodite, with some contributions by Maureen Reddington-Wilde.

Kingsley, Peter. *Ancient Philosophy Mystery and Magic: Empedocles and the Pythagorean Tradition.* New York: Oxford University Press, 1995.
  An in-depth analysis of the context and spread of these Greek mystical traditions.

Lawler, Lillian B. *The Dance in Ancient Greece.* Seattle: University of Washington Press, 1964.
  A study of the many different types of dance used in rituals, dramas, and everyday life. Includes many illustrations from pottery and sculpture.

Paris, Ginette. *Pagan Meditations.* Dallas: Spring, 1986.
  The section on Aphrodite in this book is over one hundred pages long. Detailed exploration of what she means for us here and now.

Parker, Robert. *Athenian Religion: A History.* New York: Oxford University Press, 1996.
  A much different approach from Burkert's, placing the religion solidly in its social context.

Price, Simon. *Religions of the Ancient Greeks.* Cambridge: Cambridge University Press, 1999.
  Looks at Greek myths both in a general panhellenic context and in specifics for different time periods and cities.

To the Gods of Hellas: Lyrics of the Greek Games at Barnard College. New York: Columbia University Press, 1930.
  A superb collection of poetry from student competitions. The first section of poems is dedicated to Aphrodite.

West, M. L. *Ancient Greek Music.* New York: Oxford University Press, 1992.
  For any musicians interested in creating new music in the ancient

forms, this book is packed with all the information you need to get started.

Zaidman, Louise Bruit, and Pauline Schmitt Pantel. *Religion in the Ancient Greek City.* Cambridge: Cambridge University Press, 1997.
   A good light overview and introduction, particularly for those who would be intimidated by the density of Burkert.

MUSIC

Music of the Ancient Greeks. Ensemble De Organographia. Pandourian Records, 1995.
   A selection of music from the fifth century B.C.E. to the third century C.E., from surviving musical scores, played on reconstructions of period instruments. Some of the pieces are only very short fragments, some are of suitable length to use for ritual processions. Contact Philip Neuman by e-mail at neuman@emgo.org.

A Rainbow Path. Kay Gardner. Lady Slipper, 1984.
   This is wonderful music for processionals, movement, dance and meditation. The music superbly blends many musical styles, including ancient ones.

INTERNET

(Note: Since Internet addresses are subject to change, if any of these links are not active at the time when you read this and try to access them, try doing a Web search under key words to see if they have moved. National advocacy organizations are great sources of information and you may wish to join them.)

www.abebooks.com
   The Advanced Book Exchange is a network of used book dealers whose inventory can be searched on this Web site. Anyone doing serious historical research will inevitably want some particular out of print or hard to find books. ABE is just an invaluable resource.

www.aclu.org
   American Civil Liberties Union, supporting a wide variety of civil rights.

www.au.org
   Americans United for Separation of Church and State, an educational and lobbying organization supported by many-faith communities.

groups.yahoo.com/group/HellenicPagan
A discussion group for anyone interested in Hellenic polytheism.

www.ncsfreedom.org
National Coalition for Sexual Freedom is committed to protecting freedom of expression among consenting adults.

www.ngltf.org
National Gay and Lesbian Task Force works for many specific civil rights for queer people. They are in the forefront of nationwide efforts to secure equal marriage rights.

www.numachi.com/~ccount/hmepa
A reconstruction of the Athenian civic calendar and list of Athenian festivals. Lunar dates are shown for the current year and projected back to the first Olympiad (four-year cycles counting from the first Olympic Games in 776 B.C.E.) and forward to the thousandth Olympiad which ends in 3222 C.E. This calendar also shows the phases of the moon, including the day the new crescent moon is likely to be visible.

www.sexuality.org
This along with many other Web sites has a detailed guide to safer sex practices.

PART IV

LAMMAS

Judy Harrow has a master's degree in counseling, and is president elect of the New Jersey Association for Spiritual, Ethical and Religious Values in Counseling (an affiliate of the American Counseling Association).

She began studying Wicca in 1976. She founded Proteus Coven in 1980, and has served as High Priestess of that group ever since. Proteus is affiliated with Covenant of the Goddess. Judy has held a variety of offices within CoG, including National First Officer (president) in 1984.

Judy was the first member of CoG to be legally registered as clergy in New York City in 1985, after a five-year effort and thanks to the assistance of the New York Civil Liberties Union.

She is also a member of the steering committee of the Interfaith Council of Greater New York.

Judy has written two books: *Wicca Covens* and *Spiritual Mentoring: A Pagan Guide*.

Gaia

Gaia, mother of Gods
heroes and mortals,
prolific destroyer,
parent of all you devour,
we honor you.

You give us fruit,
herbs and flowers.
You are the pure pulse
in everything.

Those verses are from an Orphic hymn, composed in ancient Greece. It's at least as old as the Bible, and far too ancient to be accurately dated. And it moves me and many others like me.

I am not a Greek; nor am I drawn to reconstruct Greek religious practices. I am a contemporary American Witch. I do not worship the Greek Goddess Gaia. Like the Greeks, I worship Mother Earth, life giver and life taker, here and now.

Humans name and worship Gods. We've created many religions in our quest to express our gratitude and love, to draw on Sacred guidance and power. Mother Earth has been given many names; we have worshipped Her in many ways, at many different times and places throughout human history. This is because the wise of all nations have recognized that our lives are utterly dependent on Hers.

The Algonquins, who lived in the northeast United States, where I live now, called Her Nokomis. My distant ancestors who rode the steppes of central Asia, called Her Umai, which is the word for placenta in modern Mongolian. Her indigenous Peruvian name was Pachamama. In India, She still is known as Bhumi-Ma. The Greeks called Her Gaia, and wrote poetry that, ancient though it is, still speaks to our hearts. All of us who speak English, regardless of our personal ancestry, can trace part of our cultural roots to classical Greece.

Until recently, all cultivated English gentlemen studied Latin and Greek. So the Greek name Gaia entered the English language, becoming the root of words such as *geo*logy and *geo*graphy, words that describe our empirical ways of understanding Earth's life. When, in time, modern science confirmed ancient insight, recognizing our home planet as a single, living, self-regulating organism, it needed a name to call her by. Gaia was an obvious choice.

Whatever scientists may have intended by linking the name Gaia to their hypothesis, and to whatever uses and abuses it might be put by popular imagination, the name does powerfully evoke a deity. Pagans were already discovering (or uncovering after years of neglect) the power of evoking and communicating with Nature as a living, personal, autonomous being. Experience suggested that such a being was more than an anthropomorphic personification or a strongly projected archetype. The Goddess was manifesting herself in her fullest, most essential form: the Earth. The scientist's Gaia resonated with Pagan intimations about the nature of deity and seemed to suggest appropriate means of building relationships. Gaia would not respond primarily to calls for salvation or expressions of praise, but responded better to life-styles expressive of ecological commitment: recycling, down-shifting, simple living, and "Green" cooperation with the environment. Doing, not believing, seems a more adequate response to Gaia."[1]

It is She that I honor, the Gaia of my own time and place, called to our minds and hearts by the modern biologist James Lovelock rather than the ancient poet Hesiod. Being a Witch, I worship Her as Witches worship. Our Wheel of the Year follows the rhythms of Earth's life cycle where I live. Our ritual Circle reminds us to celebrate the fullness of life.

ROOTS AND RESOURCES

The great blessing of the Pagan renaissance is wide knowledge. Archaeology gives us access to some of the stories, poems, and practices of the Greeks and other ancient civilizations. Anthropology relates the ways of indigenous peoples who have kept Earth-based spirituality alive much longer, some even to this day. Psychology helps us understand how ritual practices affect our deep minds, helping us connect with the Sacred. Many arts enrich our ritual skills. But the shadow side of all this wealth is information overload. No one person can take in or use all the knowledge that is now available to us, so each of us has to make choices.

[1]Graham Harvey, *Contemporary Paganism* (New York: New York University Press, 1997), p. 146.

Choice brings responsibility. We need to choose or create stories, symbols, and practices that work harmoniously together and that express our best understanding and dearest love for the Mother. Faced with all this breadth of information, we must always remember that depth of connection is what really matters. Most important of all, our worship must flow into service—especially now, when our Mother is grievously wounded and still under attack. Doing, not just believing, is the truth of our faith.

Just as I am not a Greek, I am not a biologist, archaeologist, or historian. Some of what guides me is conjectural, even controversial, within an academic setting. Still these words and images offer me and many others inspiration. I am far more concerned about the values these symbols convey—about where they might lead us—than I am about the past and where they come from. Please understand that what you read here is myth. It may or may not also be fact.

Myths are stories told by people to convey a culture's values: what is right, what is wrong, what really matters to us. We create myths of origins to explain how our people and our customs came into being. Many of these tales, read literally, are just plain impossible, whether they are found in *Genesis* or in the Irish *Book of Invasions*. Others are merely unprovable. Although it's foolish to take them as fact, these myths of origins are worth our attention because they reveal the foundational values of a culture. Myths of a lost Golden Age also say a great deal about people's hopes for a better future. For religious purposes, this is far more important than objective history.

For me, Gaia's story starts with silent stones, images, which I'll discuss, created by artists and artisans long before the emergence of written language. We have no way of proving what these ancient graven images meant to those who made them, or to those who reverently beheld them for countless generations. Nonetheless, as reproductions become available, and as we contemplate these objects in ritual and meditative states, we can reach through them back to the most primal Earth consciousness. We can be open to what each image calls forth from within ourselves. We can name and worship what we discover. We can live by what we learn.

THE LADY OF LAUSSEL

This sculpture is one of the most ancient known works of human art, created in ice-covered Europe during the Old Stone Age. The Lady of Laussel was carved in relief at the entrance to a cave in what is now France. She is broad-hipped and heavy-breasted, a picture of fertility. Her left hand lies on her belly, while her right hand holds a horn, which is decorated with thirteen incised lines.

DRAWING BY DR. RAVEN

Is she telling us that her womb is the true horn of plenty? Do the horn's thirteen markings indicate the number of lunar, and menstrual, cycles within a year? Perhaps.

Caves are openings into the body of Mother Earth. They were used for shelter, and also served as ritual chambers. The art that adorns some of them probably expressed prayers for success in the hunting and gathering by which the clans survived. Human life before animals were domesticated, before the development of agriculture, was utterly dependent upon the Mother's provision. It seems to me that relief sculpture, which seems to emerge from the rocky matrix but is really still fully attached, is a good symbol for the lifeways of hunters, gatherers, and fisherfolk.

And how independent are we, really, even now? After nine months of gestation, each of us emerged from our mother's womb. Still, we were unable to fend for ourselves for many years, completely dependent on the care we received from the adults around us. Adults ourselves now, we seem more autonomous. Few of us, however, could live apart from the interdependence of human community. The human community is as completely enmeshed within the biosphere, Earth's living body, as a fetus is in the body of its mother. Separation is a dangerous delusion.

We are cells in the body of the Mother;
We are cells in Her body.
We ourselves are the body of the Mother;
We ourselves are Her body.[2]

DRAWING BY DR. RAVEN

THE LADY OF WILLENDORF

The Lady of Willendorf is a younger image, but still ancient, created about 23,600 years ago, in the Neolithic Age, soon after the glaciers receded from what is now Austria. She is a small free-standing figurine: The people could take her with them as they migrated in search of food of all kinds.

She has no face. Tiny, thin sugges-
tions of arms lay across her generous breasts. To make sure you know that these omissions were not for lack of skill, consider her elaborately cornrowed hair and her accurately portrayed genitals. Like the body of the Lady of Laussel, her body mass suggests abundant and nurturant fertility.

The Neolithic Age saw the beginnings of agriculture, of creative interactions between the tribe and the land. Cornrows remind me of this. Much of religion since then has been an attempt to create and maintain right relationship between people and land—until we forgot, and tried to replace cooperation with force. We have wounded Mother Earth and placed Her life—and our own—at risk.

[2]Chant lyrics written by Christopher Hatton, used with permission.

Do these primal images of the Mother tell us that, in the earliest times, people gave their reverence to the Goddess alone, that one Great Mother reigned, that Her fragmentation into many specialized Goddesses later was a sort of Fall. I don't think so. From those same caves comes the proud and virile image of the Trois Frères Sorcerer, which speaks as clearly as the Lady of Laussel to the soul of the modern Pagan.

Earth gave us life. Earth nourishes and sustains us. Earth will take us back into Herself, dissolve us and use the materials of our bodies to bring forth other creatures. Earth is our Sacred Mother, but not our virgin mother. Without sexual reproduction, the constant reshuffling of genes, the miracle of evolution could not take place.

Old Europe

For a century or more, there have been speculations about a widespread prehistoric matriarchal culture. For almost as long, controversy has raged among scholars about whether any of the archaeological data support these theories. Resolving that controversy is beyond the scope of this book, and far beyond my personal competence.

Marija Gimbutas (1921–1994) was a Lithuanian refugee archaeologist who worked first at Harvard and later at UCLA. She came to believe that the culture of southeastern Europe, which she termed "Old Europe," was peaceful, egalitarian, matrifocal, and Goddess-worshipping before the Indo-European horsemen conquered the area and imposed patriarchal and militaristic rule.

In support of this theory, late in her career, Gimbutas compiled two stunning collections of prehistoric art. First came *The Language of the Goddess*, which was soon followed by *The Civilization of the Goddess*.

If the history interests you, read Gimbutas's arguments and those of her supporters and critics. For religious purposes, it's sufficient to look at the pictures. What they did or did not mean to the ancients is interesting, certainly, but what matters now, I think, are the meanings they hold, the reactions they evoke within us. The images in Gimbutas's two books, like those of the Ladies of Laussel and Willendorf, can nurture your meditations and your dreams.

Among the many people inspired by Gimbutas's work was the cultural historian Riane Eisler, who radically reframed the matriarchy theory's ideas in her acclaimed book, *The Chalice and the Blade*. Eisler notes that, when we find no evidence for male dominance in the earliest archaeological records, we infer female dominance—matriarchy—because we cannot conceive of a truly egalitarian culture.

This limitation is instilled in us by the "dominator culture," within which our habits of thought are formed and constantly reinforced. We are trained to believe that dominance is inevitable, that somebody must always be on top. Patriarchy is simply male dominance. The once and future matriarchy was, and will be, better for the people and for the Earth, many believe, because women—mothers—are naturally more sensitive and nurturant. I recall various female heads of state throughout history, however, and I doubt it. Dominance inverted is still just dominance.

But what if Eisler is right? What if once there was equality among people? Then, maybe, we can re-create a truly just and caring society. If we did it once, we can surely do it again. Eisler's term for this, not just a different form of domination but its antithesis, is *partnership*. If golden age myths are more about hope than history, if they are to be evaluated by where they might lead us, then Eisler's new perspective is truly transformative. Perpetuating the antagonism between matriarchy and patriarchy sustains distrust and conflict. Refocusing on the far more basic distinction between dominator and partnership models of society can open the way to peace.

The Partnership Way, which Eisler coauthored with her own partner, social psychologist David Loye, followed. *The Partnership Way* is a workbook, based on *The Chalice and the Blade*, full of exercises for developing the skills needed for egalitarian living. Since then, Eisler has taught extensively and written several more books. Her Center for Partnership Studies has a Web site at www.partnershipway.org.

GAIA IN GREECE

When the Indo-Europeans, including the classical Greeks, entered the stage of history (starting about 4300 B.C.E.), they also honored Mother Earth. Consider this excerpt from the ancient Homeric Hymn to Gaia:

> *The Mother of us all,*
> *the oldest of all*
> *hard, splendid as rock*
>
> *Whatever there is that is of the land*
> *it is She who nourishes it,*
> *it is the Earth that I sing*
>
> *Whoever you are,*
> *however you come across Her sacred ground*
> *it is She who nourishes you*

Classical authors such as Hesiod, Homer, and Orpheus, just like the Hebrew Moses, are figures from a time so remote that we cannot even verify their existence. What we have are enduring bodies of writing that may have been produced by individuals or by schools of poets who shared a particular perspective on Deity. It doesn't really matter.

These writings shaped the religious consciousness of Pagan Greece. Contemporary Pagans can read them meditatively. We can listen for the echoes they may raise within our hearts. We may find in these remnants of ancient, sacred poetry a path that leads back to the same Source that inspired our Pagan predecessors.

The *Theogony*, a narrative of the births of the Gods attributed to
Hesiod, dates back to the eighth century B.C.E. In this telling,
chaos came first, undifferentiated potential, followed by eros,
which was not a cute little cherub, not a personality at all, but
something more like gravity, the force of attraction that causes
matter to organize itself. Chaos and eros are the first polarity. The
first consciousness to be born of their creative interaction is Gaia,
Mother Earth. Gaia brings forth Ouranos, the starry sky, then
mates with him. All else descends from this primal pairing.

> Gaea, the "deep breasted," whose soil nourishes all that
> exists, and by whose benevolence men are blessed with fair
> children and all the pleasant fruits of earth, was thus at one
> time the supreme goddess Whose majesty was acknowledged
> not only by men but by the gods themselves. Later, when the
> victorious dynasty of the Olympians was established, Gaea's
> prestige was not lessened. It was still she whom the gods
> invoked when they made oaths: "I swear by Gaea and the
> vast sky above her," Hera proclaims when, in the Iliad, she
> answers Zeus' accusations.[3]

Earth abides and witnesses all that we promise and all we perform. Many peoples have realized this. Far away from Greece we
find the parallel tale of how, when the Buddha was seeking
enlightenment, he banished the forces of delusion by simply
touching the Earth. Notice also that our word *conjure* comes from
the Latin roots *com* "together" and *jurare* "swear." It means "to
swear with." So may we conjure Earth to help make our words
real.

NORTH AMERICA

For more than a thousand years, the ancient Earth-based spiritual
ways of Europe were hidden or dormant under the onslaught of an

---

[3]*New Larousse Encyclopedia of Mythology* (London: Hamlyn, 1959), p. 89.

intolerant monotheism. This transplanted faith placed all value in some celestial plane, leaving the Earth just a thing without intrinsic value, a commodity, a resource placed under human dominion to be wastefully or wisely used. Even so, glimmers of Earth reverence still appear in the maternal imagery of Julian of Norwich, St. Francis of Assisi's kinship with the animals, and the work of a few other tenacious nature mystics, often harassed by the religious authorities of their own times.

When, eventually, Europeans came to the New World, they found—but certainly did not value—the primal reverence for Earth that their own culture had forsaken. They perceived it as devil worship, or "savagism." Or they failed to perceive it at all.

Today, some scholars deny that Native American reverence for Mother Earth even existed before English-speaking pan-Indian movements of the 1970s named and claimed Her. Well, of course, and so what? There were hundreds of tribes, speaking hundreds of languages, some as unrelated as Malay is to Gaelic. Of course, they had different names for Her. They also had different words for their human mothers, but they all were gestated, birthed, and nursed. Native Americans also lived in some dramatically different ecologies, so they experienced the natural cycles in different ways—and represented them differently in their myths.

Of course the names and tales are different. Only a theology disconnected from Earth could impose one name and one tale across such varied experiences of life.

To say that Mother Earth is not real unless all people call Her by the same name and tell the exact same stories about Her sets a standard of proof that can never be met by a grounded religion. Moreover, if we adopt it, differences of detail will distract us from our essential unity with all Her children, human and other—and from our critical need to reconcile with Her. The story can be told in a way that emphasizes similarities, and so unites us. It can be told in a way that emphasizes differences, and so divides us.

Neither of these tellings is more factual, so I have to ask: Who benefits from telling it in one way or the other?

Across the wide range of environmental, cultural, and linguistic differences, Native American people lived in loving harmony with the natural world, and honored Mother Earth in ways that resonate in the hearts of others who love Her. Consider this beautiful invocation from Arizona's Tewa tribe:

> Oh our Mother the Earth; oh our Father the Sky
> Your children are we
> with tired backs we bring you the gifts you love
> So weave for us a garment of brightness
> May the warp be the white light of morning
> May the weft be the red light of evening
> May the fringes be the falling rain
> May the border be the standing rainbow
> Weave for us this bright garment
> that we may walk where birds sing,
> where grass is green

One of the best known, and most challenging, declarations of Native American Earth reverence comes from the prophet and dreamer Smohalla, who lived in what is now Washington State during the late nineteenth century. He said:

> It is a sin to wound or cut, to tear or scratch our common mother. . . . You ask me to dig in the earth? Am I to take a knife and plunge it into the breast of my mother? But then, when I die, she will not gather me again into her bosom. You tell me to dig up and take away the stones. Must I mutilate her flesh so as to get at her bones? You ask me to cut the grass and the corn and sell them, to get rich like the white men. But how dare I crop the hair of my mother?[4]

[4]Mircea Eliade, *Myths, Dreams and Mysteries* (New York: Harper & Row, 1960), p. 155. This statement, which has been quoted many times, originally came from a government report on the Ghost Dance religion, published in 1896.

Late in the nineteenth century, Smohalla and his people still lived entirely on what wild nature provided. Remember, though, that other Native American groups were farming even before the arrival of Europeans. They developed maize, which we call corn, from wild grasses. They taught the New England settlers farming methods appropriate to this land. By Smohalla's time, many more tribes had turned to farming or other "civilized" crafts for their livelihood. Did this necessarily take them out of right relationship with the Mother?

Is gardening a loving process of grooming and adorning Earth's body? Is agriculture creative interaction between people and land? Or are both rape, force, imposing our will upon Her, as Smohalla considered them?

We do not have the skills to live as hunter-gatherers, but we could learn them. Still we can't all return to Smohalla's lifestyle. The unbalanced growth of human population removed that choice long ago. Perhaps I could find enough to sustain me in my city's parks, but if all my neighbors did the same, the parks would soon be denuded of all life. Smohalla's way was probably not a feasible option for most people even in his own time. It certainly is not now.

Remember, however, that hunting-gathering and aggressive factory farming are two ends of a fairly long spectrum. There are things we can do collectively to live more gently upon Mother Earth. There are things we can do individually to move society in that direction. It is incumbent on all of us who profess to love and worship Mother Earth to learn what those things are and to do them.

Smohalla lived his values, and so can we. The change begins deep within, as we come to realize the interdependence of all life on Earth, and to make our decisions from that understanding.

THE ROMANTIC MOVEMENT

During the nineteenth century, brutal holocaust raged against Native Americans, and other indigenous peoples and cultures, all along the frontiers as Europe seized dominion of the world. But at the center, European culture was losing heart and spirit to the incipient Industrial Revolution. Value became synonymous with market price, rather than guiding ideals. Resistance to encroaching alienation found a voice in the Romantic movement.

In 1806, in "The World Is Too Much with Us; Late and Soon," William Wordsworth deplored a consciousness that is, sadly, still prevalent:

> The world is too much with us; late and soon,
> Getting and spending, we lay waste our powers:
> Little we see in Nature that is ours;
> We have given our hearts away, a sordid boon!
> This Sea that bares her bosom to the moon;
> The winds that will be howling at all hours,
> And are up-gathered now like sleeping flowers;
> For this, for everything, we are out of tune;
> It moves us not. — Great God! I'd rather be
> A Pagan suckled in a creed outworn;
> So might I, standing on this pleasant lea,
> Have glimpses that would make me less forlorn;
> Have sight of Proteus rising from the sea;
> Or hear old Triton blow his wreathèd horn.

Is our Pagan creed outworn? It seemed so to Wordsworth. In hindsight, I believe he was overly pessimistic. Yes, many people were, and are, just as he described. Other hearts, however, were moved by nature, then, now, and always. The Romantic poets, musicians, and artists worked to reweave our web of connection with nature, with night, with folklore, and with the realm of dreams and visions.

Ever since the Renaissance, British and Continental intellectuals had been reading classic Pagan poetry in the original languages. They had taken the Gods of Greece and Rome as a symbolic and artistic vocabulary. For some of the Romantics those symbols began to live and move again. What seemed outworn was merely dormant, neglected, choked with dust—but full of potential life.

Some sixty years after Wordsworth's wistful complaint, the old ways shone more brightly for another Romantic, Algernon Charles Swinburne. Here are some verses from his long poem "Hertha":

First light on my sources
  First drifted and swam;
Out of me are the forces
  That save it or damn;
Out of me man and woman, and wild-beast and bird;
  before God was, I am.

* * *

But what thing dost thou now,
  Looking Godward to cry,
"I am I, thou art thou,
  I am low, thou art high"?
I am thou, whom thou seekest to find him; find thou
  but thyself, thou art I.

* * *

Who hath given, who hath sold it thee,
  Knowledge of me?
Hath the wilderness told it thee?
  Hast thou learnt of the sea?
Hast thou communed in spirit with night? Have the
  winds taken counsel with thee?
What is here, dost thou know it?
  What was, hast thou known?
Prophet nor poet
  Nor tripod nor throne
Nor spirit nor flesh can make answer, but only thy
  mother alone.

If those ideas sound familiar, consider: this was what students read and discussed in English literature classes during the late nine-

teenth and early twentieth centuries. Some of those students
became the forerunners and earliest founders of the Pagan Renaissance. Robert Graves and Dion Fortune, Margaret Murray and
Charles Seymour, all contemporaries of my grandparents, surely all
read Wordsworth and Shelley and Swinburne. The poetry moved
them, just as it moved me two generations later. And yet it moves.

An instrument out of tune can be tuned again. Alienation can
be resisted and, with patience, healed.

Twentieth Century: External Influences

In his magisterial study, *Triumph of the Moon*, historian Ronald
Hutton documents all the direct roots of contemporary Witchcraft
and Paganism. His book is a slow read, not because it's dull but
because it's so very rich in information. Savor it in small bites.

It's neither possible nor necessary for me to replicate his excellent work.

Instead, I want to discuss two streams of non-Pagan thought
that have added a great deal to my own understanding of what it
means to be a contemporary devotee of Mother Earth.

Religious Studies

The first is an intellectual cluster of liberal theology, feminism,
and archetypal psychology, all of them the bane of fundamental-
ists of any religion. These may be antithetical to naive belief, but
they support thoughtful and mature spirituality.

Liberal theology starts with humility, a good old-fashioned virtue,
which reminds us that human understanding can never fully grasp
or define Deity. The Sacred is most certainly within us, the ani-
mating spark, the "still, small voice" of wisdom. But it is also far
beyond us, as we are tiny parts of a greater whole, cells in the body
of Gaia. How shall a wave presume to define the ocean?

We try, of course, because we have to, because there is a human
drive to understand, or at least to guess. People tell stories about

that which they hold Sacred, about Deity. But these stories co
from our limited understanding. We necessarily perceive the Sacred
through the limiting lenses of culture, gender, class, bioregion, and
much more. As long as we understand that our stories are conjec-
tures and metaphors, not literal facts, there is no harm in spinning these tales. It's normal and natural to the human mind.

When we get to thinking that our myths are Truth and therefore
other people's contradictory myths are devilish lies, crusade and
bloody inquisition soon follow. We have seen too much of this,
down all the centuries to our own. Fundamentalism kills: first our
own minds, then other people's bodies.

If you want to read more about liberal theology, there's an
extensive reading list on the Proteus Web site at www.draknet.
com/proteus.

Feminist thought directs our attention to the ways in which
gender, and gender privilege, condition our understandings of the
world. Riane Eisler, whose work about partnership culture I discussed earlier, is an excellent example and exponent of this relatively new intellectual tradition. For now, let me just caution you
that some Goddess worshippers simply accept and reinforce old
gender-role stereotypes, long since discredited elsewhere, and that's
not healthy or liberating for either women or men. Inverting
something is not truly the same as transforming it.

Archetypal psychology, the tradition begun by the Swiss psychologist Carl Gustav Jung, is usually misinterpreted as a denial
that the Gods "really" exist. On the contrary, Jungian theory
demonstrates that the energies and patterns we Pagans invoke in
ritual also structure the lives of total unbelievers—and even
monotheists—just as much as they do our own. There is an extensive Jungian literature about the Gods, very worth reading because
it explores their manifestations in our own time, their presence in
lifestyles utterly different from those of Hesiod or Smohalla.

I particularly appreciate the work of Christine Downing, which
is nurtured by all these streams. Downing served for twenty years

...us studies at San Diego State University in Cali-
...ow professor of mythological studies at Pacifica
...te in Santa Barbara. She has written nine books,
...explore the living presence of Pagan Gods in the
moder...

In one of these books, *The Goddess*, Downing delves deeply into the roles of seven Greek Goddesses in her own life. For each, she examines both the classical sources and their current applications. This offers us a great model of how to work in depth with any Deity, from Greece or anywhere else. One of Downing's long, juicy chapters is devoted to Gaia.

The work of Catherine Albanese is also worth your considera-tion. Her pioneering book, *Nature Religion in America*, introduced religious scholars to the idea of nature reverence as a religious path. The last chapter includes a respectful treatment of the American Pagan movement, which places us within the context of our culture.

Dr. Albanese is a bridge builder. She gives religious scholars an overview of nature religion while giving her other readers, includ-ing us, an introduction to the ideas and vocabulary of religious scholarship. Those of us who would like to advocate for Mother Earth in interfaith discourse owe her our thanks.

ENVIRONMENTAL SCIENCE AND ENVIRONMENTAL ETHICS

To effectively serve Mother Earth, our idealism must eventually be grounded in material reality. This is happening. In the twentieth century, Romantic poets were joined by experimental scientists, very different temperaments brought together by their care for our beautiful, wounded planet. Here are just a few of the many whose research, thinking, and work have helped preserve and protect at least some parts of Gaia's body.

Aldo Leopold (1886–1948) took a college degree in forestry and began his career with the U.S. Forest Service. In 1924, Leopold advocated for the creation of this country's first officially designated wilderness area, New Mexico's five-hundred-thousand-acre Gila National Forest. In 1933, he became a professor in the nation's first graduate program in game management, at the University of Wisconsin. In 1935, he was one of the small group of leading conservationists who founded the Wilderness Society.

Leopold was also a gifted essayist. Through many years in the field, he came to understand that nature in any bioregion is a whole system, self-regulating and worthy of respect. He presented this insight, and his concept of a Land Ethic, which respects the integrity of bioregional systems, in a collection of essays called *A Sand County Almanac*, originally published in 1949. Reissued, this book has become a beacon for succeeding generations of conservationists.

Aldo Leopold died fighting a forest fire at the age of sixty-two. I have no idea what religion, if any, he practiced, no basis at all for speculation. And yet, Mother Earth moved him to love and serve Her. His life sets an example for all who love Her. I honor him as an ancestor of my spirit.

I offer a salute in passing to marine biologist Rachel Carson (1907–1964). Her book *Silent Spring* sounded the alarm for my generation. The latest wave of environmental activism was called forth by *Silent Spring*, and this prepared the group mind for Gaia's next great epiphany, which was soon to follow.

In the mid-sixties, NASA was searching for signs of life on Mars. It asked British biologist James Lovelock to develop criteria for assessing life's presence in that very alien environment. His theory was that the atmosphere of a lifeless planet would be in stable chemical equilibrium, while that of a planet harboring life would be more active.

Mars was stable, and so dead, while the same analysis, applied to Earth, did indeed show constant dynamic change. But life, while producing fluctuation, would also require a homeostatic control system to keep conditions within viable limits. Such control systems are typical of living organisms. They are how our own bodies maintain their temperatures.

In 1973, teamed with the American geneticist Lynn Margulis, Lovelock proposed the idea of Gaia as a self-regulating, therefore living, organism. In 1979, Lovelock's book *Gaia: A New Look at Life on Earth* presented these ideas to the general public. It was just what the children of Earth needed to hear.

The public reaction was immediate, enthusiastic, overwhelming— and sometimes religious. Lovelock and Margulis had chosen the name of a Goddess for their theory simply because, as discussed earlier, it was the common root for the names of several Earth sciences, such as geology. When people responded to it as a name for the Goddess, Mother Earth, Lovelock was taken aback. At first, if anything, he seemed to be a bit irritable. Later, he became more comfortable with Gaian spirituality.

In his follow-up book, *The Ages of Gaia*, Lovelock devoted a chapter to the religious aspects of Gaia, in which he wrote:

> When I first saw Gaia in my mind, I felt as an astronaut must have done as he stood on the Moon, gazing back at our home, the Earth. The feeling strengthens as theory and evidence come in to confirm the thought that the Earth may be a living organism. Thinking of the Earth as alive makes it seem, on happy days, in the right places, as if the whole planet were celebrating a sacred ceremony. Being on the Earth brings that same special feeling of comfort that attaches to the celebration of any religion when it is seemly and when one is fit to receive.[5]

The Gaia theory, as it is now called, was a paradigm shift, an intellectual revolution whose importance cannot even be estimated, let alone exaggerated. Lovelock and Margulis transformed the prevailing perceptions of the Earth. However, Lovelock's *Gaia* was not the only significant book published in 1979.

---

[5]James Lovelock, *The Ages of Gaia* (New York: Norton, 1988), ch. 9, p. 205.

CONVERGENCE

By 1979, the Pagan movement was well rooted and putting up shoots all around the English-speaking world. Then on October 31, 1979, the Feast of Samhain whose theme is transformation, came the simultaneous publication of two books that were as important for Pagans as Lovelock's publication was for the environmental movement. These books were *Drawing Down the Moon* by Margot Adler and *The Spiral Dance* by Starhawk, both of which have been updated and reissued, and are still essential.

With the publication of these two books, our budding movement came into bloom. Many new people came to us, bringing their talents and skills. Our thinking began to deepen and ramify, our ritual practice to grow in art, skill, and congruence. Our emphasis shifted from spellcraft to spirituality—with a clear spiritual focus on Mother Earth. Just as this was all beginning to happen, we learned about Lovelock's work.

For us, the Gaia theory was nothing less than validation. It seemed that modern science had confirmed the existence of the Goddess we had been worshipping for many years. We went way beyond Lovelock's original intentions, of course, but his ideas became an important source of support, nurturance, and inspiration for our Earth-based spirituality.

We began to think together about what it means to live by Earth-centered values, to develop an ethic and a practice consistent with our beliefs.

Pagans, and Witches in particular, work magic for purposes we consider worthy. What purpose could be more worthy than protecting and healing our Mother Earth? One of the classic definitions of magic is "the art of changing consciousness in accordance with will." Changed consciousness naturally and inevitably flows into changed behavior. It's equally true, although less obvious, that changed behavior often induces changes in consciousness, as we learn from our new experiences. So it's a feedback loop, accessible from either end, or, better yet, from both.

We worship Mother Earth. We serve Mother Earth, each according to our own talents and temperaments. We think, talk, and write about how to serve Her more effectively. From the many well-informed and thoughtful Pagan writers, I would like to highlight two of my personal favorites.

Chas Clifton,[6] a Pagan writer and academic who coordinates the Nature Religion Scholars' Network, emphasizes the practical:

> We are not what we believe, we are what we do. Likewise, we should participate in the natural processes around us even as we celebrate them abstractly. Participation empowers us: we take control over as many aspects of our lives as possible. This desire to participate in and acknowledge natural cycles is why our festivals connect with the seasonal wheel rather than re-enacting what some person or group did some centuries ago.[7]

* * *

You cannot love the Earth before you understand something about it. Likewise, you cannot "save the planet" without starting where you are. It is a little hypocritical to be concerned about the fates of species on the other side of the globe before you know what happens to your own take-out pizza cartons after you have disposed of them.[8]

Adrian Harris, a British Pagan academic and the founder of the Dragon Environmental Group,[9] with a long record of activism, writes more about the needed transformations of consciousness.

---

[6]Chas Clifton's essay "Nature Religion for Real" is available on the Proteus Web site at www.draknet.com/proteus/forreal.htm. Other essays that he wrote or selected can be found at his own site, www.chasclifton.com. I strongly recommend both.
[7]Chas Clifton, *The Modern Craft Movement* (St Paul, MN: Llewellyn, 1992), p. 128.
[8]Ibid., pp. 126–27.
[9]See its Web site at dragon.gn.apc.org/index.htm.

Our culture is based on a certain way of understanding reality which has developed over the last two thousand years or so. What passes for common sense, as obvious, actually has a history. The way we think about ourselves is not "natural," not born into us, but learnt. What we in the West have inherited from the great philosophers and theologians of the past: Plato, Aristotle, Saint Paul, and their ilk, is a split in our reality that alienates us from ourselves. Our languages, our culture, and our "common sense" all conspire to convince us that we are self-contained entities, divided from the rest of the universe. Each of us occupies a little box, and most of us remain shut up inside our heads for our entire lives. "Common sense" teaches us to analyse our world into discrete units. I am "in here," and everything else is "out there." We are separate, unconnected, and the boundaries are set by that Sacred Cow of the West, the big "I am," the ego.

But this analytical and divisive way of knowing the world is not the only one possible. Anyone who has been part of a powerful ritual or experienced good sex can tell you that. At such times we come to the wisdom of the body; that all things are ultimately one. . . . Yet even if we accept intellectually that the split between the self and the other can be healed, . . . it is far more important to feel it, to experience it in our bodies. That is a far deeper knowing and a true healing. . . .

For me, Paganism is not so much a set of beliefs as a way of relating to the world. The wholeness I have spoken of, that oneness of everything which we can experience in moments of spiritual knowing is what I call the sacred, and Pagan ritual is both a path to the sacred and a way of honoring it. In our rituals we reconnect with ourselves, healing the rift between body and mind through ecstatic dance, chanting, and the drama of ritualized myth. We lose our ego-centered selves and achieve that somatic knowing of the unity of everything. . . .

It is a deep knowing of the sacredness of the Earth, which is beyond intellectual awareness of the facts and figures about species decimation and habitat loss. It is a feeling of unity with the Earth that we have in our gut. At such moments there is no guilt, no fear or disempowerment. We act to protect our Earth because we know, in every cell of our bodies, that our lives, our communities and our land are sacred. We act from a grounded strength which reaches beyond intellectual awareness and yet reinforces it, rooting deep within us.[10]

REFLECTION

These two approaches are entirely complementary. We have neither need nor reason to choose between them. Of course we should learn all we can about the life of our own bioregion, as well as such planetary concerns as global warming and acid rain. We should work ecstatic ritual to integrate this knowledge into the deep mind. We should live by our Sacred values, being mindful of how our choices and actions affect Mother Earth's well-being. We should act in accordance with our own talents, temperaments, and values to protect and heal Her. All this and more, of course.

But have you noticed that we need to do all these things both individually and collectively? We need to transform both personal and cultural consciousness, both individual and societal behavior. Neither can ever really be effective without the other. Right there is the false dichotomy that binds and blinds us.

Adrian Harris named it: the delusion that threatens all life now is the delusion of separation. We are ultimately and irreducibly interdependent. This truth was always before us, always in plain sight, and besides, Mother Gaia whispered it into our dreams. We caught fleeting glimpses, but never really followed Gaia's wisdom to its logical conclusion.

---

[10]Adrian Harris, "Sacred Ecology" in *Paganism Today*, ed. Graham Harvey and Charlotte Hardman (San Francisco: Thorsons, 1995), pp. 152–53.

Our religious traditions teach us that we must find the Sacred within ourselves, or nowhere. This is still true, but no longer adequate. The Sacred thread is anchored deep within each living being. We must look there first, in the understanding that this anchor point is also a portal to the Web of Life, within which each living thing is a nexus point and a shining jewel. Now, for Gaia's sake, we must find the Sacred in each other, and in the trees and fishes, and in Gaia Herself.

Like the Lady of Laussel, we are both ourselves and parts of the greater whole, and this is what we must realize. Those who believe that they are truly separate are open to the temptations of greed, of wanting more than their fair share of Earth's gifts. The Web of Life is frayed now, dangerously damaged by greedy behaviors. Until we can find and honor the sacred spark in one another, and in all our relations, all other living things, the fabric cannot be rewoven. So conjure Earth for healing.

We are brothers of the forest
We are sisters of the Goddess
We are nothing without each other
If we let it die, there'll be no other
So call Sky Father
and call Earth Mother. [11]

ATTUNEMENT

We need to learn, to think, and to dream, but we also need to do. Values and ideas may be the core structures of spirituality, but dry bones can never dance by themselves. Religion connects belief and behavior—that's the root meaning of the word. So religious lore comes in two main categories: ritual and meditative practices that help us discern, clarify, and integrate our beliefs, and ethics that guide us to live congruent lives.

[11]Song lyrics by Kenny and Tsipora, used with permission.

Polytheistic religion works on the assumption that we get close to different Gods in different ways, in accordance with the different values and energies that each particular God or Goddess represents.

Our upbringing within Western industrial society tends to estrange us from Gaia, to our own detriment and that of the Earth Herself. If you seek reconciliation and attunement with Mother Earth, and with all our relations within Her living body, here are some overall guidelines:

- ❧ Stay as much as you can in the World of Form. Pay attention to what you find right here. The Inner Planes are no less beautiful or holy, but other Deities prevail there. Gaia is the Lady of Manifest Life.

- ❧ While working with Gaia, live as simply and naturally as you can while honoring your other responsibilities.

There are many ways to get down to Earth. What follows are a few that work for me and for people I know. Start with these, but please don't limit yourself to them. As you find or create some others, please share them. The more ways each of us has to get back to the Mother, the better.

PREPARATIONS

At the beginning of any project, we gather information and equipment that we think will be useful.

First, locate some green area, however small, close enough to your workplace that you can walk there and back during lunch. This need not be a natural area. A vest pocket park will suffice. Look for a place with benches, so you can sit down for a moment, perhaps eat your lunch, without soiling or rumpling your work clothes. A few minutes out of doors will do you good. If you live in an apartment, or a house without a yard, find another small green space as close as possible to home.

Then find a larger green space, as natural as possible, within an hour's travel of your home. When you go there, wear clothing that you can move in easily, and that is easily washable, so you can sit on the ground without worry.

Go to these places as often as you can, to connect with the living Earth. You can watch the seasons change there. When the weather permits, you can meditate, read or write, sketch or photograph, feed the birds and squirrels, watch the children play, or just relax.

If you find yourself enjoying your time in nature, you'll probably soon be wanting some comfortable walking shoes, a rain parka, and one of those water bottles that comes with a shoulder strap. For summer, get some good sunscreen, sunglasses, and a light-colored hat.

Don't make a huge investment in equipment at the beginning, but do notice what you find yourself wanting: perhaps a camera or some art supplies, probably a day pack. Our objective is attunement, not asceticism. The more you keep yourself comfortable out of doors, the more likely you are to spend time there.

Keep a journal of your work with Gaia. I've recommended some books, and I'll be recommending more, but the most important book is the one you'll write, the chronicle of your discoveries. Great writing style isn't important. Spelling, grammar, and even neatness are irrelevant. The only thing that matters is recording your experiences and feelings so that you can reflect on them later. Your Gaia journal should be an inexpensive, lightweight, and durable notebook, one that can spend a lot of time outdoors with you and even take a few grass stains or raindrops.

LEARNING

Before we can care for where we are, we have to know where we are. We have to inhabit a particular place—possibly not for our entire lives, but with all possible understanding while

we are in that place. In understanding the natural order of a
place, we can begin to create our own spiritual order.[12]

In Gaia's service, there is no conflict between science and spirit.
Get to know Her as well as you can. Indulge your curiosity, and
follow your enthusiasms. Visit your local zoo, botanical garden,
and natural history museum. They probably have guided tours,
workshops, or classes that will catch your interest. Or just pick up
some field guides and look up the trees, plants, or birds that you
see in your own neighborhood. Here are some things to find out:

- What kind of tree grows closest to your front door? Is it a
  native species? If not, where does it come from?

- What wild grasses or flowers grow on your block? Which are
  native species? Are any of them traditional healing herbs?

- Where does your water come from? Where does it go from
  your drain?

- Where does your garbage go?

- How did the indigenous people of your area feed, clothe, and
  shelter themselves?

- What are the prevailing weather patterns in your area? Have
  they changed since your childhood? (Check your memories
  against the records.)

- What local resources will help you find out more about your
  bioregion? What aspect of nature in your area fascinates you
  most?

Record what you learn in your journal: highlights of workshops,
summaries of things you read, observations that you make during
your time outdoors. Be sure to record how you feel about all these
experiences. Reactions, insights, and inspirations are very important. Even more important are the questions that come up as you

[12]Clifton, *Modern Craft Movement*, p. 130.

learn, the next things you would like to explore. Learning comes first, but it is not a preparation or a preliminary. It is a constant. If we all continue to learn as long as we live, we will keep our minds young in the service of Mother Earth.

GROUNDING

Ground is a word with many meanings. According to the *American Heritage Dictionary*, the ground is the solid surface of the Earth, and also an area of land designated for some particular purpose. By analogy, *ground* also means the foundation or basis of an argument, a belief, or an action, and the underlying conditions upon which our beliefs and actions are based. As a verb, *to ground* can mean literally placing something on the ground, providing a basis for something, or supplying people with basic information.

One ancient way of blessing a newborn baby is to briefly place the naked child on the bare Earth. This simple and powerful ritual action would also be the best possible way to begin a process of reconnection with Gaia. Regrettably, few of us have access to private, secluded outdoor space where we could safely press our naked breasts against Hers. Still, we can all find somewhere to simply lay our bare hands upon Her skin and ask for Her guidance. Modern Pagans know how to make do.

Frequent, tangible, and mindful contact with the Earth is what matters. Consider, you can hug a human loved one—and feel pleasure and comfort in the contact—even when both of you are fully dressed. A couple of layers of cloth is not that much of a barrier. Even the soles of a sturdy pair of shoes allow you much more Earth contact than concrete or floorboard ever could. So, dress for comfort and safety—and get outdoors, get off the pavement. Get your body as close as you can to the irregular, resilient, living surface of Mother Earth.

Stand still and breathe. Look and listen. Walk around, paying attention to the sensations in your feet. Are you going up or down hill? Is the ground soft or firm? Try walking on a beach, on a piney forest floor, on a lawn—how do they feel different underfoot? If you feel safe, try them barefoot. (Beware of broken glass, poison ivy, disease-bearing ticks.)

Sit down, and plan on sitting for a while. Find a place where your back is supported by a rock or the trunk of a tree. If the ground is chilly, a folded-up old blanket will insulate you. Let yourself enter a relaxed and alert state of mind, sort of like meditation, but directed to the life around you rather than to your inscape. Rest your gaze on the square foot or so of ground that is right in front of you. Quietly observe all the tiny, intricate life activity in that one small area.

When you've been still for a while, you may be visited by a ladybug or a bird. A leaf or petal may fall into your lap. Mother Earth is present all around you, far more visibly than She is indoors. Feel Her presence.

Lie down. If you're in a safe place, you might nap. Sleeping outdoors replenishes the spirit. If you're under a tree, look up at the dancing leaves. Clouds by day and stars at night, Father Sky preens Himself for Mother Earth. If you feel like rolling over, don't hesitate. You are not prostrating yourself, you are snuggling up.

Once in a while, let go to gravity (and to levity) and just roll down a gentle, grassy slope.

Pay attention to your experience, both the physical sensations and the emotions they evoke within you. Remember all this, so that you can draw on it when you are back indoors. Although we live most of our lives indoors, we are still Gaia's children. Even in a skyscraper, even in an airplane, we remain within Earth's biosphere. Estrangement is an illusion.

Indoors, it helps to have some token, some anchor for your memories. This need not be anything obvious. In most workplaces, a potted plant, or even a small rock or piece of driftwood, "souvenirs from your last vacation," will not draw notice. At home, you can be as blatant as your space or taste allows. Whatever you choose, keep it handy as a visual and tactile focus.

Your mind can certainly reach right through any building to the living Earth. The classic grounding meditation is to imagine a taproot extending down from the base of your spine to the living soil, and even to the bedrock below. Draw the energy up, like nurturing water, through this taproot and up your spine. Let it form branches like a tree. The fruit can go where it is needed, or fall to ground like the leaves in the autumn to nourish the Earth again. You can do this grounding meditation as a brief stress buster, or use it as a preparation for further work.

Lately, some Pagans have been creating geologically accurate grounding meditations. Instead of talking generically about soil, water table, and bedrock, these meditations describe the actual rock strata in your area, and also a bit about how those particular rocks were formed. Doing the research for such a grounding is a good way to learn about the deep history of your own bioregion.

Your local library might not have detailed geological information, but a nearby university or government library probably will. A natural history museum is another good resource. Such information also is becoming available on the Web. Two good Web sites to start with are the United States Geological Survey (www.usgs.gov) and the Geological Survey of Canada (www.nrcan. gc.ca/gsc/index_e.html).

A nicely printed out, or even calligraphic, local grounding meditation using the information you've discovered would make a particularly thoughtful and inexpensive housewarming gift. My own favorite geologist, the erudite Dr. Raven, created a site specific grounding for my new house and also gave me the following advice about how to do the research:

Remember, you're trying to understand two related things: the vertical succession of materials beneath your home, and the various ways these materials came to be there. So it's not

just ancient rock strata. It might also be old mine workings or
the rubble of buildings that stood there before yours. Both
belong in your grounding, if you are truly describing what is
beneath you.

Geological papers normally include a synopsis of the geological history of the area in question. You may also find the
same information presented as a table of formations (a listing of the scientific names of the rock layers, beginning with
the grass roots and working down as deep as has been
observed so far) or a geologic column (the same information
presented graphically). To a geologist, these are the true magical names of the place.[13]

CLEAN HANDS

UNDERSTANDING OUR PERSONAL ENVIRONMENTAL IMPACTS

You would not expect to develop a closer relationship with
another person while your behavior was doing that person harm.
Deities are no different, as all religions know. Our loud profes-
sions of belief and elaborate ritual practices mean nothing unless
our behavior is congruent. Approach the altar only when your
hands are clean . . . or are at least, as clean as you can get them.

Here is the real beginning of reconciliation and attunement
with Mother Earth. Each of us needs to figure out how our own
behavior contributes to Her wounding or Her healing—and to
adjust our actions accordingly. To come into right relationship
with Gaia, reduce, reuse, recycle, and—most important of all—
rethink. Taking a personal environmental inventory from time to
time, starting now, is an effective structure for rethinking.

This self-examination is personal because the only thing we can
actually control is our own behavior. It is also truly collective
because no human stands alone on the Earth. All the ways we affect
the Earth, for good and for ill, happen in interaction with other

[13]Personal correspondence 7/12/02. Author requested anonymity.

people. Still we cannot advocate for the Earth, cannot urge others to take better care of Her, till our own behavior reflects our beliefs. Only then can our words ring true in advocacy or in worship.

As a Witch, I live by the Wiccan Rede, a core ethic that balances freedom with responsibility. *An it harm none, do what you will.* But the Rede is a guiding ideal, a "navigational star" that I steer by, always knowing that I will never actually get all the way there. In reality, no one can completely and absolutely avoid doing any harm. None of us is perfect, but knowledge of our imperfection does not exempt us from trying our best.

We can and should anticipate the outcomes of our actions as accurately as we can, while knowing that our best efforts can still have unpredictable and harmful side effects. Of course, when these things happen, we need to do whatever we can to set things right. Sometimes all we can do is choose what seems to be the lesser evil.

We are also responsible for the indirect results of our choices. If we roast the Thanksgiving turkey in a disposable aluminum roaster, we support strip mining. If we use disposable paper goods that were not made from recycled paper, we support clear-cutting.

Start with asking what immediate damage you do, and how this might be minimized or mitigated:

- What do you buy, and why? What are the side effects of its manufacture and use?
- Do you select recycled paper products whenever possible? Do you use the back sides of discarded paper for notes, lists, and drafts?
- What happens to the stuff you throw away? Do you really have to throw it away? Could you reuse it instead?
- Do you pass on what you can no longer use to others who need it? Do you participate in your local recycling program? More challenging: Do you buy what you need secondhand whenever possible?

- ♣ If you live in the suburbs or country, can you compost your kitchen trash?

- ♣ What do you release into the air? What are its long-term effects?

- ♣ What do you pour down your toilet or into a storm drain? Where does it go? What is the effect on the body of water that receives that drainage? Did you really need to use, and then dispose of, that liquid?

- ♣ Do you conserve water as much as possible?

- ♣ Do you know how the energy you use is produced? What are the side effects of producing that energy? Do you conserve energy as much as possible?

- ♣ If you use battery-operated equipment, what do you do with the highly toxic dead batteries?

- ♣ If you own your own home, is it well insulated?

- ♣ Is your refrigerator regularly defrosted?

- ♣ Do you walk or bike or take public transit when possible? If you drive a car, is it an energy-efficient model? Do you keep it well tuned to reduce emissions?

Consider moving toward a lifestyle of voluntary simplicity. There's a social movement supporting people in this choice, with a Web site at www.seedsofsimplicity.org, through which you can find practical suggestions for living lightly, and frugally. The adage that got our ancestors through the Great Depression can also help us heal the Earth:

> *Use it up, wear it out,*
> *Make it do or do without!*

Simple living saves money, and so gives you more choices about your work and your life. To complete this circle of blessing, you may want to contribute some of what you save to the environmental organization of your choice.

Now, probe further. What about indirect or long-range harm? And what might you do to actively help?

- ✤ If you have any investments, are they in Earth-friendly industries or technologies?
- ✤ Do you support groups that work for the environment in whatever way seems most appropriate to you: public education, land conservancy, political lobbying, or direct activism? Do you contribute time and work, or just money?
- ✤ Can you join (or start) an environmental club or committee in your area so that you and your neighbors can work together to protect and heal your own part of Mother Earth?
- ✤ Do you turn out for community cleanup days at local parks, riverbanks, and the like?
- ✤ In a city, could you commit to the care of one street tree?
- ✤ If you own land, even a small yard, do you care for it in an Earth-friendly way, without the use of polluting chemicals?
- ✤ If you observe pollution or other environmental vandalism, do you blow the whistle? More challenging: What if the polluter or vandal is your employer?
- ✤ What do you do to support your local recycling program? What do you do to support strong environmental legislation?
- ✤ If you want to have children, are you considering adoption? Will you stay within the replacement rate of one or two children per household?
- ✤ If you have children, are you helping them learn respect for nature?
- ✤ More important, are you consistently acting from love and care for the Earth so your children can learn from your example?
- ✤ Even more important, how do you think you can realistically and sustainably improve your household's impact on the environment?
- ✤ Most important, how can you do better by Mother Earth?

Record these reflections in your journal. This is an exercise you should probably repeat every few years, to monitor your own progress. If you're in a group, you may want to try writing up your findings in the form of a chart or diagram and sharing it at a meeting. We can all learn from each other's good ideas.

A personal environmental impact statement is one tool that can help us focus our love and concern for Mother Earth into practical, immediate action. Serving Her makes our love real. Knowing that our love is real helps us move away from anxiety and guilt over the state of the Earth, and toward joy.

MAKING CONTACT: GAIA AS NEIGHBOR

Bad feelings lead to burnout. Guilt, fear, anxiety, rage: all of these might well be evoked by Mother Earth's perilous condition and the wanton and callous indifference of those currently in power. These emotions, however, are poisonous to our personal mental health and even worse for our spiritual development. Nor will they sustain us in the long and careful work that Gaia needs us to do on Her behalf.

Not that we should suppress or deny these bad feelings. The polluters and greenwashers (paid advocates for industries that harm Mother Earth) would just love that, now wouldn't they? Our first need is to acknowledge our natural reactions to Earth's situation, express them, but not get stuck in them. Despair is the polluters' second best friend. Instead, let bad feelings flow and go, then reach out for the sacred sources of joy and power, of enthusiasm. We will protect and heal Gaia not because She is needy or pathetic but because She is beautiful and good. Awareness of Her presence is a blessing available to all.

Gaia lives in your neighborhood. You can get to know Her right there. The Whole Earth, that glorious photo, was taken from a terrible distance. The small violets growing through cracks in the pavement are quieter, but no less sacred. Both show Gaia's presence.

The book I want to recommend right now is *Boundaries of Home*, edited by Doug Aberley and published by New Society.[14] This is an inspiring and useful collection of essays about map-making as a way to develop understanding of our neighborhoods and our bioregions.

Map your own very local area. Each of us has different physical abilities, so first decide what is a comfortable walking distance for you. Then, on a simple street map, which you can make for yourself, draw that radius around your home. Sketch in any obstacles to walking, such as highways or unbridged rivers. Adjust the borderline to match your actual travel patterns. This is your neighborhood.

Over a week or so, walk every block within this area, looking for all the places where Nature shows Her face. Now, mark these on your map. Are there any tall old trees? Trees or shrubs that flower in spring? Rock outcrops? Places where the Queen Anne's lace comes up on the neglected edges of parking lots? Particularly lovely gardens? Parks? Friendly dogs that like to play with you? Nesting birds? Be sure to indicate the spot you chose as your own nature retreat. Maybe you'll even find a couple of others. Choices are good.

If there's room, you may want to map the human community as well. Where's the public library, the store where you get the good homemade sausage, the nice old lady who likes to chat, the block where they put up the really spectacular Yuletide lights? What is the name of your nearest school-crossing guard? If this makes your map too complex to read, draw more than one map highlighting different aspects of your neighborhood. All of them will help you understand and appreciate the place where you live.

Date your map or maps. Redo them every so often to keep up with changes in your neighborhood. Sometimes a lovely patch of

---

[14]New Society is a wonderful source of information about ecology, sustainability, bioregionalism, and related social issues. Visit their Web site at www.newsociety.com.

woods is destroyed to make room for a shopping mall, but other times a derelict, garbage-strewn riverbank is transformed into a small oasis of peace. Learn where to look for the early crocuses and what color the leaves turn in the fall. If your journal is loose-leaf, put these maps into it. If it isn't, start a folder or scrapbook to accompany your journal.

To deepen your connection with the spirit of the place, try this: identify the seven natural features of your area that most touch your heart. Celebrate each one in your chosen art form. Take a photo or write a poem or paint a picture of each one. If your art form is visual, and you like the results, adorn your home with them. If it's poetry or other writing, it belongs in your journal. If you're working with a group, share both the maps and the artwork.

Now, choose one of those natural features. If you like, you can give Gaia the choice by writing a name or short phrase for each one on a scrap of paper, then putting the scraps in a basket or bowl. Ask for guidance, make yourself receptive, then draw out one of the scraps. Or simply see which one comes up most frequently in your dreams or daydreams for a few days.

Visit the one you pick as often as you can. Observe the seasonal changes and note them in your journal. Make another picture or write another poem every full moon, more often if you feel so inspired, for at least a year. In gratitude, take care of this spot. Pick up garbage, feed birds, bring water during drought seasons, do whatever seems helpful. Whenever you visit, leave a silent blessing there, knowing you have also received one. Friendship is always mutual.

GETTING CLOSER: GAIA IN YOUR HOME

We don't have temples. Our homes are our sanctuaries, our places of rest, reflection and worship. Home is also where we cook and eat, bathe and sleep, study and practice our arts, share laughter and make love. All of these things can be done mindfully, and can help deepen our connection with Mother Earth. You can make your home into a supportive context for this or any other spiritual exploration you undertake.

If you want to invite any God or Goddess into your home, simply treat that Divine Being as you would any welcome guest. Make Him comfortable. Provide some of the things that She enjoys. Pay attention to Him. Simple good manners, thoughtfulness, maybe a little bit of creativity—these are all you need.

Just as you might make up a bed for a human guest, you can set up an altar or shrine for a Deity. Space is short in my house, so I use small knickknack shelves, which I call shrine shelves. Gaia's shrine shelf holds a reproduction of the Lady of Willendorf, a tiny wooden bowl full of dried beans and grain, a basket of pinecones, a small globe. A grapevine wreath hangs on the wall above it.

If you have a yard or garden, you can create a shrine in the garden, or make the entire garden into a shrine. The key is conscious, mindful tending. Always enter your land reverently, even if you're just going out do some routine chores. Think of how a devout janitor would enter a church. And go there often just to be with Mother Earth, as you would spend time with any honored guest.

Don't force your will upon land you have consecrated to Gaia. Work with the will of the land. Use native species that are appropriate to your own space. Is it sunny or shady, sandy or swampy? What type of soil do you have? Eating some of what grows there, and composting your kitchen scraps, creates a reciprocal relationship between land and people. Another option is to devote part or all of your yard to a backyard wildlife habitat. You can get good information about habitat creation from the National Wildlife Federation at www.nwf.org/backyardwildlifehabitat.

Maybe you want Gaia in your home and life for more than a brief visit. When you welcome a new house mate, you probably redecorate at least a little bit, so your home reflects that person's presence. Again, it's pretty similar when you ask a Deity to move in. What you do will depend on your own tastes and comfort. Here are some suggestions:

- ✥ Green accents—or maybe just throw pillows or a tablecloth; have natural materials and fibers whenever possible.
- ✥ Plants and pets—they add life to indoor space.
- ✥ Natural objects, such as stones, branches, or shells.
- ✥ Photos, drawings, or paintings of natural scenes, or closeups of natural objects that reveal the beauty of their forms and structures.
- ✥ Reproductions of ancient Pagan artwork, or the works of contemporary Pagan artists, that portray and celebrate Mother Earth.

If you have the talent and skill, make your own art. In many religions, artisans who create sacred objects do so in a meditative state and a ritual fashion. They make their craft into a personal devotional practice. Ritual and symbolic objects that you've created in a sacred, conscious manner will hold the memories—the energies—that you put into their making. When you look at them, or use them in ritual, the recollection will help your current focus.

Similarly, the natural objects you gathered yourself will anchor memories of times you spent out of doors, in direct communion with nature. Even more important, you can be sure these things were obtained harmlessly.

Some years ago, there was a Pagan and New Age fad for quartz crystals. I lost my enthusiasm fast when I found out that most of the quartz points on the market were obtained by strip mining. What would the prophet Smohalla think of that? There are some things we have to do for survival, but should not do for convenience or adornment, and must not do as part of Gaia's worship. How can we hope to honor Her by doing Her harm?

If Gaia becomes your house mate, which room will be Hers? The kitchen, I think. This is where we prepare Mother Earth's gifts for the delight and nourishment of our loved ones and ourselves.

Cooking can easily become another form of art practice, an active meditation on Her generous love. If you want to try this, start by preparing the space so you're free to concentrate on what you're doing, not distracted or frustrated. Clear the clutter. Organize your kitchen storage and work areas so that what you need is conveniently handy. Make sure you have the tools you need, and that all your tools are in good working condition. Get rid of any foods or seasonings that are past their prime. Restock your staples and spices.

Any orderly, organized workspace has an elegant, functional beauty that is intrinsic. Make it comfortable as well. I like to listen to music while I cook. I like to be surrounded by harmonious colors. You know what you like. You may also want to celebrate Gaia with a few symbolic objects. I have a small representation of a cornucopia hanging over my stove and another right by my refrigerator. The horn of plenty is our most ancient symbol of Mother Earth's ever-flowing womb, first shown to us by the Lady of Laussel.

Notice and appreciate your food all the time. Modern life has us eating a lot of hasty meals, many away from home. Even in a public place, even on the run, you can take one long deep breath for silent gratitude before gobbling down your food. You can take another deep breath when you finish to notice how good it tastes, and how much better you feel after eating it. Gratitude keeps us in contact with Gaia. (If you instead notice that your meal didn't taste so good, or that you feel stodgy or spacey after you've eaten, that's an important warning from your body and the Goddess. Pay attention and adjust your eating habits till they are functional.)

Eventually, we come home. Occasionally, we have the option of an entirely different way to relate to our food. If you want to develop a closer relationship with Gaia, make those occasions

happen more than once a week. Cook mindfully. Careful preparation is a way of showing Her that you appreciate the raw ingredients She has supplied.

Mindful cooking starts in the store. Select fresh ingredients,
locally grown and in season when possible. Organic farms are far
kinder to the Earth. Eating seasonal foods keeps you in touch with
the Wheel of the Year. If you're not a full-time homemaker, and
almost nobody is these days, you'll probably make some compro-
mises with processed foods. But try to avoid preseasoned products. Choose plain canned tomatoes instead of commercial tomato
sauce, canned puréed pumpkin instead of pumpkin pie filling.
Even as you take a few judicious shortcuts, keep as much of the
creative activity of cooking for yourself as you reasonably can.

As you work, in your clean, efficient, and comfortable kitchen,
Gaia's room, feast all your senses on your ingredients. Enjoy the
different colors, shapes, smells, and textures, as well as flavors. Be
careful and playful about how they contrast with or complement
each other in the dishes you create. Be adventurous with seasonings. Try some food you've never had before. You may want to
keep track of all these experiments.

You can have a small, intimate dinner, just you and Gaia, or a
dinner party in Her honor with family and friends. Set a nice table.
Just as you would thank a dinner guest who brought along a luscious melon for dessert, say grace to thank Mother Earth and
Father Sky for all the good food. Say grace also because it gives
you another moment to just revel in the feast that is before you.
Then eat slowly, appreciatively, savoring every bite.

You'll find support and suggestions for this sensuous approach
to food in the slow food movement, which began in Italy and is
now spreading around the world. To learn more, visit their Web
site at www.slowfood.com. I've also learned a lot from two religious cookbook writers. Fr. Robert Farrar Capon, an Episcopalian
theologian, wrote *The Supper of the Lamb* more than thirty years
ago and to my delight, there's a brand-new edition out. Edward

Espe Brown is a Zen Buddhist monk and chef. His *Tassajara Bread Book* and *Tassajara Cooking* are classics, both inspiring and useful. More recently, he produced a delightful combination of cookbook and autobiography called *Tomato Blessings and Radish Teachings.*

If I had a houseguest, I would probably throw a party. If someone new joined my household, I would just about certainly throw a party. If Gaia visits your home, or comes to stay, that sounds like a good reason to celebrate. A party in honor of a Deity is called a ritual. Here are some ideas for a celebration welcoming Gaia to your home.

Invite guests who you feel would enjoy Her, and who you think She would enjoy. You might ask them to come prepared to entertain Her and each other with song, poetry, storytelling, and so on. Decorate in ways that reflect the beauty of the green Earth. Make sacred space according to your own customs. Invite your guests to share what they've prepared in praise of Mother Earth. Bless and consecrate the object that you have chosen to be the centerpiece of Her shrine in your home. Bless and share some ritual beverage and food (rich, dark, earthy spice cake and cider sound right to me). Close the formal part of your evening, and proceed to feast.

If you really like to cook, and the group is small, perhaps you can prepare the whole feast yourself in a conscious manner. This might be the very best possible personal preparation for the rite. But be careful to not take on too much, to not overstress yourself. If the group is larger, or you aren't that skilled a cook, consider a potluck. Ask everybody who can to bring a mindfully prepared dish. (The true noncooks can always provide beverages.) When people do for each other, and show their appreciation, the web of community is woven more strongly. The web of human community is part of the greater web of Gaia's life.

GROWING CLOSER: RITUAL PRACTICE

Real love stories never end with "they moved in together and lived happily ever after." Love is not a one-shot deal. Authentic relationships require time, love, care, and—yes—effort. Again, what applies to relationships between two or more humans seems to work about the same for relationships between humans and Deities. We can do things to sustain and even deepen our connection, or we can neglect that connection until it fades from our consciousness. Relationships weakened by neglect will not survive life's challenges.

Through consistent ritual practice, we maintain contact with our Goddesses and Gods, and with the community of devoted people who have worshipped these same Beings under various names through the centuries and across the continents. As Pagans, polytheists, we are specific in our worship practices, understanding that some ways work better than others for connecting with any particular Deity.

So, whoever wants to grow closer to Gaia needs to create and maintain a ritual practice to facilitate that. If you're working with a tradition, you have access to a heritage of lore. If you're in a group, your elders can advise you. Every sincere-hearted seeker can listen to the voice of the land, as it whispers deep in their own heart and mind. And here are some of my ideas, to help you prime that pump.

Daily practice. There are some very brief and unobtrusive things that anybody can do, anywhere, every day. You can do them in the space of one deep slow breath. You can do them silently. If you do them consistently, they will work a gradual but thorough transformation in your relationship with Nature, and in your personal spirituality.

    ❧ Frame your day with tiny rituals for significant transition points such as getting up, getting home in the evening, or going to bed. Your own daily shift points may be different. Start with a good stretch. Face each of the cardinal directions in turn. Draw in that particular quality: thought from the East, passion from the South, wisdom from the West, and skill from the North. Ask for guidance and energy to do what is needful in the best possible way. At bedtime, ask for guiding dreams.

❧ When you leave your house for the first time every day, greet the first living thing you see: a cat, a tree, a neighbor, or a tuft of grass growing through a crack in the pavement. All life is sacred in Gaia's heart. A smile of acknowledgment is all you really need. As this becomes habit, you'll probably find yourself doing it whenever you leave any building at all.

❧ When you eat, offer thanks. It's good to actually say a brief grace before meals. If you're self-conscious about saying grace when eating in public, just take a breath-long pause for inner appreciation. Only Mother Nature will notice.

❧ Whenever you encounter something beautiful or marvelous, take just a moment of pleasure. Use a long, deep breath as a mini-meditation, as you symbolically "take-in" the beauty and wonder before you: jewelweed in the sunshine, a newly-wed's first dance, wind chimes, the iridescence of a city pigeon's neck, all of these things, and many more, display the Immanent Presence. By simply noticing, you maintain and deepen your own contact. This simple practice is far more important than any formal ritual.

❧ It's also true that formal ritual gives some people structure and helps them remember to notice. The Jewish tradition includes a collection of one-sentence-long prayers, simply called "blessings." These blessings start with the same words of praise for the Creator and finish with a description of whatever is being praised. We'll see some below. In psychology, this would be called a "sentence-stem exercise."

There are blessings for many kinds of food, for seeing a rainbow, for specific ritual acts and for basic bodily functions. I'm told that pious youths sometimes use the blessing for seeing a thing of beauty as a method of flirtation!

If you like, you can certainly create some "sentence-stem blessings" of your own. "Praise to Mother Earth and Father Sky for . . . the glory of this rainbow, the strength of this rock face, the laughter of these children, the sweetness of the cup of sugar I now add to this lemonade." I'm a proud child of the sixties, so I stay with my own generation's customary mantra of delight: "Oh, wow!" Do what best suits your own personal style.

Think of this as stealth mysticism. You won't miss the few seconds each small blessing takes. They won't add up to more than about five minutes in any day. But these many, randomly scattered, tiny expressions of awe will cumulatively form a flexible connection to Gaia that is far more durable than a larger, more rigid practice could ever be. If you miss one blessing, you won't lose momentum. There will always be more beauty to notice and bless.

⚶ Try doing at least some of your meditation while moving. This will help you stay in your body and in the World of Form, rather than slipping into the Inner Planes. Some of the Asian exercise forms, such as Hatha Yoga and Tai Chi, are designed to be done mindfully, working with energy as well as muscles. For a more Western or Pagan approach, try dance. You'll find a lot of great suggestions for meditations based on rhythm and dance in a book called *Sweat Your Prayers*.

Gaia's Feast Day. We should be thanking Mother Earth for each gift we receive, in the moment we enjoy it, certainly not confining Her worship to a single day. But it's also very human to set a special day aside to celebrate an anniversary or a loved one's birthday—as long as we continue to love and care for Her on all the other days.

Most modern Pagans use the Wheel of the Year as our ritual calendar. This is an evenly spaced set of eight festivals: the solstices, the equinoxes, and the "quarter days" that fall between them. Of those eight feasts, I think August Eve (July 31) is the most appropriate for celebrating Gaia.

This feast is sometimes called Lunasa, in honor of the many-skilled God Lugh. An equally familiar name for it is Lammas, "loaf mass." It was celebrated under that name for many centuries by the Christian countryfolk of Europe, who managed to hide and preserve many an ancient custom within the church.

The roots of our words can be revealing. *Lady* derives from the Old English *hlaefdige*, which means "kneader of bread." *Lord* comes from *hlafweard*, "bread keeper." These words, which later became terms for aristocracy, are rooted in generosity, not in domination or command. Our Goddess demands no sacrifice, for Her love is poured forth over the Earth. The word *Lammas (hlafmaesse)* comes from that same root.

Lammas is the traditional opening of the Harvest season, the time when the tribe asks permission of the land to reap Her generous gifts. This will always be relevant to everybody, urban as well as rural. Even those of us who don't raise even a single tomato plant are sustained in life by the land and the harvest. We all should greet Gaia, thank Her and renew our conscious bond with Her.

One wonderful possibility is for a group to bake enchanted bread together. Remember, your kitchen is Gaia's temple. Gather some like-minded friends there, later in the evening when the temperature is cooling down. Everybody chants while you take turns kneading. Consciously fold your love of one another and of Mother Earth into the dough. Later, you will share the new-baked bread.[15] Be sure that you share some also with the birds and other wild creatures in your area. I'd strongly recommend bringing a loaf to a local homeless shelter. Save a bit, too, for your picnic the next day.

Enjoy an outdoor ritual and a potluck picnic feast. In many areas, blackberries will be ripe on August Eve. It's traditional to eat something that combines wild foods, Nature's free gift, with

---

[15] This idea comes from Mycota Coven, and is shared with their generous permission.

the work of human culture—for example, wild berry shortcake. The customary Lammas water-gun fight, which began as a way to cool ourselves in the heat of a New York August, can also be consciously done as a call for rain in times of drought. Rejoice, the Harvest is here again!

GOING TO HER PLACES

We've talked about inviting Gaia home, now let's think about going to where Her presence is strongest: the garden, the park, the wilderness. For this, you'll find both inspiration and practical advice in *Awakening to Nature* by Charles Cook. Remember, though, reading about any activity, while it may be good preparation, is no substitute for the actual experience. Get outside; get off the pavement.

Many areas have hiking clubs, local grassroots organizations, often volunteer-based, that maintain trails, sponsor group hikes, even offer workshops for beginners.

Sunfish, our coven's favorite outdoorswoman, offered the following advice about hiking:

- Hikers should drink at least two liters of water per person per day, more in August. Really! Rinse out an old soda bottle and use that.

- Good hiking boots are expensive, but they last forever and are nowhere near as expensive as missed work due to a broken ankle.

- Never ever, ever, ever wear cotton socks, which lose insulation value when wet—buy the $15 wool or synthetic or the wool-synthetic blend ones.

- Take along some moleskin (cheap, and not actually made of rodents), a special skin-covering material that can prevent blisters from worsening. Apply moleskin to any "hot spots" that develop on your feet while you are walking. Moleskin can be found in the first-aid section of your local pharmacy. You also need to take a pair of scissors.

WEEKEND VISION QUEST

For a more sustained and more intense experience of contact, try a weekend vision quest. A vision quest is a short, highly intensive retreat during which the quester seeks contact with Deity or Spirit.

First, be sensible. Mother Nature doesn't want you to get hurt. Don't go wilderness camping alone unless you are an expert camper and have good equipment. Alone or with a group, bring along a cell phone so you can call for help in emergencies.

There are several safer options for neophyte campers. One is for a group of fellow seekers to camp together. There are state parks where you can reserve a site that has running water, a fireplace, an outhouse, maybe even some basic shelter. At least one person in your group should be familiar with first aid and with basic fire and food safety.

Another, if you have the privacy, is to "camp out" in your own backyard.

The third, and probably most practical, option is to do your vision quest during a Pagan gathering. Set up a campsite a little away from the main camping area. Let the organizers know where you'll be and what you'll be doing. In these years of global warming and consequent drought, you may want to return to the dining hall for your meals rather than risking a cooking fire outdoors. Endangering Gaia is not the way to come closer to Her.

Along with your camping and safety equipment, bring some field guides, your journal, a camera or sketchbook, maybe a small musical instrument. Be sure you have more water than you think you'll ever need. Do not bring any form of recorded music, books other than field guides, or any other distractions.

In Native American traditions, vision questers would typically fast. If you have any sort of blood sugar irregularities, do not fast. Even if you're fasting from everything else, drink lots of water. Within those limits, fasting is an option. However, fasting can be understood as a rejection of Gaia's gift of food. Maybe the best symbolic act is to eat only raw foods during your quest, since they

are what Nature actually provides. Whenever you eat outdoors, say
grace as usual, and also offer a libation.

Native American vision questers would also mark out a small
area and stay within it for the duration of their quest. You decide
whether this will increase your focus, or whether taking some
nature walks would help you grow closer to Gaia.

If you're with a group, you may do some group nature study,
especially if some of the people are really knowledgeable. Other
than that, try to limit conversation to what is necessary. Social
chatter is distracting. If you're at a festival, you might want to
attend any workshops that are about Nature study or Earth consciousness.

Spend as much time as possible out of doors, but don't be a
martyr. If the weather turns severe, take shelter. While you are out
of doors, you can observe the plants and animals, with or without
reference to a field guide. Or you can meditate surrounded by the
sights, sounds, and smells of Nature. You can sketch or take pictures of all that's around you. You should certainly write in your
journal about your immediate experiences and your personal
reflections and reactions.

If the weather permits, sleep out. Not in a tent, under the moon
and stars. If the weather does not permit, reschedule your weekend.
Sleeping out is the heart of the quest. Before you go to sleep, be
sure to ground yourself. Ask for Gaia's guidance in your dreams. In
the morning, write in your journal as soon as you wake. If you
remember your dreams, record them. If you don't, just write your
immediate stream of consciousness for at least fifteen minutes.
After that, begin your day with a greeting to the sun and to the life
all around you. Later in the day, you may want to read what you
wrote in the morning and see if it brings up any further reflections.

Here's a suggestion for anchoring the memories. Bring along a
cord or braid about the thickness of a clothes line in colors that
match the Earth in your area: shades of green in a New England
forest, golden tones in the California hills. Carry this cord with

you all weekend. When you see something that moves you, make a simple overhand knot in that cord. As you make the knot, the cord will form a circle that you can use as a frame. Look through this framing circle at the sight you would like to remember. When the image is clear in your mind, pull the knot tight. Do this at least twenty times, more if you like.

Bring the knotted cord home with you and use it like a rosary. Pass the knots through your fingers, taking one deep slow breath per knot, while you remember moments from your vision quest. The best time for this meditation is in bed, right before going to sleep, to invite Gaia into your dreams.

When the weekend is over, show your respect for nature by leaving your campsite in at least as good a condition as you found it. Leave some food for the animals. Give thanks. Back home, continue to pay attention to your dreams and intuitions for at least another week.

SERVICE

Ritual practices, ranging from a moment of conscious appreciation during a busy workday to a full-weekend vision quest, can create, clarify, deepen, and sustain our conscious contact with Gaia, and that feels good. But real religion is more than a feel-good exercise. If the sacred contact is real, it will necessarily change our lives. If our lives don't change, there are two possible explanations. Either we were living perfect lives all along, or we are engaging in fantasy, or even hypocrisy, but not religion.

If our hearts are moved by the love of Gaia, we will feel called from within to come to Her aid.

If people took responsibility for their own behavior, that would be enough. But some don't know and some don't care. Many have been confused and dazzled by the spin doctors and greenwashers, spokespeople for the destroyers and polluters. In the present crisis, it's no longer enough to simply live lightly. Active service is needed. But it's also true that each of us has different skills, talents, and temperaments. These become our callings, directing the form our active service will take.

DIRECT SERVICE: VOLUNTARISM

It starts with this: when you go out for a walk in Nature, take an empty plastic shopping bag. Pick up any trash you see, not just your own. Taking responsibility for Gaia's well-being, beyond cleaning up your own mess, is the basis for any other advocacy or activism.

In many communities, there are one-day cleanup campaigns. Show up for them whenever possible.

You may find more long-term opportunities for service. Does your local botanical garden use volunteer docents or guides? If it does, it probably also provides great training for them. Does your town have an environmental or beautification committee? Could the local hiking club use volunteer trail maintainers or guides? Might you write articles on nature appreciation and environmental issues for a local newspaper? Could your group volunteer to help maintain a local park?

What are the possibilities for a specific Pagan project, a proud public declaration that we love and serve Mother Earth? Here's a great example: at one time, the forests of the northeast United States contained abundant chestnut trees. The nuts provided abundant sustenance for deer and other wildlife, as well as for people. Then in 1904 the blight hit, and pretty much wiped out the American Chestnut tree, with consequences throughout the ecosystem.

Now, the American Chestnut Foundation is trying to breed a resistant strain. In 2002, Pagan landowners in western Massachusetts donated a plot of land for an experimental orchard. Another very respected Pagan elder is the volunteer orchard manager. A crew of Pagan volunteers spent two weekends last spring planting and mulching the baby trees. May their work be blessed!

Most important of all for Gaia's future: teach the children to love Her as you do. I'm a city kid myself, grateful to a series of camp counselors and scout leaders who shared their love of the green forest with me. If you have children of your own, or nieces and nephews, or grandchildren, be very mindful of the example you set for them.

INDIRECT SERVICE: ACTIVISM

No amount of voluntary action will offset the destruction wrought by the polluters. They have to be stopped, and soon. As Her defenders, some of us feel called to various forms of political action. Again, a range of options are available. We will be most effective, and most comfortable, doing what matches well with our own temperaments and talents.

- Inform yourself. The more you know, the more effectively you can advocate. Beware of deceptive greenwashing propaganda. Anybody can put leafy borders on his or her Web site full of carefully framed, soft-focus photos of four-year-old clearcuts (areas where all trees were cut, sometimes for miles), where wildflowers have grown up to cover the stumps. Greenwashers fooled even some of the search engines.

- Vote. Inform yourself about candidates' environmental records, as well as their records on other subjects that interest you. You may have to decide that a good record on one issue overrides a bad record on another. You'll usually have to settle for the lesser of two evils. For all that, voting is free of charge and free of personal risk. If you care at all, vote.

- Join and support those environmental organizations whose approaches fit your values and politics. Again, do your homework. Some greenwashing groups are now masquerading as environmental groups. Be especially careful when two groups seem to be covering the same issue, such as sustainable forest management, but one is proposing far weaker standards than the other. Often, the group proposing the weaker standards is backed by industrial interests, trying to forestall effective environmental regulation.

⚘ Speak out! Some of us feel confident speaking at public hearings or town council meetings. If you feel shy, you can help with the preparatory research. You can show up at the meetings to lend moral support, and take those who spoke out for a glass of their favorite beverage afterward. Anybody can write his or her legislators. Remember, the polluters have money to spend on glossy campaigns or on plain bribery. We have to counteract that by vigilance and diligence.

⚘ Blow the whistle! If you observe environmental violations in your area, keep track, take pictures, and, most of all, notify the proper authorities. Also, keep track of how well the authorities respond. If they drag their heels, present your observations to the local investigative reporter. (Find out in advance which local journalists seem to care about the environment.) Local environmental groups will also want to know, and may have better access to the media.

⚘ Some of us are called to direct confrontation, to putting our bodies between the corporations and the trees. Blessed be Julia Butterfly Hill, and if you don't know who she is, find out! Direct action is not for everyone. Nearing sixty, I stay home and write and train a new generation of priestesses and priests for Mother Earth. Any of us who knows somebody who is out there defending Gaia through direct action, or who is in jail for doing so, can help look after that person's home responsibilities. And anybody can contribute to legal defense funds.

⚘ And every single one of us can and should raise power for the protection and healing of Mother Earth. Doing this will also help you connect your personal energies with Hers, which is what this chapter is about

INTEGRATION: A MONTH OF FOCUS ON GAIA

From a polytheistic perspective, different Deities govern different aspects of experience. Accordingly, some Pagans find it useful to occasionally devote a month to intensive work with a particular Goddess or God. This helps us gain an understanding and open a connection that will empower and guide that portion of our lives from then on.

If you want to devote a month to your relationship with Gaia, use as many of the ideas in this chapter as you can. They will all reinforce each other, and help you come closer to Mother Earth. Let me make a few more general suggestions. First some guidelines:

- ❖ For a Gaia intensive, you'll be spending a lot of time out of doors. Pick a month in spring or fall, when the weather is moderate.

- ❖ Just as you might read guide books or study maps before setting out on a vacation, do most of the book work in advance. Realistically, you'll be keeping up your job and home responsibilities. This leaves you only just so much time. Save it for experiential work.

- ❖ Set up an altar for Gaia in your home, and a small "stealth altar" at your work place.

- ❖ Wear something green every day, even if it's just a bit of ribbon under your clothing. If you like, you can use an essential oil that smells like an herb or flower.

- ❖ Eat whole, unprocessed foods as much as possible. This will probably mean bringing your lunch to work. Include something raw (a salad, a piece of fruit) in every meal. Eat outdoors whenever you possibly can.

- ❖ Of course, you'll keep your journal during this month.

❧ Spend a minimum of an hour a day out of doors, except during severe storms. (Gentle rain is no obstacle. You may even get to see some creatures that come out only when it's wet.) You can take a walk or work in your garden or eat lunch on a park bench, whatever you like. Just stay mindful of the life around you, and enjoy being part of it.

The month will mean more to you if you give it a coherent structure, a "plot line." There are many possibilities for that. Here's one:

❧ Start at the New Moon. For the first week, learn as much as you can about how life evolved on Earth. Read Lovelock's *Gaia*, if you haven't already. Create or work with your local grounding meditation. Meditate on the miracle of evolution.

❧ During the second week, explore and celebrate the fullness of life. This is a good week to map your neighborhood. In your journal, list every living creature you observe near your home. See if you can figure out how they interact.

❧ At the Full Moon, have a potluck feast with your friends. Ask people to bring natural dishes that were mindfully prepared. Eat outdoors if at all possible.

❧ During the third week, learn about Gaia's wounds and the ongoing threats to Her well-being, especially those in your local area. This week is also a good time to work on your personal environmental impact analysis.

❧ During the fourth week, consider what you can do to contribute to the protection and healing of Mother Earth. What personal lifestyle changes do you feel ready to make? What kinds of active service can you feasibly and sustainably undertake? Be careful not to promise what you can't perform. You can always add more commitments later.

❧ If possible, conclude your month by doing a vision quest on the weekend closest to the New Moon. If you receive any insights about the commitments you plan, adjust them accordingly. Remember that Gaia witnesses vows. Speak your pledges aloud to the listening Earth just before you go to sleep on the night before you go home. (If you can't get away for a weekend in nature, make these pledges at the Gaia altar or shrine in your home. Either way, record the pledges in your journal.) Pay attention to Her responses in your dreams.

As your month ends, as you go home to live your values, remember these words of Walt Whitman:

> *I swear there is no greatness or power that does not emulate*
> *those of the earth,*
> *There can be no theory of any account unless it corroborate*
> *the theory of the earth,*
> *No politics, song, religion, behavior or what not, is of*
> *account, unless it compare with the amplitude of the earth,*
> *Unless it face the exactness, vitality, impartiality, rectitude of*
> *the earth.*

RESOURCES

Aberly, Doug. *Boundaries of Home.* New Society, 1993.

Adler, Margot. *Drawing Down the Moon.* Boston: Beacon, 1986.

Albanese, Catherine L. *Nature Religion in America.* Chicago: University of Chicago Press, 1990.

Brown, Edward Espe. *Tassajara Cooking.* Boston: Shambhala, 1986.

———. *Tassajara Bread Book.* Boston: Shambhala, 1995.

———. *Tomato Blessings and Radish Teachings.* New York: Riverhead Books, 1997.

Capon, Fr. Robert Farrar. *The Supper of the Lamb.* New York: Modern Library, 2002.

Carson, Rachel. *Silent Spring.* 1962. Reprint, Boston: Houghton Mifflin, 1994.

Clifton, Chas S. "Witches and the Earth." In Chas S. Clifton, ed., *The Modern Craft Movement.* St Paul, MN: Llewellyn, 1992.

Cook, Charles. *Awakening to Nature.* New York: Contemporary Books, 2001.

Crowley, Vivianne. "Wicca as Nature Religion." In Joanne Pearson et al., eds., *Nature Religion Today: Paganism in the Modern World*. Edinburgh: Edinburgh University Press, 1998.

Downing, Christine. *The Goddess: Mythological Images of the Feminine*. New York: Crossroads, 1984.

Eisler, Riane. *The Chalice and the Blade*. New York: Harper & Row, 1987.

———, and David Loye. *The Partnership Way*. New York: HarperCollins, 1990.

Eliade, Mircea. *Myths, Dreams and Mysteries*. New York: Harper & Row, 1960.

Giambutas, Marija. *The Language of the Goddess*. New York: Harper & Row, 1989.

———. *The Civilization of the Goddess*. San Francisco: HarperSanFrancisco, 1991.

Harris, Adrian. "Sacred Ecology." In Graham Harvey and Charlotte Hardman, eds., *Paganism Today*. San Francisco: Thorsons, 1995.

Harrow, Judy. *Wicca Covens*. New York: Citadel, 1999.

———. *Spiritual Mentoring: A Pagan Guide*. Toronto: EWC, 2002.

Hartley, William W. *Loving Nature . . . the Right Way*. Tuckerton, NJ: Partnership Press, 1996.

Harvey, Graham. *Contemporary Paganism: Listening People: Speaking Earth*. New York: New York University Press, 1997.

Hultkranz, Ake. "The Religion of the Goddess in North America." In Carl Olson, ed., *The Book of the Goddess Past and Present*. New York: Crossroads, 1983.

Hutton, Ronald. *Triumph of the Moon*. New York: Oxford University Press, 1999.

Leopold, Aldo. *A Sand County Almanac*. 1949. Reprint, New York: Oxford University Press, 2001.

Lovelock, James. *Gaia: A New Look at Life on Earth*. New York: Oxford University Press, 1979.

———. *The Ages of Gaia*. New York: Norton, 1988.

Preston, James J., ed. *Mother Worship: Theme & Variations*. Chapel Hill: University of North Carolina Press, 1982.

Roth, Gabrielle. *Sweat Your Prayers*. Los Angeles: Tarcher/Putnam, 1997.

Starhawk. *The Spiral Dance*. San Francisco: HarperSanFrancisco, 1999.

CONCLUSION

Maybe you simply read through this book, like an armchair traveler reading about exotic places you may never see. Even so, I don't think you just wasted your time. If you read thoughtfully, you learned a few things about the contemporary Pagan revival.

We aren't devil worshippers and we aren't flakes. We are as serious about our religion as other folks are about theirs. We are intelligent, educated, curious, and devoted to our path. We are successfully rediscovering or reconstructing the old ways. Our knowledge, our skill—and our numbers—are growing every year.

Oral traditions were interrupted. Written records were lost or destroyed. Our knowledge of ancient beliefs and practices will always be incomplete. And yet, we find we have access to all the same Sources from which the ancients learned. Deity speaks to all those who care to listen, as always.

If you did some of the rituals, meditations, and exercises described here, perhaps Deity spoke to you, a still, small voice within your innermost being, filling you with awe and joy. There's more. There's plenty. This well may have been choked with debris after centuries of neglect, but it never ran dry. It never could. Once the channel is clear, we find the living water still there, sweet and abundant as ever.

As you get to know the ancient Gods, I offer this advice:

- ⚹ In the words of Tradition, as within, so without.
- ⚹ In plain English, with Gods just as with people, love the one you're with.

You cannot become acquainted with the ancient Gods without getting to know yourself better. May this book serve you well as you walk your path. Blessed be!

—Judy Harrow

INDEX

Speaking out, 282
Spell(s)
  Book of the Dead and, 10
  bringing justice, 34
  In-Drinking, 64–67, 69
  for protection, 139–40
Spiral Dance, The (Starhawk),
  249
Spit (spittle; spitting), 46–47
Sprinkle, Annie, 203
Starhawk, *The Spiral Dance,* 249
Stories. *See* Myths; *and specific
  stories*
Sumer (Sumerians), 170, 182–84
Supper of the Lamb, The (Capon),
  270
Swallowing, 47
  In-Drinking Spell, 64–67, 69
Swans, 193, 199
Swastika, 135
Swinburne, Algernon Charles,
  243
Sylvanus, 113
Symposia, 204

Tai Chi, 274
Táin Bó Cualnge, 105
Tales. *See* Myths; *and specific tales*
Tassajara Cooking (Brown), 271
Tattoos, 220–21
Tefnut, 19, 29, 46, 85
Tellus, 95
Temples, 94
  Aphrodite, 177
    map, 171–78
    Paphos, 182, 194
    Uruk, 185
Terpsikhore, 196
Tewa Indians, 240
Thalia, 186

Thankfulness, Ma'at Ritual for,
  68
Theogony (Hesiod), 164, 165–66,
  189, 238
Theological assumptions,
  xi–xii
Thessaly, 177
Thomas, Dylan, 73
Thoth, 19, 24, 30, 85
Three, Brigit and, 127–28
Tobar Bríde, 142–43
Trance work. *See also*
  Meditation
  Anubis, 38, 39–40
  Visit to the Necropolis,
    40–45
Transgendered beings, 184,
  190–91
Travelers, Anubis as Protector of,
  32, 37
Trees, 133–34, 194–95, 256,
  280
Triple goddess, 128–29
Triumph of the Moon (Hutton),
  244
Trois Frères Sorcerer, 235
Trojan War, 95, 164, 167
  archaeological evidence,
    169–70
Troy, 165, 167, 175
Truth, Ma'at Ritual and, 67–70
"Truth and Falsehood," 22–23
Tuatha Dé Danann, 103–4
"Two Brothers, Tale of the,"
  11–18
Tydings, Alexandra, 203

Ucetis, 98
Ucuetis, 116
Umai, Her, 230

Uniqueness of people, xii
Urns. *See* Vessels
Uruk, Temple of, 185
Utu, 183

Vault of Remembrance, 43–44
Vault of the Future, 44
Vault of the Past, 41–43
Venus, 179–80
Venus of Willendorf, 234–35
Vessels (urns)
    breaking of, in rituals, 50–51
    for loved one, 35
Vesta, 93, 94
Vestalia festival, 94–95
Vestal Virgins, 93–96, 155*n*
Vestments, 117–18, 193–94
Vignettes, Egyptian, 100
Vision quest, 277–79
Volcanoes, 191
Voluntarism, 280–81
Voluntary simplicity, 262–63
Voting, 281

War
    Ares and, 190
    Brigit and, 120
Washing (bathing), 142–43,
    203, 207

Water, Brigit and, 98–99,
    126–27, 142–43
    tobar Bríde, 142–43
Web sites, 225–26
Weekend retreats. *See* Retreats
Wente, Edward F., Jr., 11–12
Wheel of the Year, xiii–xiv,
    274–75
Whistle-blowing, 282
White, Brigit and, 129–30, 145
White animals, Brigit and, 107–8
White Cow, 108, 132
Whitman, Walt, 285
Wiccan Rede, 261
Wiccans, xiii, 6
Wilderness Society, 247
Willendorf, Lady of, 234–35
Wordsworth, William, 242
"World Is Too Much with Us;
    Late and Soon"
    (Wordsworth), 242

Xenophon, 176

Yoga, 274

Zephuros, 189
Zeus, 164–65, 167
Zoos, 256